HIKING FROM PORTLAND TO THE COAST

Hiking from Portland to the Coast

An Interpretive Guide to 30 Trails

JAMES D. THAYER

OREGON STATE UNIVERSITY PRESS • CORVALLIS

Maps and photographs by James D. Thayer except as noted.

Library of Congress Cataloging-in-Publication Data

Names: Thayer, James D., author.
Title: Hiking from Portland to the coast : an interpretive guide to 30 trails / James
    D. Thayer.
Description: Corvallis : Oregon State University Press, 2016.
Identifiers: LCCN 2016029572 | ISBN 9780870718779 (original trade paperback :
    alk. paper)
Subjects: LCSH: Hiking—Oregon—Guidebooks. | Hiking—Oregon—Portland
    Region—Guidebooks. | Trails—Oregon—Guidebooks. | Oregon—Guidebooks.
Classification: LCC GV199.42.O7 T52 2016 | DDC 796.5109795—dc23
LC record available at https://lccn.loc.gov/2016029572

♾ This paper meets the requirements of ANSI/NISO Z39.48-1992
(Permanence of Paper).

Every effort has been made to assure the accuracy of the information in this book,
but changes inevitably occur over time. Corrections and updates are welcome and
can be sent to Jim Thayer at jim@thayers.org.

Oregon State University Press
121 The Valley Library
Corvallis OR 97331-4501
541-737-3166 • fax 541-737-3170
www.osupress.oregonstate.edu

Contents

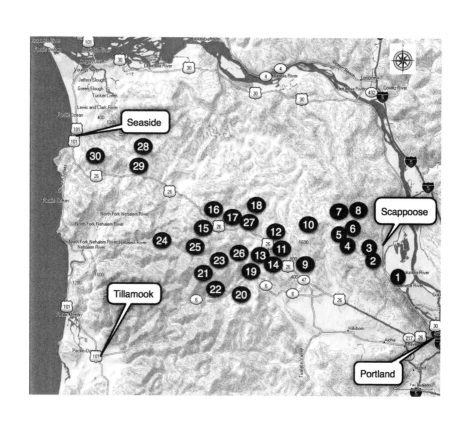

Preface

The challenge that this book attempts to resolve presented itself to me one wintry day in 2007, after I published *Portland Forest Hikes*, my guide to the more esoteric trails in and around Forest Park. While researching that book I discovered and explored many paths along the wildlife corridor that connects Forest Park with the Coast Range. But standing at the edge of the vast forest that covers Oregon's northern coastal mountains, I was reminded of a project dating back to the late 1980s. A group of us, mostly associated with the Friends of Forest Park (now Forest Park Conservancy), had proposed developing long-range trails that would connect Forest Park with several destinations on the coast. The Conservation Fund, headed by its western representative, Keith Hay, came to our assistance and funded the first scoping study to consider this outlandish plan. The outcome of the study was to propose several trails connecting Portland and the coast.

The first trail identified was the traditional canoe route used by Lewis and Clark to reach Astoria. Keith Hay later wrote the guidebook for that water route. But the second and third trails linking Forest Park and the coast remained aspirational. For several decades these trails, with one ending near Seaside and the other near Tillamook, remained dotted lines across a map—suspiciously straight in all that welter of constantly shifting nature.

I knew how unrealistic these lines were, and I also knew that as long as they remained mere placeholders for future generations to fulfill, they were in imminent danger of becoming impassable due to relentless residential development in the rural belt surrounding Portland. More and more people were building their dream homes in the remote hills between Portland and the coast, and each one of these private reserves further limited the corridor through which our proposed trails would have to transit. Already much of northern Washington County was fenced off and posted to prohibit any pedestrian access.

The situation became even more problematic after Weyerhaeuser began charging access fees for selected tracts of timberland in the Coast Range. As I stood looking west toward Saddle Mountain, I realized that the faster we gained momentum on developing these regionally significant trails, the better the chance we'd actually accomplish what we envisioned. So, I began to map existing forest roads, "skidder tracks," old rail grades, and even game trails in the northern Coast Range. It took me about a decade, but in the end I had mapped two feasible routes from Portland to the coast. One led to Tillamook; the other to Seaside.

Hiking from Portland to the Coast began as a portfolio of trail descriptions infused with a rich layer of local lore, natural history, and historical anecdotes from the region. As I walked many hundreds of miles crisscrossing the Coast Range, I accumulated a trove of stories and anecdotes pertaining to the places through which these trails passed. With each new story I became more convinced that a mere recitation of trail instructions wouldn't do justice to the rich history of the northern Coast Range.

For many Oregonians the northern Coast Range is an unfathomable confusion of nameless peaks, shadowy valleys, and furtive rivers rushing to their destiny. Slicing through it is US 26, the Sunset Highway. On either side of the highway, travelers see thick commercial forests, with occasional glimpses of vast clear-cuts denuding whole mountains, and blue or yellow gates that prevent cars from penetrating up the many nameless gravel roads that disappear into the forest gloom.

Several years ago, I explained to a friend that I was writing a book about the forests and trails that stretched from Portland to the coast. "Aside from describing trail routes, what more is there to say?" he asked. To him the Coast Range was a vast expanse of forest that was occasionally visited by hunters, fishermen, and loggers. Where in these remote forests were the dramatic stories that might interest people? he wondered.

Five Pieces of Practical Advice for the Oregon Hiker

While Oregon is undoubtedly one of the most scenic states in the nation, it is also one of the most deadly when it comes to getting lost in the woods. Since 1997, 189 men and 51 women are unaccounted for as a result of walking into our forests. It's easy to get lost in the dense coastal mountains. Since then, 89 percent of those reported lost walked out of the woods unharmed, 8 percent perished, and another 2 percent were never seen again.

This trail guide includes walks that can easily be accomplished by even the most inexperienced hiker. But it also includes some longer and more difficult hikes that could be classified as strenuous and require some degree of orienteering skill. So my first bit of advice is to choose a hike that corresponds to your party's skills, endurance, and way-finding abilities. It's better that you overestimate the difficulty of these hikes than find yourself cold, wet, and lost.

With the initial warning that this book contains some admittedly difficult hikes, let me begin this guidebook to your next adventure by offering five pieces of advice that will make your time in the woods more enjoyable, safer, and survivable in case of unforeseen mishaps.

CARRY EMERGENCY SUPPLIES TO SUSTAIN YOU OVERNIGHT

From about May to the end of September I usually carry a lightweight waist pack with minimal overnight provisions, including medical supplies, emergency high-energy food, a bivy sack (lightweight shelter), a tube tent, a poncho, a space blanket, string, a couple of small bungee cords, a Leatherman tool, and a whistle. The main purpose of these items is to help me stay warm, dry, and nourished. The little waist pack has enough room to also hold a map, my small camera, some lunch, and snacks for Zoe, my dog. Most of this stuff resides permanently in my pack, which is always ready to grab on the way out the door.

Once the colder weather sets in, I switch to a larger waist pack. All the aforementioned items except the tube tent get transferred into the larger pouch, and I add an extra pair of wool socks, a tiny one-man tent, and a Jetboil stove. That takes care of the primary challenges—staying dry and warm.

For added safety I also carry a GPS device that shows the landscape in topographic format—mainly for recording where I've been—and a satellite beacon with which I can alert my wife if I'm in trouble. Each message also provides my location. Keep in mind that phones usually don't work once you descend into the valleys, which is when you are most likely to need them.

MAKE GOOD DECISIONS

The second challenge is making good decisions. Oregon's cold, wet climate induces hypothermia in those unfortunate enough to get stuck in the woods without adequate protection from the damp. Hypothermia is no joke! Its main symptom is a tendency to become befuddled, make poor choices, and refuse to reassess the situation as things go from bad to worse. It's also very insidious, because the very first symptom can be denial that you might be suffering from hypothermia. The best strategy is to conserve body heat zealously. Toughing it out and trying to barrel through the wilderness is almost always a poor decision, sometimes even fatal.

Maintaining a consistent estimation of which risks are acceptable, and which are not, is often a moving target when operating far out in the woods. Take, for instance, the risk of traversing a slope full of newly cut trees. These logs are not anchored and could slide, pinning anyone in their path. Crossing such a slope is potentially very risky. Considering this scenario near the beginning of my hike, I would immediately reject the idea of crossing this log-strewn slope. But now consider the same proposition after having walked five hours to get to the edge of this slope, and knowing that your car is just beyond it. Naturally we downgrade the risk ahead of us, because we're aware of the effort and time it will take to retrace our way to get back to the car. Risk is a relative measure and it's influenced by the investment already undertaken. Retaining a valid estimation of risk in these situations is very important in avoiding potential harm.

REMEMBER THAT THE PACIFIC NORTHWEST IS UPSIDE DOWN!

Hikers in the Pacific Northwest should learn to heed a basic element of local geography. The old adage holds that one should follow water to reach civilization. This does not apply to the commercial forests of the Pacific Northwest. The reason is simple: logging roads in the Pacific Northwest are built across the tops of the mountains, not along the valley floors.

In the Pacific Northwest timber is harvested by pulling it *up* the slope to a landing pad built at the top of the ridge or mountain. That means that all major roads in the forest run along the heights. To find people and roads you must ascend the slopes, not descend them.

The narrow ravines that drain the Coast Range are often filled with a penetrating wet fog, chilly pools, and slippery rocks. In addition, it is virtually impossible to avoid the thorny vegetation located at the bottom of these ravines. To make matters worse, many of these mountain streambeds descend over waterfalls or are clogged with gigantic logjams. Stay away from these chilly chutes and climb up to find the logging roads that crisscross the ridgetops of the northern Coast Range. It may take a while, but you'll walk out alive if you climb up.

UNDERSTAND LOGGING ROADS, FOREST GATES, AND PERMITTING REGULATIONS

Commercial forest tracts are often gated. Understanding the significance of these gates can be essential to a successful hike in these working forests. Many timber companies support limited recreational access to their lands. These forests are usually gated with blue gates that are accompanied by a sign announcing the users' recreational rights. But not all landowners permit access without prior permission. Typically, landowners who want to restrict access, including recreational use, do so by posting the boundaries with No Trespassing signs. Another way to prohibit public access is to use

Weyerhaeuser has recently begun requiring permits to enter its timberlands. They are available once per year on May 18th and 19th.

yellow metal gates. Unless expressly open (e.g., for rifle season), I avoid these intentionally private forests.

It is generally safer to park outside a gate and walk in. The trailheads of the hikes in this book are public and physically accessible by car without entering a gated area. If you should somehow get stuck behind one of these gates, contact the local county police department. They often have duplicate keys.

Weyerhaeuser has recently implemented a recreational fee for access to their timberlands in both Washington and Columbia Counties. Weyerhaeuser states that these fees allow them "to offset costs incurred . . . especially for road maintenance to protect water quality."

Needless to say, these permits have stirred quite a controversy because of the imposition of a fee for access that was freely available to Oregonians since pioneer days. The limited availability and high cost of these permits has resulted in restricting access to hunters, ignoring the huge market for other recreational use among casual hikers, cyclists, and equestrians. Several efforts are being pursued to make these permits more accessible and priced to reflect the limited use that casual hikers might require.

The trails in this book that may currently require valid permits are identified in the trail descriptions.

BE AWARE THAT LOGGING CAN CHANGE THE SCENERY

Some of the descriptions in this guide are perishable. Please note that place descriptions that rely on visual cues like "tall timber" or "young forest" can change appreciatively over time or—in the case of a clear-cut—quite suddenly. Logging has a way of radically changing the optics of a trail. Active logging ensures that the places described in this book are constantly evolving. That's why I regularly reference the cumulative distance from the trailhead. In this way, the changing landscape cannot mislead you, since the distances remain the same.

One final admonition: be aware of where active logging is occurring. The telltale signs that say "Trucks entering the road" warn that logging trucks are actively using the logging roads. During the workweek I avoid entering actively used logging roads because many log-truck drivers drive as if they own the road—which they do.

Mount Hood.

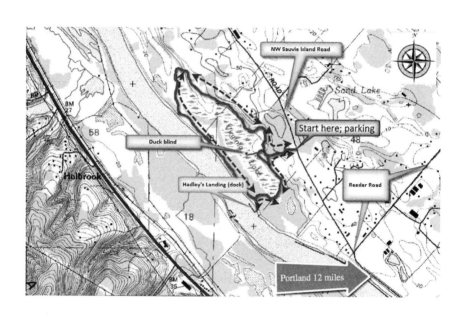

NW Sauvie Island Road

Sand Lake

Start here; parking

Duck blind

Hadley's Landing (dock)

Reeder Road

Holbrook

Portland 12 miles

1. Sauvie Island Loop

BRIEF DESCRIPTION: This hike is a great way to begin this collection. It's easy to find, short, and full of wildlife, interesting plants, and a variety of habitats, including oak savannahs, wetlands, and tall stands of riverside cottonwoods. Much of the route along the river is under cover of trees, so this can be a very enjoyable route to the Multnomah Channel on a hot August afternoon.

DISTANCE: 2.75-mile loop

ELEVATION CHANGE: 46 feet

TRAIL CONDITION: Wide, well-maintained trail with markers identifying common animals, birds, and habitats

APPROXIMATE DURATION: About 1 hour for full circuit. The shortest route to Hadley's Landing takes 15–20 minutes.

TRAVEL TIME FROM PORTLAND TO TRAILHEAD: 25 minutes. On summer weekends expect delays crossing onto the island.

DRIVING DIRECTIONS: The bridge to Sauvie Island is about 10 miles from NW Portland via US 30. After crossing the bridge, continue north on Gillihan Road for 2 miles, where the intersection with Reeder Road veers off to the right. Stay left on Gillihan Road and continue 0.6 miles farther, passing the Oregon Department of Fish and Wildlife office on the right. Soon you will see a wide parking area on your left. Turn into the parking area, which is marked with an official Oregon Parks and Recreation sign announcing the Wapato Access Greenway. A Sauvie Island parking permit is not needed for this parking area, unlike many other locations on the island.

SPECIAL ATTRIBUTES: Great for bird-watching and the occasional deer viewing. Hadley's Landing has a nice dock for boaters and a riverside picnic area. If you're just there for a quick canine dip in the water, use the southern approach to shorten the trip down to one-third of a mile each way.

TRAIL LOG: After parking, proceed through the gate. The initial portion of the trail meanders along the edge of a clearing. A small path scoots off to the left. This is a shortcut that heads directly to Hadley's Landing, and is worth investigating when the berries are ripe in August and early September. Otherwise, stay on the main trail and after 0.2 miles you will arrive at a covered picnic area. Here the trail splits. The trail headed south around the lower end of Virginia Lake (really a marsh) splits off to the left of the picnic structure.

The route heading north is visible on the right side of the picnic structure. It continues to traverse the gentle slope on the eastern side of the marsh, affording numerous views of the wetlands. Watch for great blue herons, brilliant western tanagers, various ducks, grebes, and the occasional deer poking through the muddy bottoms. In the wet season there are lots of frogs in the underbrush. At its northern end, the trail crosses the marsh on a footbridge before turning south to parallel the Multnomah Channel. About 1.6 miles past the picnic structure it meets the southern route at a three-way intersection. The right-hand option leads to Hadley's Landing. The left-hand option leads along the southern end of the marsh and back to the parking lot.

The remaining portion of the loop back to the picnic structure is about 0.4 miles long, but before turning homeward, take a short detour to Hadley's Landing, located just 375 feet from this junction. This wide trail extends southward parallel to the Multnomah Channel. Almost immediately you will encounter a picnic area. Beyond it, a slanted catwalk leads out to a floating dock. Most days there are about a half-dozen fishermen angling for catfish in the murky waters of the channel. Take the time to enjoy this little piece of paradise amid the quiet stirrings of the river's sluggish back channel.

Returning up to where the northern circuit meets the southern route, turn to the right and follow the wide trail 0.4 miles back across the southern edge of the marshlands. You'll pass a wildlife viewing blind on the way, and farther along encounter a side spur on the left that leads out to a viewing area in the marsh. At one of my visits to this vantage point, a great blue heron lifted off from the reeds and flapped its way aloft like some overloaded cargo plane struggling to gain altitude. Only about 50 feet from the platform a doe stood at the edge of the shrubbery; we eyed each other warily until she picked her way daintily through the reeds and disappeared into the bushes.

Moving on, return to the main loop trail and after about 260 feet you'll be back at the picnic structure. From here it's only 0.2 miles back to the parking lot. I find myself revisiting this short but scenic excursion regularly.

"Sauvie" Island?

The island at the confluence of the Willamette and Columbia Rivers is known as Sauvie Island. It's a favorite spot for Portlanders to cycle, to hunt waterfowl, or even to go skinny-dipping in the summer months. This low-lying island was named after Laurent Sauvé, the cowherd who spent only a short time on the island.

But perhaps it should be called Wapato Island.

Sauvie Island was once the most densely populated location north of Mexico City.

WAPATO ISLAND

Today this island serves mainly as an agricultural and recreational foot-
note to the Portland area, but not so long ago it was the epicenter of human habitation in North America. The interior of the island is covered
with shallow lakes and pools in which an onion-like plant thrives. Known
to Native Americans as *wapato* and as broadleaf arrowhead (*Sagittaria
latifolia*) to the Europeans, this underwater tuber was a favorite treat of
the native peoples. The popularity of this aquatic onion, and the torrents
of migrating salmon nearby, had the effect of concentrating the Native
American population, making the Lower Columbia the most densely
populated area in the entire North American continent. It is thought that
prior to the 1770s the Lower Columbia supported a population of more
than sixty thousand Native Americans, who consumed as much as forty-
one million tons of salmon annually as well as vast quantities of wapato.

In 1806, Lewis and Clark stopped by the village of Cathlapotle, located in what is now the Ridgefield National Wildlife Refuge, just north
of Vancouver. There they camped at a local portage where the Native

Americans carried their canoes to an inland pond. In their journals they described what they found:

> In this pond the nativs inform us they Collect great quantities
> of pappato, which the womin collect by getting into the water,
> Sometimes to their necks holding by a Small canoe and with their
> feet loosen the wappato or bulb of the root from the bottom ...
> and it imedeately rises to the top of the water, (then) they Collect
> & throw them into the Canoe, those deep roots are the largest and
> the best roots.

According to the local tribes, the very best roots were to be found on the island they called Wapato Island, and which we know as Sauvie Island.

> Wappatoe Island is ... high and extreemly fertile ... with ponds
> which produce great quantities of the ... bulb of which the
> natives call wappatoe ... we passed several fishing camps on
> Wappetoe island ....
>
> — Meriwether Lewis, March 30, 1806

NATHANIEL WYETH'S FORT WILLIAM

The three decades preceding and following the visit by Lewis and Clark were devastating for the native populations living in the area. From the 1770s and intermittently through the 1830s epidemics of smallpox, syphilis, measles, and tuberculosis killed most of the local Native Americans on the island and all along the Lower Columbia River. By the time Nathaniel Wyeth, the first American fur trader, arrived, the island was nearly deserted.

In 1834, Wyeth established Fort William along an ancient trail that crossed the island and the Tualatin Mountains to access the Willamette Valley. However, the venture was fated to fail as most of the beaver in the region had already been trapped, and efforts to rely on trade in agricultural goods proved fruitless. It didn't help that Wyeth's Hawaiian laborers promptly decamped, taking most of his horses. This was compounded by a murderous dispute involving the fort's gunsmith and the tailor over the affections of a local Native American girl. The fact that the island was often submerged in the swollen river waters contributed to its unhealthy environment. After seventeen of his men died of "bilious disorders," Wyeth finally abandoned Fort William, writing in his journal that they were "living off of trash and dogs."

LAURENT SAUVÉ

In 1837, Dr. John McLoughlin, the chief factor of the Hudson's Bay Company, entered into an arrangement to supply the Russian settlements in Alaska with butter. This led to the establishment of a dairy herd on the island at the site of the ill-fated Wyeth venture. Around four hundred cows were swum across the Columbia River from Fort Vancouver. According to some sources, McLoughlin chose James Logie, a young Orkneyman, to run the operation. But James had a sweetheart back in the British Isles, so Dr. McLoughlin gave him leave to return to the remote Orkneys to fetch his betrothed, the sixteen-year-old Isabelle. Even though the newlywed couple made their way back to London as quickly as possible, they missed the sailing of the annual supply ship. So the couple had to wait until the following year to make the crossing. During James's two-year absence, Dr. McLoughlin assigned another Hudson's Bay employee, Laurent Sauvé, to care for the herds. Aside from this temporary assignment, not much more is known about the island's namesake.

JAMES AND ISABELLE LOGIE

In 1842, James and Isabelle took up residence on the island. They began to develop dairy operations there, as well as in a secondary location across the Tualatin Mountains in the vicinity of Dairy Creek. Isabelle must have been a remarkable woman to travel so far from home at eighteen and take up residence in Oregon's formidable wilderness. It wasn't long before the resident doctor of the Hudson's Bay Company recognized her skills and trained her in the medical knowledge of the day. Thereafter she was tireless in tending to the desperate medical afflictions of the natives, who were gradually being exterminated by European illnesses against which they had no resistance. The Logies remained at the center of the island community, and they eventually assumed ownership of the dairy after the Hudson's Bay Company moved its headquarters to Victoria. In 1854 James was stricken with typhus, and despite valiant efforts to get him medicines from Portland, he succumbed to the disease that had already taken so many of the island natives.

Even though James spent a dozen years building up the dairies and establishing a new community on the island, the name that came to be associated with the island was Laurent's surname, not his. But for the love of a lass on the distant Orkneys, we'd now be visiting Logie Island instead of Sauvie Island.

Green gate exit to
Gilkison Road

Portland 19.8 miles

Bob Johnston cabin

Intersection with path
going up; take left turn
going downhill

Start here;
parking off
Rocky Point
Road.

US 30 at base of Rocky Point Road
Junction with Skyline Blvd at summit

2. Jackson Creek

BRIEF DESCRIPTION: This walk follows a gravel road down from Rocky Point Road to the ruins of the Bob Johnston cabin. The road continues past the cabin, but it becomes more overgrown as it enters the thickets near Jackson Creek. However, if you follow the track it will deposit you on upper Gilkison Road near the entrance to the Vedanta Society Retreat. For an easier hike simply proceed as far as the ruined cabin.

DISTANCE: 1.4 miles one way to Gilkison Road

ELEVATION CHANGE: 382 feet

TRAIL CONDITION: Mostly gravel, but the lower trail is muddy and some-what untamed. Wear waterproof footwear in the wet season.

APPROXIMATE DURATION: 1 hour round trip; add time to explore the old homestead

TRAVEL TIME FROM PORTLAND TO TRAILHEAD: 45 minutes

DRIVING DIRECTIONS: From NW Portland, travel about 17 miles north on US 30 to the bottom of Rocky Point Road. The trailhead is located 2.77 miles up Rocky Point Road.

Another way to reach the trailhead is via Skyline Boulevard. Rocky Point Road is the northernmost road through the Tualatin Mountains that intersects with Skyline Boulevard. The trailhead is located about 0.45 miles below the intersection of Skyline Boulevard and Rocky Point Road.

Rocky Point Road is a very windy road. Near the top, the north side of the road is forested. Just within the forested area, note a private driveway on the north side of the road (right side if you're coming up from US 30). Just beyond it is an old logging service road. This is the trailhead. There's plenty of room to park near the gate. Beyond the gate the trail heads due north, dropping gently down the slope.

SPECIAL ATTRIBUTES: This trail is the lynchpin that connects the closer-in trails that traverse the hillside above Burlington, past Logie Trail to Rocky Point Road. Rocky Point Road has been extensively clear-cut, but it does present a panoramic view of the Portland area and Mount Hood. Just beyond this trail a vast network of commercial logging roads covers the eastern slope of the Tualatin Mountains, providing pedestrian linkages all the way to the coast.

TRAIL LOG: Beyond the gate the trail heads due north, dropping gently down the slope. In the fall you should keep a sharp watch along the verge of the forest, as I have occasionally found chanterelles along this part of the trail.

Log cabin

Continue in a generally northwesterly direction; you will eventually enter a cleared area at an elevation of 1,125 feet. At the north end of this clearing (about a half mile from the start) a ruined log cabin is set among the trees. The cabin bears a plaque commemorating Bob Johnston, who evidently cared for this once-idyllic cabin on behalf of Boy Scout Troop 221. Local folklore has it that after Johnston's death the cabin stood empty for several years, and ultimately burned down after attracting transients.

Descent to Gilkison Road

The clearing around the old homestead is a pleasant destination on its own, but to continue all the way down to Gilkison Road, follow the road farther downhill.

Below the cabin the road swerves through a series of bends before emerging at the base of a small clear-cut area. This is an area much frequented by deer, elk, and even cougars. I once spotted a cougar track on this stretch of the road. Keep in mind that I have spotted an actual cougar only once in all my hundreds of solo walks, and there has never been a fatal wild cougar attack in Oregon. So there is no need to be afraid—just resist the temptation to pet large stray cats you might encounter.

Farther down the trail along the bottom edge of a small clear-cut, the road turns into a trail that squeezes through bushes and enters a stand of alders. At this point, the main trail continues in an uphill direction—this is not the direction to follow as it leads to private residences. It's definitely not a place to enter without prior permission!

Instead, look for a smaller trail that branches off to the left just after you've entered the alder grove. This less-distinct path bends downhill through the ferns and descends the hillside. Take this trail downhill. On your right you will be able to hear the splashing of Jackson Creek as it wends its way downhill paralleling the somewhat overgrown path. Just continue to press onward and you will be rewarded as the path reasserts itself and turns in a westerly direction. After another 300 feet the trail turns back to its original north-northwest direction and begins dropping more steeply as it approaches a green gate where the track intersects with Gilkison Road.

Should you decide to leave a second car at the bottom end of this hike, find this lower entrance by driving on US 30 past Rocky Point Road and

The cabin on the Sophie Mozee homestead.

turning left onto Watson Road (just past the Columbia County line). Take the first left after Joy Creek Nursery: Gilkison Road. Follow Gilkison Road to the end of the public road. A mossy green gate set into the woods marks the bottom of the Jackson Creek hike.

Another option is to continue into the Vedanta Society Retreat. Follow the directions provided in chapter 3 for that extension.

Peeling Back the Layers

The way that legends and stories attach themselves to places is not well understood. But it is indisputable that sprinkling in some local lore can bring an otherwise anonymous landscape to life. This certainly is true of the Sophie Mozee homestead located near Rocky Point Road.

The ridge-hugging trail ascending Dixie Mountain has served people since the beginning of human migration across this continent, and animals well before that. Like nearby Logie Trail, this route over the heights was used by the original travelers through these parts. They came down from Puget Sound and crossed the Columbia where a large swampy island split the river and it became shallow enough to swim or float across. In those days, the island was situated in the middle of the river and the main stem of the river wasn't as deep as it is now. Reaching the western shore, these early migrants would follow the path left by those that had passed before. In this manner they crested the Tualatin Mountains near Dixie Mountain and descended into the Tualatin Valley. From there they could follow the Willamette Valley all the way south into the Siskiyou Mountains on to-day's California border.

Until they were felled by contagion, early inhabitants used these paths with regularity as the Calapuyans and other tribes traded with the Chinooks all along the Lower Columbia. Even after the original inhabitants were displaced, these travel routes continued to see occasional use as the pioneers looked for ways to cross into the fertile Willamette Valley.

One of the earliest settler routes from the Lower Columbia into the Tualatin Valley was first traveled by the legendary Presbyterian circuit rider, Jason Lee. In 1834, Lee and a companion blazed their first trail into the Tualatin Valley, going right up the ridge between Raymond Creek and Jackson Creek. The horse trail led up the spine of the ridge, where the faintly visible Indian trail had passed. Traveling along the ridges meant that the terrain was mostly unimpeded by fallen logs and avoided the brush-clogged ravines.

Along the way Jason Lee's trail passed a plateau, which later became the site of a remote log cabin that had its own dark history.

So let's peel back the layers of history a bit further.

Originally this place was the homestead of Sophie Mozee. Like many of the original pioneers she eventually abandoned her claim, leaving only her name attached to this pretty little glade on the side of Dixie Mountain. After Mozee's departure, it appears that the place stood empty into the winter of 1894. But around that time a number of nearby homesteads began to experience petty thievery, which soon escalated into several instances of more serious burglary. No one knew who was to blame until one day a nearby homesteader left his freshly cooked dinner on the table while he went out to get some water to drink. Upon his return he found a heavily armed stranger helping himself to the steaming dinner. Given the precarious circumstances, the settler put on a brave face and hosted the stranger until he had had his fill, whereupon the stranger slipped off into the woods. Aside from confirming that someone fitting his description was occasionally stocking up on food in Scappoose, the trail had gone cold.

But then there was a lucky break in the case. Maybe it was cabin fever, or maybe it was just the collapse of an outlaw partnership, but it appears that the burglar and his henchman had a falling out. The burglar's mate escaped and went straight to the St. Helens police. According to the informant the chief burglar was an escaped convict called John Bain, and he was as bad as they came!

Bain was murderous from the get-go. He was just a teenager working in a butcher shop when he killed a Chinese American man with the meat axe he was wielding. He served out his time, but apparently the experience hardly left an impression on him because soon thereafter he killed both of his own children. Once again he was convicted, but this time he escaped and had been leading a lawless existence ever since.

Soon after news of Bain's activities, Constable Ed Fowler found himself mounted and en route to Dixie Mountain. One can only imagine what went through the constable's mind when he rounded the corner on Rocky Point Road and there was John Bain, on foot and armed with a rifle. Needless to say, the constable didn't care for the odds in that encounter, so he tipped his hat and continued on up to Dixie Mountain.

It can surely be surmised that the residents of that distant hilltop community weren't entirely thrilled at the prospect of participating in a midnight foray against a hardened and determined criminal. But eventually Constable Fowler was able to accumulate half a dozen stalwart souls to help him apprehend the villain. At midnight six of them slipped out of their homes and made their way quietly down Rocky Point Road and down the track that led to the Mozee place. There they took up positions all around the cabin, hoping to surprise Bain when he came out to wash in the morning.

It was a long, chilly wait, but finally the sun rose and began to light the isolated clearing. Just inside the shadowy forest fringe, the posse stood huddled in their coats, clutching their rifles and nervously peering at the cabin from which they expected Bain to step at any moment. All eyes were on the cabin, when suddenly Abe Nelson, one of the posse, noticed John Bain striding out of the forest with a sack over his back. At once, Bain saw him and the others, who were now nervously fingering their rifles. Defiantly, he ordered them off the premises and told them that they had "better get out—damn quick!" But by now the posse was lining up opposite Bain. The constable quickly rose from his crouched position and pointed his revolver at Bain, demanding, "Throw up your hands!" To which Bain replied, "No! Go to hell!"

Reportedly he stood looking at the posse for a long moment, sizing up his chances with this ragtag bunch of farmers. Then he dropped the bag, brandished a revolver, and started shooting in every direction. Jumping around wildly to avoid being hit, Bain emptied his revolver at the posse and then sprinted for the woods. Abe Nelson, who had first spotted Bain, now drew careful aim at the zigzagging fugitive and got off one last shot as he vanished into the shadowy gloom. The posse was about to follow in hot pursuit, but at the constable's advice they decided to avoid the forest and instead search the cabin, where someone had been spotted through the window.

Battering down the door, which was locked from within, the group ransacked the cabin. Finding no one, they decided to postpone the search for Bain in hopes that he might succumb to the wound that Abe Nelson thought he had inflicted. Besides, it was considered too dangerous to venture into the outlaw's home turf where he might have hidden caches of guns that could result in more grievous harm. In any event, a few days later Bain's friends came looking for him, only to find him lying dead just inside the forest. Though mortally wounded, Bain had retrieved a shotgun from a hidden stash and had been waiting for his pursuers when he finally bled out.

And thus the story ends? Not quite.

Many years later, a logging crew was cutting wood near Rocky Point Road. It was the custom among the loggers to swap stories and yarns to pass the cold nights in the bunkhouse, there being precious little else they could do in those "unplugged" days. It was during one of these long evenings that William Gentry volunteered a story about his first visit to the area. It seems that while cruising down the Columbia River aboard one of the ubiquitous steamers, Gentry had made the acquaintance of a fellow who had a cabin near Dixie Mountain. Together they disembarked in Scappoose and made their way to the cabin with plans to go hunting the next morning. After climbing up to his cabin, they supped on venison and shared a double bunk. But in the morning, Gentry awoke to an empty bed and an absent host. He was about to fix breakfast when all hell broke loose outside, with gunfire resounding all around the solitary glen. Seeing no chance of escape, Gentry locked the door from the inside and pried a board from the foot of the boarded-up chimney. Slipping inside, he replaced the wooden panel and climbed up onto the "chimney bench," where he crouched in utter silence while the posse combed the inside of the cabin. Waiting until everyone had long since left the area, William Gentry quietly slipped out the door and ran all the way down the hill.

While most of his audience thought the tale to be an entertaining yarn, but not entirely believable, one listener knew it was true. Sitting among the loggers was Robert Service Jr., who was also intimately acquainted with the gun battle with Bain. Service's own father had participated in the shootout. In utter astonishment Service now heard Gentry recount the details of that dramatic gun battle—a tale he'd heard so often from his father. Finally, the mystery of the mysterious figure in the cabin window had been solved.

Today, all that remains is the old chimney where Gentry hid, and a few poles that served as the frame of the roof. It seems that during the 1950s and 1960s the place became associated with a Boy Scout troop. Near the ruined cabin, a plaque commemorates Bob Johnston, a Boy Scout leader known to his friends as Hock. He was just fifty-five when he died. We don't know much about him, except that he called this place his "Hilton." To him this particular clearing in the woods was the height of luxury.

These are but a few of the stories that have been passed down to us from the slopes of Dixie Mountain, but this slim sampling of travelers' tales will have to serve for all the unheard voices of those that struggled over these mountains.

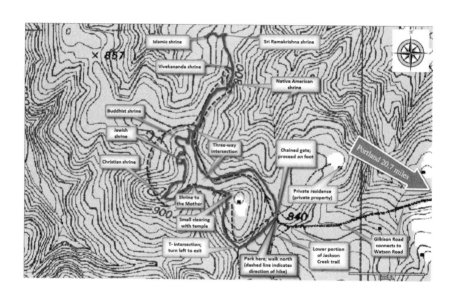

Islamic shrine

Sri Ramakrishna shrine

Vivekananda shrine

Native American shrine

Buddhist shrine

Jewish shrine

Three-way intersection

Christian shrine

Chained gate; proceed on foot

Portland 20.7 miles

Shrine to the Mother

Private residence (private property)

Small clearing with temple

T- intersection; turn left to exit

Gilkison Road connects to Watson Road

Lower portion of Jackson Creek trail

Park here; walk north (dashed line indicates direction of hike)

3. Vedanta Society Retreat

BRIEF DESCRIPTION: This gentle stroll in the woods follows a series of hillside trails on property owned and maintained by the Vedanta Society of Portland. Numerous small temples dedicated to sages and saints from many of the world's religions are scattered around the 120-acre property. A temple building, complete with a golden spire, is located on the summit of a small hillock at the center of the property.

DISTANCE: 2.35 miles. To shorten the hike, focus on the Spirit of the American Indian shrine and perhaps the shrine dedicated to Sri Vivekananda before returning the way you came in; this will cut the overall distance to just over a mile.

ELEVATION CHANGE: 180 feet

TRAIL CONDITION: The path is well maintained. This loop is one of the easiest hiking routes included in this guide.

APPROXIMATE DURATION: Plan to spend about 60–90 minutes to give yourself time to explore the wide variety of small temples scattered about the grounds.

TRAVEL TIME FROM PORTLAND TO TRAILHEAD: 35 minutes

DRIVING DIRECTIONS: Travel north from NW Portland on US 30 for 18 miles and turn left onto Watson Road, located immediately after crossing the county line. Follow Watson Road until it splits. Stay left and follow Gilkison Road to the end, where a cul-de-sac has three roads leading off in various directions. Park your car thoughtfully to avoid blocking gates or other cars. Take the center route, a gated forest road. A private driveway to the right does not permit access. The yellow gate to the left is the main entrance to the retreat—you will eventually return by way of this driveway.

SPECIAL ATTRIBUTES: Unique wooden shrines are set in an aging stand of timber. The relatively undisturbed forest supports an excellent variety of flora and fauna.

NOTE: I have asked the Vedanta Society whether the public is welcome on their retreat grounds, and those responsible have assured me that access is permissible, although they encourage visitors to remember that they are entering private land and to be mindful of the privilege being extended. Members of the society have added explanatory signs that help guide visitors.

TRAIL LOG: Walk up the gravel road heading north. You soon enter an older forest. This area was partially logged around the 1860s and then again in the early 1930s, making the current stand approximately 80 years old. Note the giant old stumps with the moss-covered slits that originally held the springboards on which the loggers stood to wield their long crosscut saws, often referred to as "misery whips." In those days, it took the loggers all day to cut a single tree.

Cast your eyes downward and you will encounter many Oregon natives, including baneberry and false Solomon's seal, amongst the large bunches of sword ferns and Oregon grape. On the roadway you can find lots of wild ginger and carpets of shamrock-like Oregon oxalis. In the bogs visible on the forest floor are skunk cabbage and camas lilies—a favorite staple of the long-absent Native Americans. A profusion of mushrooms, both edible and not, can be spotted as you traverse the property, including honey mushrooms, chanterelles, the prized lobster mushroom, and the pretty (but inedible) amanita mushrooms.

One-tenth of a mile up this gravel road, head right (north) at the Y. After another 0.1 mile, another Y is marked with signs indicating various shrines. Turn right to follow this unimproved forest road 0.2 miles to the Native American shrine. Approaching this shrine from behind, all you can initially see is the back of an eagle's wings. A short trail leads down to where you can slip under the wing and emerge in front of the shrine. Of all the shrines, the Native American shrine stands out as the most remarkable. Built in 1977 to resemble a gigantic crouching eagle, the shrine spans almost 50 feet from wing tip to wing tip and rises 30 feet into the air. For many years a Lakota shaman named Brave Buffalo consecrated the shrine. He would travel from eastern Oregon to reassert the presence of the Native American spirit in this majestic forest setting.

The eagle's head, carved in the dramatic Haida Indian style, looms over the visitor as it keeps a watchful eye on Sauvie Island—once the site of the largest permanent Indian community north of Tenochtitlán, or Mexico City.

To visit the remaining shrines, retrace your steps back up to the forest track immediately above and behind the Native American shrine. Turn right to continue down the trail. Soon you will spot three more shrines: the towering shrine to Sri Vivekananda, the Islamic shrine, and the shrine dedicated to Swami Ramakrishna. From the Swami Ramakrishna shrine retrace your steps back up the forest track all the way to the signpost at its intersection with the gravel forest road. At the crossing, turn right and proceed north about 240 feet along the gravel road. There a sign indicates a path leading

The Spirit of the American Indian shrine casts its watchful eyes over Sauvie Island, the ancestral home of the Chinook.

left to the Biblical Trail and the Buddhist Way. Follow this path, which climbs up a wooded slope to a tidy little Buddhist shrine. The winding path continues to the Jewish shrine and then narrows as it leads to the Christian shrine. Near the end of this circuitous path you will pass by the Shrine to the Mother, the oldest of the shrines on the property.

Just beyond the Shrine to the Mother is a three-way intersection. Almost directly across from where you emerged you will see a small footpath, the Mother's Trail, heading up the hill. To reach the temple, ascend this trail. At the top of the hill you will emerge into a mossy clearing. In the center sits a small building topped with an onion-shaped golden steeple.

Since this temple is often used for spiritual retreats, I usually try to keep my distance and skirt along the edge of the forest. Following the edge of the clearing to the right you can descend the driveway, which will quickly lead you down off the knoll. At the base of the hill turn left and follow the road downhill for about 100 feet to another split in the road. Turn left again at the bottom of the slope to find the main gate to the retreat. Walk around the gate to get back to your starting point, and parked car.

This is an awesome and magical place. I usually feel as if I am leaving with a little more than I brought.

The Case for Proliferation

In 1936 an unfamiliar religious group bought 120 acres on the slopes of Dixie Mountain. This surprising acquisition was organized by a small chapter of the Vedanta Society, a group devoted to the study of Hindu philosophy.

Hinduism was and remains virtually unknown to most Oregonians. The first widely noticed encounters with this Indian religion had only occurred about four decades earlier when the first swami arrived to introduce Hinduism to Americans. Swami Vivekananda was graciously received from San Francisco to New York. He never came to Portland. Undeterred, the Portland members of the Vedanta Society, who followed Vivekananda's teachings, purchased a recently logged tract of land on the heights above Scappoose as the site for their future spiritual retreat.

The Vedanta Society members elicited little notice among the residents of Scappoose, then a very rural community that had only just begun to receive electric light. Most locals confused them with Buddhists, and virtually no one understood the ancient panoply of exotic gods they worshipped. By 1954 they had begun to convert the tract's original homestead cabin into a small Hindu temple—the first of its kind in the Pacific Northwest.

But there were challenges to overcome. Multnomah County objected to granting the Vedanta Society tax-exempt status for the entire tract, and would grant an exemption for only a limited area around the temple. Society members disagreed with this narrow interpretation of which lands were religious. They argued that the entire property and its groves of trees were an integral part of what the retreat was intended to be—a place for positive contemplation in the midst of impressive natural beauty. In court, the county argued for a much narrower definition of this special status. But the Vedantists took that in stride, and began building meditation seats and scattering small wooden shrines dedicated to a wide range of beliefs and perspectives all across the property. The proliferation of their shrines effectively created clusters of spiritual "spheres of influence" that saturated the entire property with its sacredness. In the end the Vedanta Society won its legal appeal, but not before they had spread their shrines over the entire property in such a way that it would be difficult to argue that one area was more religious than another. It may have been an early example of sprawl, but it was entirely spiritual.

This place has a real aura about it. Maybe it's the many intricate shrines, or maybe it's the gracefulness of Douglas firs when they mature, or the eighty years of serving exclusively as a garden for thought and spiritual discovery. I encourage you to visit, and perhaps let your spirit grow as you wander through this garden of meditation.

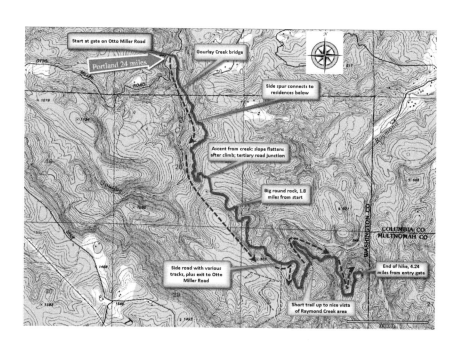

Start at gate on Otto Miller Road

Gourlay Creek bridge

Portland 24 miles

Side spur connects to residences below

Ascent from creek; slope flattens after climb; tertiary road junction

Big round rock, 1.8 miles from start

COLUMBIA CO
MULTNOMAH CO

Side road with various tracks, plus exit to Otto Miller Road

End of hike, 4.24 miles from entry gate

Short trail up to nice vista of Raymond Creek area

4. Gourlay Creek Grade-Line Road

BRIEF DESCRIPTION: This is one of three parallel logging roads traversing the eastern slope of the Tualatin Mountains between Raymond Creek and South Scappoose Creek. I have chosen this particular route because it's the grade-line route, which means that it is generally level (to accommodate the log trucks hauling their heavy loads). This grade-line road passes through younger stands of trees and multiple ravines nearly all the way to Gilkison Road. The road also sports numerous side trails that cross this long expanse of hillside. Consider using a bicycle if you want to reach the southern end of the route and still get back to your car without blisters and exhaustion. Permit required on Weyerhaueser land. Visit www.wyrecreationnw.com.

DISTANCE: 8.5 miles round trip

ELEVATION CHANGE: 634 feet

TRAIL CONDITION: This route follows a well-graveled logging road. It's hard-surfaced all the way and accessible in all weather conditions.

APPROXIMATE DURATION: 4.5 hours

TRAVEL TIME FROM PORTLAND TO TRAILHEAD: 1 hour

DRIVING DIRECTIONS: From NW Portland drive north on US 30 to Scappoose. Turn left just beyond the gas station at the intersection of US 30 and Bonneville Drive. Then take an immediate right onto Old Portland Road, which parallels US 30. After 0.6 miles, turn left on Dutch Canyon Road and follow it west along South Scappoose Creek. Stay on Dutch Canyon Road all the way to the bridge near the road's end (4.6 miles from US 30). Cross the bridge; immediately thereafter the pavement ends. Follow this dirt road (Otto Miller Road) uphill 0.4 miles and park at the second blue gate on the left side of the road.

TRAIL LOG: From the gate (elevation 450 feet) the road descends for 0.33 miles to the Gourlay Creek Bridge, which, at 356 feet, marks the lowest point of the walk. In the spring you can find big-leafed sandworts (*Moehringia macrophylla*) blooming in huge bunches along the creek.

As you cross the creek there is a notable example of logger humor: a collection of ghoulish artifacts attached to a large hemlock tree. When I passed by, there was a "bloody" plastic leg (the kind you buy at a practical joke store) nailed into the trunk. Also dangling from this display was a cast-off antler, a rubber mask, and the obligatory moonshine jug. A big alarm clock was there to remind log-truck drivers that time is crucial when you're trying to deliver as many loads to the mill as possible. Atop this tableau was a pair of knee-high lace-up calk logging boots, leaving no doubt about the provenance of this impromptu artistry.

Just beyond the bridge the road splits three ways. Follow the main road, which proceeds directly up the hill. For the next 1.1 mile this well-worn dirt road gradually climbs out of the Gourlay Creek valley. About 0.75 miles from the bridge a spur road splits off to the left and doubles back to ascend the ridge above this road. About 100 feet before reaching this spur road, you may spot a big patch of devil's club (*Oplopanax horridus*) growing below the shoulder of the road. Note the spiky thorns that adorn the branches. Give devil's club a wide berth for two reasons. First, you want to avoid painful contact with the spikes that cover the stalk and leaves of this plant. Second, this plant does not tolerate human interference well and often takes years to reestablish itself—hence its location where most humans will not venture.

The road climbs steadily, curving back on itself until it crests the side of the Gourlay Creek valley at an elevation of 810 feet. At this point the road splits. One road heads off in a northeasterly direction and eventually links up with a trail along lower Gourlay Creek. The main branch of the road bends to the right and continues to climb the slope, albeit at a much less intense angle.

Follow the main road south another 0.2 miles, gradually climbing to an elevation of 876 feet. Keep to this road as it bends in and out of ravines. A large round boulder alongside the road makes an excellent landmark with which to check your progress: it is 1.8 miles from the blue gate. Continue southward, paralleling the headwaters of Raymond Creek, which flow along the bottom of the slope to the left. The road continues along at a fairly level grade for another 0.7 miles. Here it intersects with a logging road descending off the slope on the right.

Continue on; the road dips into a little valley complete with a small pond and a huge old-growth stump. Flocks of finches like to frequent this sheltered nook, and their gregarious chirping echoes through the forest. The road bends around and emerges onto a long ridge at an elevation of 730 feet. At this ridge intersection, the main track turns left and follows the ridgeline north. Yes, you will be walking north to go south! Eventually, the road turns around and heads south.

An alternative route ascends the hill to the right. Even though the path ultimately peters out, there are several nice viewpoints overlooking the Raymond Creek valley and the eastern face of Dixie Mountain. (Enjoy the

The Gourlay Grade-Line Road traverses the eastern slope of the Tualatin Range.

view, then head back if you want to save yourself the 1.3-mile trip to the end of the grade-line road.) If you're intent on following this traverse to its ultimate end, head north along the aforementioned narrow ridge. The road follows the ridge to its end and then descends to overlook Raymond Creek at an elevation of 500 feet. Finally, the road turns and climbs a small peak to an elevation of 800+ feet, 4.3 miles from the blue gate. When I first came here a few years ago this hilltop was deeply forested and gave me little visibility across Raymond Creek south toward the Vedanta Retreat. Today, the newly barren hill affords good views of the surroundings.

There has been considerable logging in this area, but the upper Raymond Creek watershed seems to still be intact. It is possible to cross over to the Vedanta Retreat by circumventing the knoll and following the ridge upward for about a half mile. Drop off the ridge on the east side and descend to the bottom of the ravine. On the eastern side of Raymond Creek look for any tracks that climb the heavily vegetated hillside. Crossing Raymond Creek entails bushwhacking through 0.75 miles of dense forest with a thick understory, an active creek, and steep, unstable slopes. This bushwhack is not for the fainthearted. I recommend enjoying the long hike to Raymond Creek and back—without overdoing it by engaging in a dubious scramble across this thorny jungle.

A Cautionary Tale and Some Advice

Locally, a story is told of Albert Lange, who walked more or less the same route just described. While out hunting with his two dogs he traversed this mountainous terrain, encountering thick vegetation, ridges, canyons, thickets, fallen trees, and patches of deep snow. Near the end of the day he emerged from this trek at Rocky Point Road, where he met Abe Cornelius, one of the original settlers on Dixie Mountain.

Abe invited Albert to share some food before his long hike back to Dutch Canyon, but Albert demurred. Soon thereafter Albert's dogs treed a coon, which Albert shot and skinned. Later he was also able to kill a deer and dress it near the Sophie Mozee homestead. With light fading and carrying a heavy deer carcass, he now started for home.

When Albert failed to return home that night, a search party tracked his progress through the rough-and-tumble terrain. They found the spot where he shot the deer and from there they followed his tracks toward Dutch Canyon. His movements were now clearly showing signs of fatigue and possible hypothermia. At one point he fell off a log and rolled down the hill. The searchers followed his increasingly erratic journey, and discovered that he'd fallen into deep snow and failed to rise.

It is reported that when the search party finally located him, his dogs had their noses in his armpits, still trying to encourage him to rise. So loyal were the dogs to their dead master that the rescuers had to fight them off before they were able to approach the deceased Albert.

Few among us would be able to traverse such thick wilderness for six to seven miles. But the story of poor Albert goes to show that even the experienced woodsman can succumb to hypothermia, given enough incrementally poor decisions in the wilderness. The woods around here don't look dangerous—there aren't swamps or cliffs, poisonous animals or vicious predators—but once you're wet and cold, hypothermia can kill you just as surely.

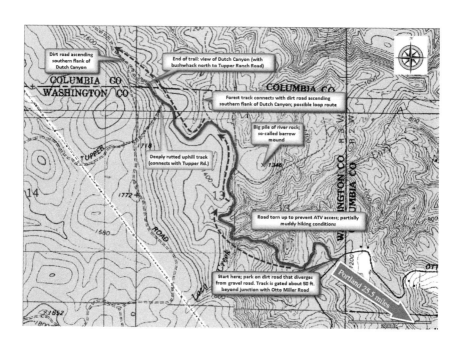

Dirt road ascending southern flank of Dutch Canyon

End of trail: view of Dutch Canyon (with bushwhack north to Tupper Ranch Road)

Forest track connects with dirt road ascending southern flank of Dutch Canyon; possible loop route

Big pile of river rock; so-called barrow mound

Deeply rutted uphill track (connects with Tupper Rd.)

Road torn up to prevent ATV access; partially muddy hiking conditions

Start here; park on dirt road that diverges from gravel road. Track is gated about 50 ft. beyond junction with Otto Miller Road

Portland 25.5 miles

COLUMBIA CO
WASHINGTON CO

COLUMBIA CO

5. Barrow Trail

BRIEF DESCRIPTION: With deep forest vistas and a beautiful view of Dutch Canyon, the Barrow Trail is spectacularly beautiful. The trail traverses the Tualatin Mountains, crossing several creeks, including the aptly named Lazy Creek. In summer it's a feast of huckleberries, thimbleberries, native trailing blackberries, salal berries, blueberries, and even some salmonberries. And in the fall, this area is full of mushrooms. Although it's muddy in wet weather, this trail remains one of my favorites. Permit required on Weyerhaueser land. Visit www.wyrecreationnw.com.

DISTANCE: Approximately 4 miles round trip

ELEVATION CHANGE: 342 feet

TRAIL CONDITION: The trail has been torn up, apparently to discourage the ATV crowd and four-wheel drive enthusiasts. While the heavily carved-up trail makes it virtually impossible for wheeled vehicles to maneuver, the deconstruction degrades the trail marginally from a walker's perspective. But it should be mentioned that the trail can get muddy, with wide puddles; tread carefully to avoid getting your feet wet, or wear waterproof boots!

APPROXIMATE DURATION: 3 hours, 15 minutes

TRAVEL TIME FROM PORTLAND TO TRAILHEAD: 45 minutes

DRIVING DIRECTIONS: From NW Portland drive north on US 30 to Scappoose. Turn left just beyond the gas station at the intersection of US 30 and Bonneville Drive. Then take an immediate right onto Old Portland Road, which parallels US 30. After 0.6 miles, turn left on Dutch Canyon Road and follow it west along South Scappoose Creek. After 4.6 miles (from US 30), turn onto Otto Miller Road at the bridge crossing South Scappoose Creek. Note your odometer reading as you cross the bridge, as it will help you identify the location of the side trail that marks the beginning of the Barrow Trail.

The trail begins as a spur diverging from Otto Miller Road 2.5 miles from the bridge at an elevation of 1,282 feet. The forest road is just above two remote residences that sit atop the ridge surrounded by open pastures and beautiful eastward views. After passing these residences the road runs alongside an upland pasture. At the west end of the pasture the main route enters the forest and turns slightly left to ascend the slope. As you enter the forest, note that there is also a somewhat less traveled track proceeding straight ahead. Instead of staying on the well-graveled Otto Miller Road, follow the side road. Since the track can be muddy during the wetter seasons, park near the intersection with Otto Miller Road.

TRAIL LOG: The hike begins with a gradual descent. After 0.2 miles, you'll pass a yellow gate usually awash in muddy tracks. Cross Lazy Creek (0.4 miles) and climb uphill through a stand of older trees, where you'll encounter the first ditches designed to keep ATV enthusiasts away.

The trail turns abruptly to the southwest and begins weaving in and out of the multiple ravines that cross the eastern slope of the Tualatin Mountains. Most of the trees in this tract are middle-aged stands of Douglas firs and hemlocks. The trail itself is covered with pine duff and moss, and surrounded by Oregon grape, salal, vine maple, and a profusion of huckleberries.

At 0.8 miles into the hike, the trail crosses its last stream. A small pond choked with fallen trees and vine maple spills across the trail route. Cross the pond's outlet by balancing on a pile of small logs. Over the next third of a mile, the trail ascends about 100 feet until it emerges into a small clearing dominated by a huge pile of rocks. This artificial hill reminds me of ancient British burial mounds, which is why I have named this route the Barrow Trail. In reality, it is probably a pile of leftover road-building rock. Skirt the rocks, passing the hillock on the right, and head north on the older forest road that extends past the "barrow."

A few weeks after the first autumn rains these forests break out in successive flushes of mushroom blooms. The early October rains usher in the *Russula* genus—typically reddish in color with wide gills. These mushrooms are utterly devoid of gastronomic appeal since they turn into slime when cooked. Later in October you can expect to see *Lactarius* species, or "milky caps," some of which are worth eating. About the same time various species of *Boletus* will begin to pop up through the duff. Most of these spoil quickly, but if used soon, they can be good for soups. I focus almost exclusively on chanterelles, because they are by far the most delicious. They begin to appear in late October and early November and last until the first frosts bring the mushroom season to a halt.

A short distance past the rock pile, the forest road will arrive at a brutally muddy intersection, where it looks like several gigantic metal monsters have dug deep muddy trenches into the soft earth. Just how anyone can navigate a vehicle through this slough is beyond me.

Stay on the right-hand edge of this spectacular morass. Don't follow the off-highway-vehicle (OHV) tracks uphill, but instead keep angling gently along the slope. Here an older forest road (unscarred by OHV activities) traverses the slope on the older forest road. No doubt our motorized friends

Barrow Trail ablaze with brilliant vine maples.

ignore this short moss-covered roadway, because it ends abruptly at the edge of the tall timber.

Pause at the end of this road to enjoy a panoramic view of upper Dutch Canyon. Rabinski Road cuts midway across the opposite slope. Higher up on that opposing slope portions of the Pisgah Home Road are visible. In the distance, look for Bald Mountain, Buck Mountain, Mount St. Helens, and Mount Adams. Stop to sit on a log and relax; the view can be breathtakingly beautiful, especially in stormy weather when you can watch the forces of nature sweeping up and down the canyon.

The return trip is back along the same road.

Lords of the Lower Columbia River

Prior to the epidemics that swept through this region, no less than sixteen Chinook villages were stretched along the Lower Columbia River from the mouth of the Columbia Gorge down to the Cowlitz River. It was home to more than three hundred thousand Native Americans, of whom more than sixty thousand lived in the vicinity of Sauvie Island. This was the highest population density on our continent north of Tenochtitlán (Mexico City).

With a population density of nearly 3.1 people per square mile, Sauvie Island was the pre-Columbian equivalent of Manhattan.

The tribes who lived along the Lower Columbia had little use for horses, as the forests were far too dense to traverse with the cumbersome horse and, besides, their highways were the rivers and streams that crisscrossed Oregon. The Chinook were often called the canoe Indians since this was their primary way of getting around. In fact, early observers interpreted their short bandy-legged physique as an evolutionary adaptation to this ubiquitous mode of transportation. Though they didn't have horses, the Chinook did accumulate a breed of husky-like dogs whose only apparent purpose was to alert the village to the presence of intruders.

The Lower Columbia Valley and the Willamette Valley were rich in ryegrass, tarweed plants, camas onions, and aquatic wapato plants. Five different species of salmon regularly migrated up the Columbia along with steelhead, cutthroat trout, and smelt. The river was teeming with sturgeon, lampreys, sea lions, seals, and waterfowl, along with a wide variety of shellfish at the coast. Elk, deer, bear, beaver, grouse, raccoon, sea otters, mink, marten, muskrat, and many other smaller mammals were abundant in the surrounding forests and tributaries.

As bountiful as nature may have been, it was still a laborious process to collect adequate supplies of food and firewood, maintain fishing equipment, repair weirs, patch nets, and engage in extensive plant and berry gathering—not to mention the time and effort needed to mount successful hunting sorties. There was plentiful food, but it took extensive and regular attention to ensure that each of nature's bounties was harvested efficiently. The framework within which these benefits and responsibilities were shared was known as Illahee.

It would be difficult to understand the busy Lower Columbia in the pre-contact times without mentioning the pivotal role that the Chinook Indians played. Originally these Salish-speaking people occupied the western slopes of the Rockies in the vicinity of Lake Pend Oreille in northern Idaho. About a thousand years ago, some of these Salish speakers literally drifted down the Columbia, finally coming to rest on the wide sandy shores of the Lower Columbia River.

The Chinook culture and tribal power dominated the Lower Columbia River from a series of villages that lined the river from Willapa Bay, on the coast, to Cathlapotle, a large prosperous village located near present-day Vancouver, Washington. The Chinooks were by far the most advanced cultural and economic force in this region. Anthropologists consider them to be one of the few examples of an advanced hunter-gatherer society. The Chinooks were unique because they were the only tribe able to sustain extensive specialization without ever adopting agriculture.

This was probably due to the fact that the mainstays of the Chinook diet grew all around them. And none of these plants were cultivated in the traditional sense. Rather, the plants were tended, harvested, and even cooked where they grew. Family groups would spend much of the year following the harvest cycle, visiting their hereditary camas patches, wapato ponds, and huckleberry thickets. On their rounds, they would camp in the vicinity of the harvest areas and tend them for several weeks. Underground pit fires were used to cook the camas onions into loaves that could be transported and preserved until winter. It has been estimated that each family harvested nearly twelve acres of camas onions to produce a year's supply of greens for a multigenerational family of five.

PACIFIC COAST TRADERS

The Chinook were consummate traders. They monopolized the trade between the interior populations and the traders plying the Pacific coast. Not only did they act as the middlemen in these exchanges, they even defined the language of trade. Made from a mixture of European languages and Chinook, Chinook [*Wawa*] was the accepted jargon of commerce in the Pacific Northwest.

In the late 1700s, European "coasters" began trading up and down the coast. This increased contact between the southern tribes concentrated near the Columbia River and the more bellicose tribes on Vancouver Island and beyond. The mainly British and American coasters began ferrying slaves northward on behalf of their Native American customers, along with other trade goods purchased from the Chinooks. The flourishing of this slave market was an outgrowth of the increased fur trading along the Oregon coast that helped the Tillamooks and other more aggressive tribes locate potential targets. Given the convenience of transporting groups of slaves on European vessels, the Tillamooks and other native raiders soon picked up the pace of their raids.

The Chinook didn't just handle others' goods; they also specialized in their own assortment of trade goods, including dried salmon, armored cloaks made from elk hide (*clamons*), and waterproof hats. The trade in clamons was very lucrative for the Chinooks. These especially hardened leather vestments could stop arrows and even deflect musket balls. It is reported that when Meriwether Lewis first encountered Chief Comcomly

Overlooking Dutch Canyon and Buck Mountain.

of the Lower Columbia Chinooks he was shaking a spent musket ball out of his clamons—a nice theatrical touch.

ILLAHEE

The Chinook world was made up of a network of kinship-based villages. This tribe's understanding of homeland, as expressed in its concept of Illahee, was not predicated on a physical location, or even a finite amount of enclosed space. The Chinook were surrounded by a network of kinship ties between individuals that reflected varying degrees of familial proximity. This was similar to our conception of family.

It was no more possible to put a boundary around this homeland than it would be to draw a boundary line enclosing your first and excluding your second cousins from your family. Home was a "relative" concept to the Chinookans, not a finite place on a map.

Efforts by the European traders to impose a territorial definition of homeland were frustrated by this non-geographic approach to organizing tribal affiliation. The dramatic die-offs following the waves of pestilence that swept the Lower Columbia exacerbated European efforts to establish territorial assignments. Some tribes were so completely extirpated that not even the memory of their village name survived. Some groups continued to dwindle in their traditional winter encampments; others fled; and some were assimilated into new groupings. But in the face of the 95 percent mortality rate, the essential familial structures collapsed. Tribal memories were lost, and the rhythm of Native American life was so completely uprooted that all prior links existing under the Illahee framework vanished.

David Thompson, the British-Canadian explorer, complained that the Chinook were "bungling blockheads" for not establishing a standardized system for trading or allotting ownership to parcels of land. Apparently each different village priced goods according to their whim, making it more difficult for Thompson to engage in efficient negotiations. The Illahee framework, which allocated usufruct rights so efficiently among the tribal members, was never designed to distinguish geographic rights. The concepts of Illahee and property were mutually exclusive. Resolution of this contradiction was mooted by the almost complete extinction of the Chinookan peoples by the middle of the early nineteenth century.

Between the pressures exerted by this lopsided commercial relationship, the ravages of increasing slave raids, and the disastrous epidemics, the Chinookan population of Illahee shrank from fifteen thousand to fewer than two thousand between 1830 and 1845. At the same time they also lost almost 80 percent of their reservation lands. And today, scarcely anyone has heard of Illahee.

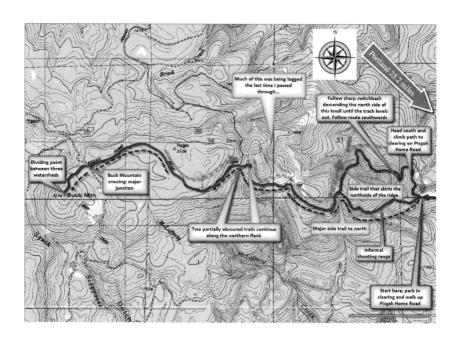

Much of this was being logged the last time I passed through...

Follow sharp switchback descending the north side of this knoll until the track levels out. Follow route southwards

Head south and climb path to clearing on Pisgah Home Road

Portland 25.2 miles

Dividing point between three watersheds

Buck Mountain crossing: major junction

Side trail that skirts the northside of the ridge.

Two partially obscured trails continue along the northern flank

Major side trail to north

Informal shooting range

Start here; park in clearing and walk up Pisgah Home Road

6. Buck Mountain via Pisgah Home Road

BRIEF DESCRIPTION: This trail traverses the north slope of Dutch Canyon using the old Pisgah Home Road, and takes you to the summit of Buck Mountain. The return route meanders down a back trail to reach the car from the north side of the ridge. I rarely encounter anyone along this ridge, and the gradual grade makes it a relaxing walk with lots of panoramic views of Dutch Canyon and the Columbia River.

DISTANCE: 8.15 miles round trip (includes scenic footpath)

ELEVATION CHANGE: About 700 feet, with the highest elevation being the summit of Buck Mountain at 2,137 feet

TRAIL CONDITION: Graveled logging road, some portions with rougher grade stone, but dry and hard all the way. In the winter expect deep puddles, but the base of the road is well rocked so getting stuck is unlikely.

APPROXIMATE DURATION: 5 hours

TRAVEL TIME FROM PORTLAND TO TRAILHEAD: 55 minutes

DRIVING DIRECTIONS: From NW Portland drive north on US 30 to Scappoose. Turn left on Bonneville Drive (opposite the Shell gas station) and immediately turn right on Old Portland Road. Turn left on Dutch Canyon Road, and follow it until it crosses a small creek and turns left (at the intersection with Watts Road). Immediately thereafter turn right onto Mountain View Road, which ascends the hill. (Set your odometer to zero as you begin to climb Mountain View Road.) Follow this road for a bit more than 2 miles; at its intersection with West Road, it turns into Heimuller Road. After another half mile pass the intersection with Smith Road. Continue uphill another 2 miles and turn left onto Pisgah Home Road. The pavement ends about 200 yards onward at the intersection with Grouse Lane. Beyond the pavement this road has large potholes and rocky patches, so drive slowly and stay out of the ruts to spare your car's underside.

Pass a private driveway ascending upward to the right. Shortly thereafter the road passes next to a clearing that spans the breadth of the ridge. The main road begins to climb more steeply here, so I usually choose to park in the clearing, which is 5.75 miles from the bottom of Mountain View Road (0.7 miles from the end of the pavement). Check your odometer to confirm the distance covered. Set your pedometer or initiate your GPS now since the instructions beyond this point will reference this clearing as the starting point.

Caution: There is an informal shooting range near the clearing where I park my car, but the hiking route passes behind the target shooters so their contribution is mainly the noise of gunfire. As is usual with many of these backcountry roads, the chances of encountering target shooters or hunters increases during the fall hunting season, but otherwise it's pretty quiet in these hills.

OUTBOUND TRAIL LOG: I have calibrated the different locations along the route by providing the distance from the recommended parking spot on the ridge. Once you have parked, follow Pisgah Home Road uphill toward Bald Mountain and then to Buck Mountain. The ridge along which this road ascends has seen much recent logging, so many of the paths and game trails that once paralleled the road and led through the forest along the spine of the ridge have been obliterated. Eventually, they may become useful again as the new growth fills in the open spaces. But for now I recommend using Pisgah Home Road and avoiding the side roads, most of which are short tracks providing access to various slopes being logged.

Just beyond the parking spot the road begins to climb more steeply and becomes noticeably rockier. On either side, impenetrable vegetation at least 15 feet tall presses into the roadway. After about 100 feet, the route passes near a shooting range frequented by hunters sighting-in their guns. Unfortunately, this place has been noticeably littered, reflecting poorly on its usual denizens. But just a half mile farther you'll be rewarded by splendid views over Dutch Canyon, with the Columbia River rolling like a wide black ribbon beyond, and mists rising off the Ridgefield National Wildlife Refuge. Take a moment to consider the Columbia River basin spread out before you. What you're looking at was the ancestral home territory of the Chinook tribe, where not so long ago wooden longhouses crowded the shores and canoes crisscrossed the waterways in all directions.

0.75 miles from parking spot: The road curves to the right and in the elbow of that bend be sure to note a small trail heading off in a northeasterly direction. If you want to shorten this hike dramatically, this would be the best way to loop back to your car, using a path that traverses the north side of the ridge.

0.9 miles: Ignore the northern option and continue up the road, past the crook of the bend. Climb out to a big landing that boasts some pretty tremendous views of the Lower Columbia River. Peering far to the east you may be able to spot where the river emerges from the Columbia Gorge and

Eastern end of Pisgah Home Road with Mount Adams in the distance.

the crisp silhouette of Mount Hood looming above it. On the northeastern horizon are Mounts Adams, St. Helens, and Rainier (blocked by the ridge). Directly below, South Scappoose Creek sluices its way down Dutch Canyon. Near the top of that creek, a long ridge blocks the end of Dutch Canyon. This ridge is the spine of the Tualatin Mountains, which begins in Portland's West Hills, climbs through Forest Park, and eventually merges with the maze of coastal mountains that begin just beyond Dutch Canyon.

1.2 miles: Follow Pisgah Home Road past its intersection with Rabinski Road, which climbs up from a lower elevation.

2.2 miles: The road ascends to an elevation of 2,000 feet and then levels out. A spur road on the right leads to a radio tower. The area directly around the radio towers has been recently logged.

"Pisgah Home Road," what an odd name!

The name refers to the mountain from which Moses first saw the Promised Land. But the local story is even more interesting.

Apparently, "Pisgah" also refers to a faith-healing movement started around 1900 by Finis Yoakum at his house in Los Angeles. The home originally housed eight indigent persons. It was founded "to give free care to drunkards and outcasts" who wished to reform. The effort grew into a major social initiative that inspired Good Samaritans as far away as Portland, where "Mother Lawrence" took up the challenge. Hattie Lawrence seems to have copied the Pisgah Home concept when she established a Portland-based Pisgah Home to take care of the "down-and-out old men," and it was said that the Portland police regularly brought her men who had been arrested for drunkenness. Needing a place in the country where her aged wards could do physical labor and restore their health, she acquired a piece of land above Scappoose in 1919. Apparently, she and her "down-and-out" men built an impressive three-story shake-sided building on the logged-off land. It was surrounded by gardens and tended by then men, who hoed and busied themselves with horticulture. In 1937 Mother Lawrence died in a car accident and the social experiment was abruptly abandoned. The only hints of its prior existence are the fruit trees about two miles from the trailhead.

2.3 miles: At a four-way intersection, continue to follow the main track, and proceed toward Buck Mountain. As you emerge from the taller timber you will be crossing the top of the ridge at 2,091 feet.

3.25 miles: The main route heads northward, then bends in a westerly direction, where it soon meets another four-way intersection. This strategic intersection, which I have dubbed the Buck Mountain Crossing, marks the western end of Pisgah Home Road. On this hike you will be approaching the Buck Mountain Crossing from the east. The northern approach road (on the right) links Pisgah Home Road to Bacona Road (see chapter 10). That route also provides access (via Tater Mountain) to the Banks–Vernonia Highway. The road entering the crossing from the south (your left) climbs up from South Scappoose Creek. Directly across the intersection a newer logging road climbs up the denuded hillock, which is all that remains of the once densely forested Buck Mountain. One might say that it has earned its name since it's now "buck naked." The logging road splits a short distance up the barren slope.

From the top of Buck Mountain (elevation 2,096 feet) you're rewarded with a 360-degree panorama. To the west you can see all the way to Saddle Mountain, which overlooks the Pacific Ocean. To the east you can see the Columbia River spilling out of the Columbia Gorge. Most impressive of all is the stalwart army of volcanoes marching evenly spaced across the eastern horizon. At the northern end of this procession, Mount Rainier dominates the environs of Tacoma. To the northeast, Mount St. Helens and Mount Adams rise above the Washington Cascades. Directly to the east, Mount Hood's sharp profile seems more like a surreal icon than the real thing.

Finally, my favorite is the elegant spire of Mount Jefferson rising above the lodgepole pines of central Oregon. Take some time to look around you; this view was entirely obscured when Buck Mountain was fully forested. In time the trees will regrow and eventually this astounding vista will be swallowed up by a new generation of forest. But for now, swallow your disappointment at the devastation that human harvesting has left behind and appreciate the majestic view that has been temporarily bequeathed to us.

But there's more to this peak than meets the eye. As impressive as this panorama may be, it hides a more profound significance.

The summit of Buck Mountain is a natural division that separates three distinct watersheds. This peak forms a triple watershed that separates the rivers flowing south into the Willamette from those that flow eastward into the Columbia River and those flowing west down the Nehalem River and directly into the Pacific Ocean.

As you peer west from Buck Mountain, you will see that a small valley separates Buck Mountain from another mountaintop immediately to the southwest. Between these twin summits is a marshy area from which the first dribbles of water coalesce into the headwaters of South Scappoose Creek, which flows directly into the Columbia River.

On the western edge of this marshy area another tiny rivulet flows westward into Panther Creek, the highest tributary of Dairy Creek. Dairy Creek flows down into the Tualatin Valley near North Plains. Eventually, it joins the Tualatin River, which flows into the Willamette River.

To the north a low line of hills defines yet another watershed. Unlike the water flowing out of the basin below your Buck Mountain perch, the water on the northern slopes of these hills flows into a series of small misty ponds (Gunners Lake). Small streams escape from these shallow pools to feed the northeast fork of the Nehalem River, which eventually flows into the Pacific Ocean at Nehalem Bay.

Stand for a moment and appreciate your surroundings. From Buck Mountain it is possible to peer into the successive green folds of the Coast Range and spot the telltale shape of Saddle Mountain straddling the western horizon. Every local native knew that Saddle Mountain marked the western border of these wild mountains. Below its twin peaks lies the Pacific Ocean. To the east, Multnomah Falls is a distant cleft at the entrance to the Columbia Gorge. These two points are visual icons representing the breadth of the Chinookan homelands. It was a world bounded on the one side by the Pacific Ocean with its seafaring tribes, including the Tillamook, the Tlingit, the Nisqually, and the Clatsop people. On the eastern horizon the Chinook influence diminished as the Gorge closed in and the treacherous rapids of the Columbia River restricted travel into the dry and open lands of the Klickitats and the Nez Perce.

Buck Mountain provides a panoramic view across the entire breadth of Chinookan experience. This remote hillock is an eyrie that presides over a subtle parting of the waters. Tarry awhile and let your essence trickle down Panther Creek and into the gentle waters of the Tualatin. Watch the rivulets combine as they slip down Buck Mountain to splash into Scappoose Creek before swirling out into the mighty flows of the Columbia.

INBOUND TRAIL LOG: The return trip entails mostly backtracking along the route you followed during the ascent. You haven't much time to waste since you have more than 4 miles to go—the distance from Buck Mountain to the car.

4.3 miles: Cross through the four-way intersection and head back down Pisgah Home Road.

7.08 miles: Pass the side trail noted during your ascent. As the road skirts a ravine, a distinct trail disappears into the trees just as the road passes the elbow of the bend. This narrow but well-trodden path is plainly visible heading into the woods.

You can elect to stay on Pisgah Home Road, or if you're feeling adventurous you can explore this alternate route. The narrow footpath will take you down the north face of the ridge. Don't worry that you're now seemingly headed in the wrong direction, because eventually the path will swing back around again and head in a southeasterly direction, returning you to Pisgah Home Road.

7.9 miles: At this point the pathway, descending in an easterly direction, will abruptly make a U-turn and resume its descent heading north. At this U-turn, a somewhat overgrown track joins the path from the right. This side spur looks tempting; it appears to head back to the ridge and Pisgah Home Road on the other side. In fact it does, and I originally used this route, but it's terribly overgrown and tough to bushwhack through. Do not attempt to rejoin Pisgah Home Road using this old logging track; it is far too difficult. Instead follow the main road down a bit farther.

8.15 miles: The pathway widens as it curves around and meets a more substantial track coming up the hill from the left. Turn right and follow this wider track as it heads south. After 500 feet this track splits. Take the right-hand option, which climbs the slope up to the clearing where your car is patiently waiting.

Moonshining on the Lower Columbia River

Usually the banks of the Nehalem River were the very epitome of pastoral peace and quiet, especially down on the old Warren Smith farm near Pittsburg. In particular, the chickens sauntering around their pen in the small clearing beside the Nehalem were very satisfied. Every day they were served a delicious mash that soon had the whole roost clucking contentedly and bumping into each other as they waddled dizzily around their pen. Some had even been known to fall off the ramp leading inside.

But on this particular Monday afternoon in mid-April of 1929, the rooster and his chickens were suddenly interrupted in their usual pursuits when cars began flying down the dirt road with sirens blaring. Several Columbia County police officers, aided by state and federal prohibition officers, exploded out of their cars and began rushing the apparently undefended chicken shack. The chickens temporarily stopped their purposeful examination of the bugs and grubs crawling around their coop. Despite the intoxicating effects of his breakfast mash, the rooster did not have a warm and fuzzy feeling about this unexpected activity. Rising on his toes, he began to wind up to his best and most impressive cock-a-doodle-doo. But Sheriff Weed and Deputy Calhoun, along with their state and federal phalanx, stampeded the chicken shack and all the panicked poultry fled, squawking in confusion.

The prohibition officers, Sheriff Weed, and Deputy Calhoun bounded up the stairs to confront H. W. Dalplian and his son-in-law, Lester McConkey, both of whom were apparently still busy distilling the current batch of moonshine in their 300-gallon Kentucky-style still.

In addition to the considerable distillation equipment found on the premises, the squad also secured another fifteen vats that held more than 2,300 gallons of mash in various stages of conversion into alcohol. They confiscated 50 gallons of yeast, 50 gallons of malt, and several sacks of sugar. The arresting officers also reported that they secured a "considerable quantity" of finished and bottled moonshine in a separate building. There was no estimate of how much market-ready booze they confiscated. Thankfully, no one took note of the chickens' participation in all these shenanigans, and consequently the birds were allowed to remain in their pen—under indefinite detention.

It appears that during the prohibition days of 1916–1933, moonshining was prevalent in the mountainous regions of northwestern Oregon. Unlike their southern brethren, who used corn, Oregon moonshiners used rye and added cane sugar. It was said by some of the more successful moonshiners that this approach produced a better product, and it was quicker—always a consideration when you're trying to stay ahead of the law.

One anecdote tells of an enterprising moonshiner who built his operation into the charred remains of a massive old-growth stump. When it gave off steam during the distillation process, it simply appeared as if the tree was still smoldering. Another entrepreneur built his "store" underneath a bridge on Bonny Slope. From time to time, a car would casually stop on the bridge. The driver would open his door and tap on the wooden planks. A panel would slide open revealing the proprietor. Money would exchange hands as bottles of booze were hoisted aloft.

Aileen Itzen recalled one typical instance in which a moonshiner in Clatsop County was held in the highest regard because of the excellence of the home brew he produced. An overambitious district attorney forced the Clatsop County sheriff to arrest this culprit. Having no choice, the sheriff did his duty, but alongside the newspaper story that announced the arrest there was a lengthy apology by the sheriff for having to arrest the much esteemed moonshiner. In another case, the Clatsop County justice of the peace deliberately shot an elk out of season so that he would be disqualified from having to testify against his neighbor in a pending moonshining investigation.[1]

There were plenty of isolated barns and remote compounds and an abundance of forests in which to hide moonshining all across Columbia County and the northwestern corner of Multnomah County. The Bill Smith gang, with a still on the Multnomah/Columbia County line, dominated most of these operations. In Dutch Canyon, gang members George Davies and "Peanuts" Austin were apprehended operating an 80-gallon still on South Scappoose Creek. According to the arresting officer, the operation was about four miles from Scappoose, located deep in Dutch Canyon. Being a bit averse to unnecessary labor, Peanuts and George made sure that it was possible to easily transfer their illicit goods to cars for immediate distribution. This was probably their undoing since the arresting officer noted the convenience of "an excellent road [that] leads right to the steps of the shack."

Dixie Mountain also had its share of illicit distillers who maintained operations buried deep in the tangled headwaters of Crabapple Creek or Raymond Creek. And there were also several reports of a "six-gun totin' Tessie" who had set up camp behind the Sophie Mozee homestead and was guarding her still with all the caliber she had.

Though we're tempted to romanticize this desperate way of life, we should keep in mind how much this criminalization of liquor heaped misery on the poorest and most marginalized segments of the community. Help of any kind was hard to find for the wives and children left behind when the bootlegging father went to jail. Even the charitable organizations and the county health services were reluctant to help support these indigents, lest their aid be construed as encouragement to those who relied on outlaw income. The typical sentence for a moonshiner (usually the owner of the land) was $500 and a thirty-day sentence. His assistant would just get a $500 fine, but was typically unable to pay, and would end up languishing alongside his boss in the county jail.

Notes

1. Stella Bellingham Satern, *The Nehalem River Valley: Settling the Big Timberland* (Portland, OR: Binford & Mort, 2006), 137–8.

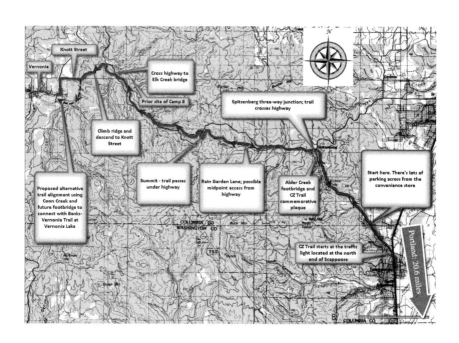

Knott Street

Vernonia

Cross highway to
Elk Creek bridge

Prior site of Camp 8

Spitzenberg three-way junction; trail
crosses highway

Climb ridge and
descend to Knott
Street

Proposed alternative
trail alignment using
Coon Creek and
future footbridge to
connect with Banks-
Vernonia Trail at
Vernonia Lake

Summit - trail passes
under highway

Rain Garden Lane; possible
midpoint access from
highway

Alder Creek
footbridge and
CZ Trail
commemorative
plaque

Start here. There's lots of
parking across from the
convenience store

CZ Trail starts at the traffic
light located at the north
end of Scappoose

Portland: 20.6 miles

7. CZ Trail

Part 1—Scappoose to Spitzenberg junction

BRIEF DESCRIPTION: This road, once privately owned by Crown Zellerbach, parallels the Scappoose–Vernonia Highway. The trail actually goes down to the banks of the Columbia about 2 miles east of US 30, but I have chosen to begin the trail description starting at its intersection with US 30. Initially it runs straight through fields and next to homes before ascending slightly up the slope of the valley. From there it traverses the valley all the way to the westward turn at the Spitzenberg junction about 5.8 miles distant. All this section has been cleared and a new bridge at Alder Creek provides smooth hiking all the way through to the highway crossing at Spitzenberg.

DISTANCE: 5.8 miles one way

ELEVATION CHANGE: 520 feet

TRAIL CONDITION: Mostly hard surface, very gradual ascent

APPROXIMATE DURATION: 2 hours, 15 minutes

TRAVEL TIME FROM PORTLAND TO TRAILHEAD: 30 minutes

DRIVING DIRECTIONS: At the northern end of Scappoose, turn left at the last traffic light and head west on the Scappoose–Vernonia Highway. The Crown Zellerbach (CZ) Trail starts at this intersection and runs parallel to the highway. For the first 2 miles the CZ Trail heads northwest. It skirts fields, crosses a brook, and bypasses occasional homes and trailer parks. At the end of this relatively flat and open landscape the valley narrows. Here you'll find the B&B convenience store, and on the northeast side of the road there is ample parking at the official CZ trailhead. I recommend starting your hike at this point.

SPECIAL ATTRIBUTES: Historical records describe how Elmer Everett Nickerson, one of the early settlers in the Nehalem Valley, took two days to go from St. Helens to Vernonia, probably with a loaded wagon. A note dated November 1891 records Nickerson complaining that the rains had made the trail "almost impassable," a description used liberally in the wet season to express the condition of the rural roads in these mountains. Another report, no more than a month later, described the mud and water as being "nearly boot deep between Vernonia and St. Helens."

In February the following year, an unidentified horseback rider passing through on his way from St. Helens to Clatskanie wrote about the conditions and the communities that he found along the way.

> St. Helens is the only place on the route that had the appearance of a city. You have excellent services and sidewalks clear through the city. In Columbia City the road was recently slashed of brush. Here too was an excellent schoolhouse, an old sawmill, a wood dock, a two-story hotel, some moss-covered tumble down houses and some very neat cottages.

The history of this trail begins in 1906 when Fred and Simcoe Chapman decided to construct a railroad to help them bring their timber to the banks of the Columbia River, from which point it could be transported to market. They constructed a rail line up North Scappoose Creek past Camp 8, a major logging depot. In 1910 they built a 1,712-foot-long tunnel to avoid the excessively steep grades in the upper reaches of the valley that gave them access to the big timber located in the Nehalem Valley.

In 2004, Columbia County purchased the Crown Zellerbach logging road from the Hancock Timber Company with grants from the Oregon Department of Transportation and Oregon State Parks. They planned to ultimately convert it to a hiking trail, which I can happily report is now practically complete.

TRAIL LOG: Just beyond the spacious trailhead, the CZ Trail enters the woods, traversing the northeastern slope of the North Scappoose Creek valley. The trail runs straight up the valley, crossing several side roads as it proceeds through a mixed forest of alder, broadleaf maple, Douglas fir, and hemlock.

A little bit (0.3 miles) beyond Alder Creek, the trail turns west and crosses the Scappoose–Vernonia Highway. Immediately north of the CZ Trail crossing is the junction of the Scappoose–Vernonia Highway and Cater Road. Cater Road leads (via Sykes Road) into St. Helens. On the southwest side of the highway crossing is an open area suitable for parking. This marks the Spitzenberg junction, the end of the Scappoose-to-Spitzenberg segment of this trail.

Part 2— Spitzenberg junction to summit

BRIEF DESCRIPTION: This trail ascends to the summit of the Scappoose–Vernonia Highway from the Spitzenberg junction. The CZ Trail parallels the

CZ Trail descending from the summit near Scaponia Park.

highway most of the way, but toward the summit it diverges from the high-way and travels through coniferous woods with views of thickly forested hills and bucolic farmlands down in the valley. Consider bicycling this trail from top to bottom rather than hiking from the bottom up.

DISTANCE: 5.36 miles one way

ELEVATION CHANGE: 680 feet

TRAIL CONDITION: Gravel road; gentle slope

APPROXIMATE DURATION: 2.5 hours (Riding bikes from the summit to Spitzenberg junction shortens the trip to less than 1 hour.)

Travel time from Portland to trailhead at Spitzenberg junction: 45 minutes

Travel time from Portland to summit trailhead: 55 minutes

DRIVING DIRECTIONS: Take US 30 from NW Portland to the north end of Scappoose and turn left at the last traffic light in Scappoose. Follow the Scappoose–Vernonia Highway from Highway 30 for 6.6 miles to the Spitzenberg junction.

To reach the summit, stay on the Scappoose–Vernonia Highway and travel about 5 miles past Spitzenberg to where the road starts to drop down into the Nehalem Valley. You will pass over a short wooden bridge before coming to a wide junction with a dirt road climbing straight up into the forest. The main road bends to the right and then starts to descend. Park anywhere along the verge of this big clearing. To the north side of the junction, a big pile of rocks prevents ATVs from entering the ramp that leads down to the CZ Trail.

SPECIAL ATTRIBUTES: Much of the CZ Road rests on the Portland and Southwestern Railroad grade originally built by the Chapman brothers to extract their timber from this valley. In time, the Portland and Southwestern Railroad became one of the major timber-hauling railroads operating in the northern Oregon Coast Range. The first train ran in 1906, and the railroad continued to be built in a "log as you go" fashion, reaching Chapman, their main base of operation, around 1910. The Chapman brothers had high hopes to extend the railroad all the way to Nehalem Bay, but the cost of extending the line up to the head of the North Scappoose Valley exhausted their finances and they sold out to Henry Turrish, who took on the task of extending the line into the Nehalem Valley by whatever means possible.

Switchbacks up the eastern slope of the valley were considered, but eventually it was decided to reach the Nehalem Valley by tunneling through the summit. Plans were drawn up in 1918, and the tunnel was bored in 1919. The following year the internal support construction was completed to help shore up the walls and ceiling. The tunnel was quite long—1,712 feet—and it stood 22.5 feet tall and 16 feet wide. The beams that supported the ceiling and walls were 12 by 12 inches, while the "lagging" boards between the beams measured 4 inches by 6 inches. The space above the curved arch of the beams was filled with scrap wood to hold the ceiling rock in place. The material through which the tunnel was bored was not solid rock, but mostly sandstone, so the entire length of the tunnel had to be lined.

In 1926 the Clark and Wilson Lumber Company bought the railroad line. In 1944 the rail line and tunnel were sold to the Crown Zellerbach Corporation. The following year the railroad was officially abandoned and replaced by the CZ Road. Eventually Hancock Timber Company acquired the road and the abandoned tunnel, only to sell it to Columbia County in 2004.

TRAIL LOG: The best way to cover this trail is to start at the summit and walk (or bike) back toward the Spitzenberg junction (5.36 miles). If you want to do a shorter version, ride down to Rain Garden Lane (3.3 miles). In either case, leave another car at the downhill destination. But to maintain consistency with other hikes, this trail log is presented in an east-to-west orientation (going uphill).

The trail is clearly visible from the open area at the Spitzenberg junction. The track soon turns north before resuming its overall westward direction. On the north side of the road several older homes date back to the days of the original logging camps established by the Chapman brothers in the early 1900s. From the north, Cedar Creek flows off of Bunker Hill and passes under the trail near the Chapman settlement. The route now climbs gently up through pastures of lounging cattle.

The trail continues to parallel the road as the route ascends the narrowing valley. About 1.5 miles from Chapman the trail intersects Rain Garden Lane, a small road that serves a cluster of homes at the west end of the valley. Just beyond Rain Garden Lane, pass through a yellow gate. The remaining 3.3 miles to the summit now diverge from the highway, and the views turn from bucolic farm scenes to a nearly mature forest of western hemlock, Douglas fir, and bigleaf maple. Riding this trail in late October is like descending a brilliant yellow avenue.

You will recognize the summit because the path leads directly under the highway. A side trail leads up to the roadway. This is a lovely trail on foot or on a bicycle!

Part 3—Summit to Elk Creek

BRIEF DESCRIPTION: This segment of the CZ Trail descends west from the summit all the way to Elk Creek, where the trail crosses the county road and climbs over the ridge to Vernonia. The trail passes through mostly forested areas with some open areas (e.g., Camp 8) along the way. The hike follows the CZ Road, which has been restored by Columbia County. It will soon connect directly with the Banks–Vernonia Trail, which circles the old millpond in Vernonia.

DISTANCE: 5.54 miles one way

ELEVATION CHANGE: 643 feet

TRAIL CONDITION: Gravel base, slightly descending, with more forest duff near the summit

APPROXIMATE DURATION: 3 hours

TRAVEL TIME FROM PORTLAND TO TRAILHEAD: 55 minutes

DRIVING DIRECTIONS: Take US 30 from NW Portland to the north end of Scappoose and turn left at the last traffic light in Scappoose. Follow the Scappoose–Vernonia Highway from Highway 30 for 11.4 miles (about 20 minutes) to where it starts to drop down into the Nehalem Valley. You will pass over a short wooden bridge before coming to a wide junction with a dirt road climbing straight up into the forest. The main road bends to the right and then starts to descend. Park anywhere along the verge of this big clearing. To the north side of the junction, a big pile of rocks prevents ATVs from entering the ramp that leads down to the CZ Trail.

SPECIAL ATTRIBUTES: By August of 1919 Henry Turrish had completed the tunnel under the Nehalem Divide, but it took another year to extend the western side of the track to the hamlet of Pittsburg. About 2.3 miles from the western portal, a tall trestle was erected and survived into the 1970s. In 1943, Crown Zellerbach acquired the rail line and converted it into a logging road. The tunnel could not be converted for log trucks, so a road was built to cross the summit above the tunnel. The tunnel has fallen into significant disrepair since that time. Entering the tunnel is not recommended. Parts of the tunnel are submerged in stygian pools of indeterminate depth.

TRAIL LOG: There is ample parking at the turnout at the summit of the Scappoose–Vernonia Highway. The ramp down to the CZ Trail begins at the east side of the turnout and drops down to the east of the bridge that carries the automobile traffic on the county road. Once down to the logging road, turn left to pass under the bridge and continue walking west.

The 100-foot-high trestle. The upper elevations of this valley can be absolutely brilliant in early fall. At the base of this valley the trail crosses Hawkins Road. This is also a good midway access point for those who need a shorter (3.1-mile) hike, or who want to double back to the summit, making it a 6.2-mile round trip.

As it runs west down the East Fork Nehalem River, the CZ Trail parallels the county road quite closely. A quarter of a mile east of the Hawkins Road junction is the entrance to Scaponia Park on the southwest side of the county road. Another quarter mile brings you to an idyllic little meadow with a lovely log cabin under a copse of big conifers.

As you approach the meadow, you are walking where the highest wooden trestle built in these parts once stood. This 100-foot-tall wooden edifice remained standing well into the 1970s, when it was torn down during the development of Scaponia Park.

Camp 8. About 2 miles from Hawkins Road or 5 miles from the summit, the CZ Trail enters a flat plain flanked by the mountains on either side. Here the Clark and Wilson Railroad erected Camp 8 to serve as their base camp. Probably built in 1928, the site soon became a burgeoning little town.

Originally, logging companies had housed loggers in railroad cars parked near the logging sites. The companies tightly controlled these railroad-logging camps, and workers could escape their quarters only from Saturday evening through Sunday—if they could afford the trip to town. By the 1920s the companies began to build detached homes where the workers lived in a company-owned community; they commuted to their work sites on the trains that hauled out the wood. In the early thirties loggers were earning about four dollars per day. Grace Brandt Martin, the schoolmistress at the nearby Wilark Camp in 1931, described the typical accommodations:

> The weather-beaten shack that we are to occupy has never
> been painted on the outside, just like all the others I saw
> around the camp. In the small kitchen there is a sink piped
> for cold water and the only places for storing things are a few
> crudely built shelves. The bedroom is about the same size as
> the kitchen, so there is just enough room for a double bed,
> dresser, and my wardrobe trunk. No closet, naturally, but a
> makeshift place to hang clothes has been built in one corner.

Crossing over to Elk Creek. At Camp 8, or at that broad expanse that now remains, leave the main trail that follows the East Fork Nehalem River and cross over the river to the county road, using what remains of an old railroad bridge. Once across the East Fork Nehalem, cross the county road and enter a forest road at the mouth of Elk Creek. This track leads over the ridge to Vernonia.

Part 4—Elk Creek to Vernonia

BRIEF DESCRIPTION: This segment of the trail crosses a long spur that separates Vernonia from the East Fork Nehalem River. There are nice views looking north to Bunker Hill. Currently, the trail drops off the hill at the end of East Knott Street in Vernonia.

DISTANCE: 2.56 miles one way

ELEVATION CHANGE: 465 feet

TRAIL CONDITION: This portion of the trail was still undergoing changes at the time of publication. Plans were being considered to realign the descending trail via the Coon Creek Road and to build a pedestrian bridge at that point to connect with the Banks–Vernonia Trail. This description relies on the existing connection at the end of East Knott Street.

APPROXIMATE DURATION: 1 hour one way

TRAVEL TIME FROM PORTLAND TO TRAILHEAD: This trailhead may be approached from two directions: (1) from Portland via US 26 and OR 47, it's about 1 hour; or (2) from Portland via US 30 and the Scappoose–Vernonia Highway, 1 hour, 10 minutes.

DRIVING DIRECTIONS: Using option 1, drive through Vernonia on OR 47 heading east. At the Pittsburg highway junction turn right onto the Vernonia–Scappoose Highway. Travel 3.3 miles from this turn to reach the junction with the CZ Road. At this eastern end (Elk Creek side), the CZ Trail segment is hard to miss with its wide pull-off area on the south side of the highway and "Elk Creek" signage near the bridge.

Using option 2, approaching the area from Scappoose, you'll find the Elk Creek trailhead 17.4 miles from the start of the Vernonia–Scappoose Highway (at the north end of Scappoose). Alternatively, it's 5.5 miles west of the summit of the Vernonia–Scappoose Highway.

The best access at the western end of the trail (Vernonia side) is the cul-de-sac at the end of East Knott Street, located on the eastern edge of Vernonia. If you're using option 1 and coming via US 26 and OR 47, you'll pass through Vernonia. A bridge crosses the Nehalem just east of Vernonia Lake. Cross the bridge, turn left and head north 0.9 miles. There you turn right onto East Knott Street. Drive to the end of the road to see where the trail follows an old logging road up the ridge. If you're using option 2 and approaching from the east, East Knott Street is 3.5 miles from the Pittsburg junction. It's a straight gravel road on your left.

SPECIAL ATTRIBUTES: There are plans under discussion to divert the trail from its current alignment with East Knott Street to a more southerly point that can be directly connected to the Banks–Vernonia Trail, which runs along the other side of the Nehalem River. Instead of descending from the wooded ridgeline onto East Knott Street, the trail would turn south and reach the Nehalem River at its junction with Coon Creek. The county is studying how a bridge at this location might expand the network of regional trails by tying these two long-distance trails together with the proposed Salmonberry River Trail, effectively tying a giant circle around the broader northwest environs of Portland.

TRAIL LOG: Approaching Elk Creek on foot from the north, you will enter a vast clearing. Cross a flat area north of the river, the former site of Camp 8. Wild grasses dominate a wide expanse dotted with bushes and rock outcroppings. Hug the main track to find the bridge over the East Fork Nehalem River. It's about 5.42 miles from the summit. On the south side of the Nehalem, the road crosses a meadow and emerges onto the Scappoose–Vernonia Highway. Across the way, on the south side, is the familiar wide shoulder and a yellow gate. Beyond is a new bridge crossing Elk Creek. After crossing Elk Creek (elevation 650 feet) the road hugs the hillside, twisting southward and westward for 1.2 miles as the route passes through middle-aged conifer stands to the summit at 1,115 feet elevation. To the north are views of seemingly endless woodlands. A bit more than an eighth of a mile onwards you will encounter a three-way split in the road.

At the summit, pass another spur road heading north along the ridgeline (it heads down to Pittsburg). Continue on the main road until you come to a three-way split; turn right and continue to follow the gravel road. You will pass two more spur roads leading off to the right (northward). Take the second spur road, 2 miles from the Elk Creek Bridge. This marks the beginning of a sharp descent to East Knott Street. At 2.5 miles you will arrive at the end of East Knott Street in Vernonia.

Kerfuffle in the St. Helens Schoolyard

When Judge McBride became the St. Helens schoolmaster in 1866, the school was a low-slung log cabin located alongside a swamp which, according to the pupils, "was prolific of green slime, mosquitoes and ague."

At the time, St. Helens had only about seven families, which meant that many of the children walked in from the surrounding wilderness. The Knox family sent over their contingent of pupils from Sauvie Island by skiff. Both the Perry kids and the Watts children hiked down from their homesteads—always accompanied by a large dog designed to keep any curious cougars at bay. Given the small amount of land that had been tamed by that time, it was not uncommon to encounter Oregon's big cats, and the early settlers relied on big dogs to protect themselves and their families from these predacious cats.

But once arrived at school, the dogs were kept in the schoolyard where they spent their time engaged in ferocious contests of growling, brawling, and otherwise making such a ruckus that it was all but impossible to keep the children engaged with their schoolwork. Judge McBride had never allowed such uncouth behavior in his court, nor was he about to tolerate it by canines in his school. So he finally responded to the mayhem with a decree that he conveyed homeward with the children. From that day forth all the dogs were to stay at home and not accompany the children to their school.

But that did not sit well with the families whose residences lay beyond the fringe of the forests, and whose youngest now had to brave the journey without their trusted canine minders. The outcry was immediate and unconditional; they would not abide by the prohibition since it put the lives of their children at considerable risk. While the immediate environs of St. Helens were relatively free of dangerous animals by that time, the situation was quite different for the outlying residences. For the homesteaders, cougars were a constant threat to their livestock, their pets, and their children. This uneasy coexistence of mountain lions and people was not ameliorated by the cats' unnerving tendency to track humans—a phenomenon that endures into the present day.

For a week, the battle raged. McBride thundered outrage and demanded a suitably contemplative and uninterrupted atmosphere in which to conduct his instruction, and the dogs continued to attend school with undiminished pugilistic fervor. But just when McBride thought things couldn't get worse, the yowls and growls escalated into a crescendo. All hell had broken loose outside! Everyone rushed out the door to find the dogs ranged all around a giant cedar that grew from the center of the schoolyard and towered over the rustic cabin. McBride and his students came to a sudden stop as they followed the dogs' rapt attention to the drama unfolding overhead. There, directly over the roof of the little school, hung a huge black bear.

There was no getting around the situation, so Judge McBride marched down the hill to the nearest farmhouse, borrowed a rifle, and promptly dispatched the bear, which landed at the front door of the school. The issue of dogs attending school was never mentioned again.

Postscript: Despite numerous encounters since the days of the pioneers, no human has ever been killed by a wild cougar in Oregon.

CZ Trail.

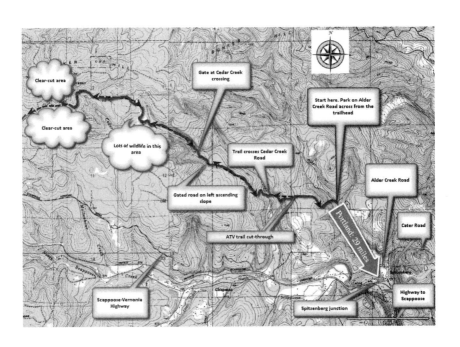

Clear-cut area

Clear-cut area

Lots of wildlife in this area

Gate at Cedar Creek crossing

Start here. Park on Alder Creek Road across from the trailhead

Trail crosses Cedar Creek Road

Alder Creek Road

Gated road on left ascending slope

Cater Road

ATV trail cut-through

Portland: 29 miles

Scappoose-Vernonia Highway

Highway to Scappoose

Spitzenberg junction

HIKING FROM PORTLAND TO THE COAST

8. Bunker Hill

BRIEF DESCRIPTION: From the beginning, settlers in the Nehalem River basin had recognized that the best route in and out of the Nehalem Valley was along the slopes of this ridge and then down into the hills above the Columbia River. This trail traverses Bunker Hill from east to west and concludes near the crest of Bunker Hill. It comprises almost 5 miles of ups and downs, ins and outs, clear-cuts and tall stands of timber. Permit required on Weyerhaueser land. Visit www.wyrecreationnw.com.

DISTANCE: 4.67 miles, one way

ELEVATION CHANGE: 1,094 feet. A swift rise and fall at the beginning, but most of the route is gently inclined as it rises toward the summit of Bunker Hill.

TRAIL CONDITION: Mostly smooth logging roads with a short stretch of ATV trail used as a connector

APPROXIMATE DURATION: 2 hours, 15 minutes

TRAVEL TIME FROM PORTLAND TO TRAILHEAD: 50 minutes

DRIVING DIRECTIONS: Take US 30 north to the northern end of Scappoose and turn left to follow the Scappoose–Vernonia Highway for 5.8 miles. Turn right onto Cater Road and follow it for 0.34 miles. Turn left onto Alder Creek Road, heading west. Reset your odometer and take this paved country road past several cute rural cottages and small farms. After 0.9 miles the road splits; take the left-hand option. Continue until you've driven 1.08 miles. Here you will encounter a gated spur on your right, and another slightly farther on, also to your right. Park anywhere that doesn't block traffic.

SPECIAL ATTRIBUTES: These Columbia County heights support a wide variety of wildlife, including plentiful deer and occasional elk, cougar, and bear. I have not seen any of the latter two species here, but have observed their tracks. This trail is the northernmost trail described in this book. It abuts a large tract of wilderness along the southern shore of the Columbia River so it's reasonable that our more reclusive neighbors have taken shelter in those remote areas. Although not described in this volume, there are plenty of unique destinations in these northernmost forests, including Camp Wilkerson, Carcus Creek Falls, Northrup Creek, Wickiup Mountain, and the old pioneer trail up Fishhawk Creek to Woodson.

TRAIL LOG: The trail begins at the parking spot located on Alder Creek Road. Instead of going up the track heading to the right, cross the road and begin to ascend the older gated logging road that heads up the hillside in a westerly direction.

This road appears to be an old railroad alignment, judging from the grade and the wide gradual curves. The rock underfoot is large, but its solidity has preserved this path during an intervening century of infrequent use. At the end of this stony causeway the track seems to evaporate, but if you look carefully you will see an ATV trail cut through the alder grove flourishing at the end of the road. Follow this twisted path through the alders for just a few minutes and emerge on another logging road that approaches from the opposite direction. Follow that dirt road downhill. At the bottom, a local roadway crosses the route. Cross this intersection and reenter the forest; then cross Cedar Creek. The junction with Cedar Creek Road is 1.13 miles from the start of the hike.

From there it is easy to follow this forest road. Occasionally, pickup trucks or other high-clearance vehicles will travel along this route, but encounters with others are rare. Eventually, 2.17 miles from the starting point, this forest road emerges into a recently harvested area. A road leading off to the left connects with a logging road network linking these roads directly to the Scappoose–Vernonia Highway. But our route avoids this option; continue on the main track (leftish bend). At about 2.36 miles into the hike, the trail will turn in a northerly direction, re-crossing Cedar Creek. A yellow gate keeps unwanted vehicular tourism at bay.

Immediately through the gate turn left and follow the dirt track up the gradual slope. This is a remote region with virtually nothing beyond it except for mountains and thick forests. So keep your dogs close. In general, dogs are an excellent way to repel bears. However, I am concerned that my dog might inadvertently flush a bear and/or its cubs, and I don't relish the thought of having a mother bear barreling down the trail at me. Nevertheless, despite my acute awareness of bear country, I have seldom encountered bears on my solitary hikes. I try to make lots of noise when I am in doubt about who's around. Keep your dog close and the dog will most likely bring it to your attention if there are any interlopers in the vicinity.

In 2013, I was walking quietly up Cedar Creek when I spotted fresh cougar tracks not far in advance of me. It was a bit eerie to know somewhere out there was a large cat keeping his eye on me. Some people think that a gun is the answer to every threat; in this case having my dog along was more than enough to dissuade any petulant cat or bear.

After 3.6 miles, the road passes by a spur road that bends off to the right, dropping down into a small dell. This intersection is near the summit

Mount Hood as seen from Buck Mountain.

of the climb. There are often deer afoot in this area. Bypass the spur road and continue on up until you come out at the edge of a larger, older clear-cut (3.72 miles) that is still cropped enough to allow you to see the large basin sloping up the hill to the west right under the brow of Bunker Hill. A spur road leads off to the left, and another on the right is discernible through the growing understory of bushes. Keep following the main trail, which winds its way through this older clear-cut and up the slope. As the road approaches the western end of the basin, there remains a small copse of trees on the right side of the trail (4.45 miles). Hidden among the trees is a small woodland pool that was a favorite swimming spot for my previous Siberian husky. Like her predecessor, Zoe now recognizes the spot and takes the opportunity to soak for a few minutes in this shadowy pool.

Just a little farther along, the road comes to a three-way intersection. Not so long ago this juncture in the forest (4.67 miles) was an idyllic sylvan glade. Sometime during 2013 this shady intersection ceased to exist. Now the area is stripped of vegetation. Gone are the stately conifers amid the deeply scented forest shadows. The transformation can be quite shocking, even for a veteran hiker. The first time I hiked this trail after the logging companies had been through, I couldn't recognize the spot. I stood in a sunbaked, dusty intersection in the middle of a huge clear-cut for several

minutes until the memory of the previous cool mountain glade slowly fil-
tered back. As I oriented myself, I remembered the vanished trees that had
crowded overhead. It was the same place; but it wasn't.

To continue on to the Bunker Hill summit, continue west. From here,
this road is called Tunnel Road. To reach the summit at 2,082 feet in elevation, take a right turn about a half mile from the three-way intersection just
described. Climb up the slope and veer to the left to follow a logging road
westward along the ridgetop. This hilltop is the summit of Bunker Hill, 5.82
miles from Alder Creek Road, where you left your car.

The return trip is simply the reverse of the outbound sequence.

A Perilous Country

Veterans of the Civil War emigrating to the West were finding that the
prime real estate along the banks of the Willamette and Columbia rivers
had already been snapped up. So some of the more venturesome homesteaders began scouting out land on the far side of the Tualatin Mountains,
principally in the Nehalem Valley. Sidney Wood, who in 1856 put his family and all his worldly possessions on a boat and rowed four miles up into
Westport Slough, established the earliest route into the valley. It came to
be known as Wood's Landing, or more recently, Woodson.

What really put this backwater homestead on the map was the nearby
Indian trail that ran over the mountains into the Nehalem Valley. Following
Olson Creek over a low saddle, the pioneers could descend Fishhawk Creek
to its confluence with the Nehalem River. Word got out, and soon settlers
began to show up at Wood's establishment looking for the "easy" route
into the valley. From Portland, it took a day to travel down to Wood's
Landing by steamer. Staying overnight at the Woods' home, the prospec-
tive settlers would then depart over the eight-mile trail into the valley.
Typically, the families would stay behind, and the settler would return to
fetch them with a team of oxen and a cart.

Everything that came into and went out of the Nehalem Valley was
carried, often by people. In the summertime, it was not uncommon for the
farmers to milk their cows after supper and then strap on a pack board to
carry the butter to Wood's Landing, a distance of more than nine miles.

Two fellows making this crossing once drove a pregnant sow over the
Woods' trail. Following the footpath into the valley was not too difficult,
but persuading their bulging companion to bushwhack through the

undergrowth proved quite impossible. This was soon solved as a neighbor neatly dropped three cedar trees into the river and proceeded to assemble a raft, complete with a little corral to hold the pig. Eventually, the intrepid settlers continued their journey rafting down the gentle Nehalem with their porcine princess regally basking on her floating sty. Within weeks she had given birth to a healthy litter of piglets, meaning the settlers now had something of value to sustain them through the next winter.

My favorite anecdote about the Woods' hospitality involved a visit by a Nehalem Valley resident who stopped by to enjoy a drink or two. Eventually, his consumption far exceeded that estimate and the pioneer was no longer able to walk. The solution to this problem was simple in those days. The unconscious guest was carried out to the sledge he had arrived on, the horses were turned to face the trail, and with a slap on the rump they were encouraged to drive themselves home. Unfortunately, as this scene was unfolding, Mother Nature was delivering a massive snowstorm that not only covered the trail, but also uprooted trees all through the Tualatin Mountains, effectively severing many of the narrow tracks through the wilderness. Sure enough, one of these massive trees fell right across the roadway, blocking the horses' progress. The horses stopped and waited for further instructions, which were unfortunately not forthcoming from the unconscious passenger. He eventually awoke, nearly frozen to death. A few hours later he reappeared at Wood's Landing somewhat distraught at having awoken deep in the forest covered by a foot of newfallen snow. With another liberal application of whiskey the near-death experience was forgotten, and eventually the pioneer was able to secure the help he needed to clear the route of downed trees.

By the 1870s the increased homesteading in the Nehalem Valley made it obvious that a more direct route was needed to St. Helens, the county seat where all the homesteads were recorded. In the spring of 1879 the pioneers mobilized fifty men to cut a road sixteen miles from Pittsburg to Bunker Hill. The men supplied their own provisions and camped along the route. Another group was organized from the St. Helens side, and on June 1879 the two groups met at Bunker Hill.

Exactly six months later, a torrential rainfall turned these slopes to mud. The subsequent midwinter storm ravaged the north coast and caused horrific damage to the forests, especially along the route of the recently completed road to St. Helens. When the surveyors returned from assessing the storm damage they were grim faced. The cyclone had dropped more trees across the new road than had originally been cut for the road, and this in the midst of heavy snowfall! It took a repair expedition several days to finally cut their way through. Unfortunately, their relief provisions, coming from St. Helens, got stranded near Yankton. The struggling axmen shivered through several more hungry days and nights to finally break through. The local postman, caught in the same deluge, resorted to shooting the locks off the mailbags and warming himself over a fire stocked by a continuous supply of handwritten correspondence.

By the early 1900s a mining operation had been established on Bunker Hill. Not much is known about the mine except that one day two miners were walking along Bunker Hill Road to return to their diggings. Noticing marks alongside the track that indicated something being dragged into the woods, they followed the bloody trail until they came upon the corpse of a man lying concealed behind a log. Since no one seemed to know the deceased, a coroner's jury was assembled and the circumstances were investigated. It transpired during the course of the investigations that the unfortunate man was Joseph Schulkowski, a homesteader who had been on his way to St. Helens to prove up on his homestead.

In order for a homesteader to acquire the 160 acres allotted by the Homestead Act, applicants had to "prove up" that they had built a home, made improvements, and lived on the land for five years. Once these improvements were established they were entitled to take ownership of the allotment. It seems that the unfortunate Mr. Schulkowski was on his way to do just that. While the homesteader had been building his shelter, he had taken refuge with his neighbor, John Schieve. And it was from John Schieve's house that he had set forth on his trek into St. Helens.

Schieve was questioned about the circumstances of their parting. Inconsistencies in the account bothered the coroner's jury. Where was the deceased's money belt, which he was known to carry? Who had rifled his pockets? Ballistic evidence matched the bullet found in Schulkowski's body to the rifle Schieve owned. Horsehairs matching that of Schieve's horse were also located at the murder site. It took the jury fourteen hours to find Schieve guilty in the first degree, and he was hanged on July 2, 1902.

This would be the only hanging to occur in Columbia County, ever.

Cyclists on BV Trail.

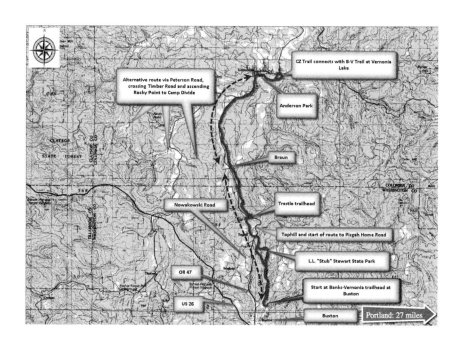

CZ Trail connects with B-V Trail at Vernonia Lake

Alternative route via Peterson Road, crossing Timber Road and ascending Rocky Point to Camp Divide

Anderson Park

Braun

CLATSOP STATE FOREST

Nowakowski Road

Trestle trailhead

Tophill and start of route to Pisgah Home Road

L.L. "Stub" Stewart State Park

OR 47

Start at Banks-Vernonia trailhead at Buxton

US 26

Buxton

Portland: 27 miles

9. Banks–Vernonia Trail

BRIEF DESCRIPTION: The Banks–Vernonia Trail (B-V Trail) runs 24 miles from the rural community of Banks in Washington County all the way to Vernonia, located in Columbia County. The forested hillsides here are a delight in any season, and it's a popular year-round bike trail. This description of the B-V Trail begins at the Buxton trailhead, 6.5 miles northwest of Banks. The main reason for this shortened version is that the first few miles of the B-V are mostly flat and as straight as a ruler. This stretch is OK on a bike, but tedious on foot.

Planning documents issued by the state agencies involved in the construction of the Salmonberry Trail suggest that connector trails will link it to the B-V Trail, which traverses the same slope, but at a higher elevation. Separately, a connection to the CZ Trail is planned along the eastern side of Vernonia Lake, with a bridge spanning the Nehalem near the bottom of Coon Creek.

DISTANCE: 15.84 miles from Buxton trailhead to Vernonia, including one full circuit of Vernonia Lake

ELEVATION CHANGE: 1,000 feet

TRAIL CONDITION: The route is mostly paved. With the numerous trailheads along the way, it is easy to enjoy the trail in bite-sized segments. It is ideal for family outings, especially on bicycles. The slope is very gradual, except on the northbound descent from Tophill down to OR 47. For young, inexperienced bike riders, this downhill stretch can pose a challenge. For most riders this is a perfectly normal downhill stretch. A soft shoulder along much of the trail caters to equestrians.

APPROXIMATE DURATION: On foot, 5 hours; cycling, 3 hours

TRAVEL TIME FROM PORTLAND TO TRAILHEAD: 35 minutes

DRIVING DIRECTIONS: Travel west on US 26 for 25.5 miles from the Sylvan exit (Exit 71B). Turn right onto Fisher Road, just past the Apple Valley airfield. Take Fisher Road north 0.7 miles; as it emerges from the small cluster of buildings that comprise the once-bustling village of Buxton, the road bends slightly to the right, becoming Bacona Road. Proceed along Bacona Road for another 0.6 miles and turn right into a trailhead area with gravel parking and an old railroad shed. Walk a dozen yards south to reach the railroad bed as it proceeds northward. A word of caution: readers of my Foresthiker.com website have alerted me that the Buxton trailhead has experienced frequent car break-ins. (It's set back from the main road and is less visible to passing traffic.) If you're concerned about pilferage, park at the Manning parking lot alongside US 26.

SPECIAL ATTRIBUTES: The Spokane, Portland and Seattle Railway branch line, on which this 21-mile trail was constructed, was originally laid down between 1919 and 1922. It hauled timber from deep within the Tillamook State Forest using widely distributed collection points on Rock Creek, in the Wilson River drainage, and from encampments along the Salmonberry River such as Cochran, Enright, and Belding. For almost forty years as much as $1 million of timber was extracted per year using this line, but by the 1950s the forests had been completely harvested and/or burned and the railroad line was closed in 1973.

TRAIL LOG: I have chosen to begin the trail description at the Buxton trailhead (mile 7) instead of the Manning trailhead (mile 3), or the Banks trailhead (mile 0), because I find the hilly portion of this trail to be more interesting than the long, straight stretches between Banks and Buxton. The mileage indicators used for this trail description start in Banks and are consistent with most other published accounts of this route. The orientation of this description is from south to north, ending in Vernonia.

Buxton trailhead. Warnings are posted at the Buxton trailhead about bear and cougar sightings. It is unlikely that you will see either of these woodland denizens. Bears and cougars have apparently been using this corridor to travel in and out of the Nehalem Valley for some time. As early as 1873, when the Salem–Astoria Military Road was being constructed, the records mention a "scarey camp" near Buxton, where tremendous storms and panthers kept the surveyors awake all night long.

From the Buxton trailhead (milepost 7) to the entry road into Stub Stewart State Park is about 3.5 miles. An alternate route diverges from the main trail a bit more than 2 miles from Buxton. The main trail from Buxton exhibits a very gradual climb, rising 634 feet over the 3.5 miles to the park. Much of the trail parallels OR 47 as it climbs the valley and ultimately leads over the top of the ridge and down into the Nehalem Valley. The well-maintained and paved B-V Trail passes through a thickly forested hillside and along tall railroad embankments and trestles that cross the frequent ravines. Arriving at the entrance to Stub Stewart State Park, the trail crosses the paved access road leading to the park.

Stub Stewart State Park. To access this trail directly from Stub Stewart State Park, park at the Welcome Center and walk or bike down to where the trail crosses the park entrance. A number of trails from the park connect with the B-V linear trail in this section, including the Horseshoe Trail.

Buxton trailhead for the Banks–Vernonia Trail.

To continue on toward Vernonia follow the trail north to Tophill, located at the summit of these hills. About 0.75 miles from Stub Stewart, the trail passes over the Nehalem Highway (OR 47) on a narrow footbridge. A third of a mile onward the trail crosses Nowakowski Road, a potential link with the proposed Salmonberry Trail. The graveled B-V Trail proceeds across Nowakowski Road and climbs to the crest (elevation 1,000 feet), then drops 200 feet to reach the Tophill trailhead, located just north of the old railroad trestle that towers over the highway. Note that this downhill stretch, though insignificant for any regular bike rider, may prove difficult for those inexperienced with downhill bike riding.

This trestle is of significance geologically because the cliffs at either end harbor rich fossil deposits from the Oligocene epoch, including fossil crinoids. This is one of twelve sites noted in a 1957 Department of Geology and Mineral Industries report on fossil-bearing locations around US 26.

Tophill trailhead. The Tophill trailhead, just north of the trestle, is at the boundary of the Tualatin River watershed and the Nehalem River watershed. The hill at Tophill also marks the transition out of countryside traditionally occupied by the Calapuyan Indians, who dominated the Willamette Valley. The Upper Nehalem was lightly visited by the Clatskanie Indians. The Clatskanies were mainly hunters, but they also benefited from the active salmon runs on both the Clatskanie and Nehalem Rivers and the abundance of berries on the hillsides. The Calapuyans and the Clatskanies burned parts of these valleys every few years to encourage revegetation, which attracted deer and elk and kept strategic pathways open through what otherwise would quickly turn into an impenetrable jungle.

The Clatskanie Indians
The Clatskanies had a fierce reputation, and they appear to have forced tribute from travelers passing through their stretch of the Lower Columbia. The men of the Hudson's Bay Company who established the first outposts on Sauvie Island considered them so dangerous that they would not pass down the Columbia in groups of fewer than sixty armed men. Indeed, it is reported that the Clatskanies had planned to attack Lewis and Clark in Fort Clatsop, but were thwarted at the last minute by the Clatsops, who came to the explorers' rescue. In 1810, Captain Nathan Winship tried to establish the first settlement in Columbia County, but attacks by the unfriendly Clatskanies, as well as flooding, forced him out. Originally, the first settlers that entered the Nehalem Valley and the Westport area found Chief Chewan presiding over a community of several hundred Clatskanies. Soon thereafter, epidemics reduced their numbers into the single digits and the survivors fled north to be adopted by another tribe.

The word *Clatskanie* was used by these Native Americans to signify a place where people lived alongside swiftly running water. The fact that this moniker might apply to several communities alongside swiftly flowing streams eluded early Caucasian mapmakers. This is why a river near Astoria is also called the Klaskanine River. By this same logic, alien mapmakers in the future might name all our large metropolitan areas as "Downtown."

From the Tophill trailhead the route crosses to the east side of OR 47 and, after a couple of ascending zigzags, resumes its nearly level run along the hillside for just over 4.5 miles. Along the way it crosses McDonald Road. Second-growth Douglas fir, hemlock, bigleaf maples, alders, and the ubiquitous vine maple populate the hillside. Trillium, Oregon grape, and (in the late fall) mushrooms abound.

Beaver Creek trailhead to Vernonia Lake. This last segment of the B-V Trail, between the Beaver Creek trailhead and Vernonia, is practically flat. The trail initially runs through the woods, but then it parallels OR 47 into Vernonia. The B-V Trail goes through Anderson Park and continues on to form a short loop (3.4 miles) that encircles what was originally the log pond for the Oregon-American Lumber Company, now known as Vernonia Lake.

A footbridge over the Nehalem to connect to the CZ Trail is being considered—possibly near the mouth of Coon Creek.

Grange Dances

By now our pathway into the Coast Range has begun in earnest. We have passed the last skinny valleys snaking into the increasingly crowded mountains. Life in these remote valleys and villages could be lonely, and having a place for the extended community to meet was hugely important. At the grange, families gathered, loves were won and lost, rivalries thrived, and stories were traded through the long nights. The grange was a social landmark that served a vital purpose for rural settlers.

The national movement that helped to establish the network of rural granges across this nation was founded in 1867, after the conclusion of the Civil War. The country's agriculture was in dire shape, and farmers were desperately needed to rebuild and to pioneer the lonely stretches of the frontier. The Oregon State Grange was soon established to help rural communities work together more effectively.[1] The grange movement consistently supported technological improvements for the small farmer. They stood for better roads, flood control, and rural electrification. But there was another side of the grange that was just as important. The granges also encouraged the enlivenment of the local community by throwing unforgettable country dances!

It is difficult for many of us to understand the isolation of the rural Oregonians who pioneered remote homesteads in the Coast Range or the Nehalem Valley. They rarely got to see their neighbors, who might live fifteen to twenty miles away through dense forest inhabited by cougars, feral pigs, and bears. Visiting took determination and stamina and sometimes required an overnight stay. Social life was hard to sustain when the roads were hip deep in mud, the skies were dumping oceans of water, and a foggy half-light persisted from dawn to dusk.

The establishment of a grange hall was considered quite an accomplishment and a validation of a community's advancement from a collection of bachelor flats to the foundation of a new town. In fact, there was considerable rivalry between the citizens of Vernonia and those of Yankton about who built the first grange in Columbia County. The opening of a local grange was a big deal and was celebrated all along the Lower Columbia.

In 1915, when Beaver Homes (sometimes referred to as Redtown) opened its grange, "an excursion boat was run down from Portland. On it was a piano, and a full orchestra, horses and hacks to supplement the company's rigs and a crowd of celebrators bent on dedicating the hall in dancing."

Most of these country dances went all night long, not simply because dancers had the stamina to do so, but because an earlier finish would have resulted in people trying to walk home through dark cougar-infested forests dressed in their best party clothes—so they simply stayed and danced until dawn. Many a latecomer was guided to the grange by the raucous sounds of the fiddle piercing the pitch-blackness of the night. And as one approached the two-story structure, warm light glowed from its many windows and the commotion of the enthusiastic dancers could be heard right to the edge of the forest.

The stairs going up to the dance hall were lined with muddy overshoes, lanterns, and the occasional nosebag full of oats for a horse's trip home. The evening having already progressed, most of the younger children were down for the count. All around the hall, they slept curled into armchairs, stretched out on benches, or nestled in piles of lap robes and coats. Like such events the world over, the festivities would have started before the onset of darkness, with the fiddler warming up, the boys screwing up their courage, and the young ladies eyeing their prospects across the room. A fresh coat of wax on the floor ensured that the younger crowd was soon spinning and twirling on the slippery surface.

Away from the energetic exertions of the unattached, the older women gathered around the tables filled with cakes and pies, home-baked bread, and locally famous delicacies that appeared only once a year at this event. Tucked away from the dance floor and just beyond earshot of the women, the men hunkered down to some serious poker fueled by an ample stock of buttons reserved for this purpose. At midnight there was a break when the ladies served a feast of cooked ham, buns, pies, cakes, and pickles, washed down with lots of coffee—all for a dollar per family![2]

After dinner, they'd put down another layer of wax and announce, "This will be the ladies' choice." Out from the kitchen stormed the matrons, just in time to catch their husbands, who were attempting a mass exodus to avoid the inevitable. All the wives and sweethearts would grab hold of their men, while the unattached girls would rush any boys who could actually dance.[3] The others then sought out any uncle or neighbor to dance a quadrille with a "right and left through," or "circle eight with a full allemande." Now the pace would pick up and the fiddler would strike up a Paul Jones or a feisty tag-waltz. Even the old-timers would get pulled into the vortex by their beaming wives, and soon all were immersed in the exuberantly whirling dance.[4]

But woe betide those who tried to drink alcohol, for these affairs were entirely sober. And if you got caught, you were not just expelled from the dance, but were also likely to lose your job on the morrow.

Today, the granges still operate under similar circumstances. Pinochle, bunco, and bingo are prominent on their calendars, and many still hold social events several times a year. One of my favorite annual events is the Strawberry Shortcake Festival put on by the Dixie Mountain Grange every year on Father's Day. Complete with a kaleidoscope of handmade quilts for sale, red gingham tablecloths, and kids tending to the tables, this event reminds us of how we used to live in small, tight-knit communities, before the Internet came to our rescue.

Notes

1. *Columbia County History*, vol. 1 (St. Helens, OR: Columbia County Historical Society, 1961), 52.
2. *Columbia County History*, vol. 2 (St. Helens, OR: Columbia County Historical Society, 1962), 53.
3. *Columbia County History*, vol. 12 (St. Helens, OR: Columbia County Historical Society, 1973), 18, 22.
4. *Columbia County History*, vol. 6 (St. Helens, OR: Columbia County Historical Society, 1966), 20.

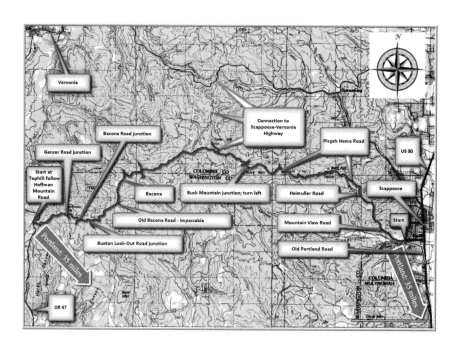

Vernonia

Bacona Road junction

Genzer Road Junction

Connection to Scappoose-Vernonia Highway

Pisgah Home Road

US 30

Start at Tophill: follow Hoffman Mountain Road

Bacona

Buck Mountain junction; turn left

Heimuller Road

Scappoose

Old Bacona Road - impassable

Mountain View Road

Start

Portland, 35 miles

Buxton Look-Out Road junction

Old Portland Road

Portland, 35 miles

OR 47

10. Hoffmann Road to Scappoose via Bacona

BRIEF DESCRIPTION: This "trail" is actually a remote ridgetop road that is suitable for hiking, biking, equestrian use, or travel by car. It runs the length of the hills that border the northern edge of Washington County. The road is well rocked and thus accessible year-round, but this rocky base can also contribute to a rough ride along some of the stretches. The eastern portion of this route uses the same route as the Buck Mountain hike. I have driven this historic road on several occasions using my Honda Odyssey. The overall ride was rough and required careful navigation to avoid scraping the underside of the car. No doubt cars with greater clearance would fare better, but in either case expect a very bumpy ride.

DISTANCE: 16 miles from Tophill to the paved portion of the Pisgah Home Road, just west of Scappoose.

ELEVATION CHANGE: 280 feet. Elevation at the Tophill end is 1,010 feet, and it's 1,290 feet at the Pisgah Home Road end. The high points are just south of the village of Bacona (2,076 feet) and just east of the Buck Mountain Crossing (2,064 feet).

ROAD CONDITION: Rough roadbed, requiring careful driving and slow speeds to avoid rocks, frequent potholes, and occasional branches and rocks strewn across the roadway

APPROXIMATE DURATION: I recommend driving this route. By car it will take a bit more than an hour, assuming you can maintain 15 mph on this road.

TRAVEL TIME FROM PORTLAND TO TRAILHEAD: Approach this route from either end, at Tophill or via Pisgah Home Road, which begins behind Scappoose. Travel time to Pisgah Home Road is about 45 minutes via US 30 and Heimuller Road. Travel time to Tophill is also about 45 minutes via US 26 connecting to OR 47 and continuing to Tophill.

DRIVING DIRECTIONS: The Tophill trailhead is located at the intersection of OR 47 and Hoffman Road. Tophill can be accessed by driving north on OR 47 from US 26 to the top of the hill.

The eastern trailhead is located at the intersection of Grouse Lane and Pisgah Home Road. From NW Portland drive north on US 30 to Scappoose. Turn left on Bonneville Drive (opposite the Shell gas station) and immediately turn right on Old Portland Road. Turn left on Dutch Canyon Road, and follow it until it crosses a small creek and turns left (at the intersection with Watts Road). Immediately thereafter turn right onto Mountain View Road, which ascends the hill. (Set your odometer to zero as you begin to climb Mountain View Road.) Follow this road for a bit more than 2 miles; at its intersection with West Road, it turns into Heimuller Road. After another half mile, pass the intersection with Smith Road. Continue upward another 2 miles and turn left onto Pisgah Home Road. The pavement ends after about 200 yards, at the intersection with Grouse Lane.

SPECIAL ATTRIBUTES: This historic road separates Columbia County from Washington County and passes the site of Bacona, a remote village first settled during the late 1870s by four Danish families: the Nelsons, the Jeppesens, the Hoffmans, and the Petersens. The Hoffmans operated a sawmill employing eight people that supplied railroad ties to the nearby railroads. The village is located high above the Tualatin River basin, and for that reason it attracted late arrivals seeking areas in which they could homestead. In the early 1900s at least twenty farms operated in the area, raising cattle, hay, and potatoes. But the elevation of Bacona, at 2,012 feet, made agriculture a risky proposition. Nonetheless, the original families were able to produce the essentials, including fruits such as plums, prunes, apples, and cherries. But the marginal conditions meant that they were never able to produce enough of a surplus to make their farms sufficiently profitable to import the varieties of goods available on the valley floor.

Often the residents had a rough go of it getting through the winter months. One of the families, the Wellers, were said to have only fifteen dollars per month to feed nine people three times a day! For breakfast they had oatmeal and cooked dried prunes or canned loganberries along with hard biscuits made of flour, water, and baking powder. For dinner they ate more biscuits, onions, and potatoes—fried together. Predictably, most of the families eventually moved down into the valley where they could find steady work and were not entirely reliant on the slim pickings and short growing seasons at the top of this long ridge.[1]

TRAIL LOG: Directions are given from Tophill heading east toward Pisgah Home Road.

Because of its strategic location at the summit separating the Tualatin and Nehalem watersheds, the hamlet of Tophill also serves as the western terminus of a rugged mountain road that follows the crest of the mountains stretching along the northern edge of Washington County. It consists of just a handful of visible houses with various farm implements and detritus scattered about.

Loki, James Benson, and author en route.

Two roads intersect with OR 47 at Tophill. Nowakowski Road leads downhill in a southwesterly direction along the base of Cape Horn Mountain. (Several of the alternative routes described in the next section begin along Nowakowski Road.) The other road, Hoffman Road, leads out of the hamlet on the eastern side of OR 47. This rocky road heads up a ridge traversing the side of Hoffman Mountain. Ascend this road slowly and carefully. Drive so your wheels sit on the ridges between the ruts. Otherwise, your car will ride too low and not have enough clearance for the hump rising between the ruts.

After 1.75 miles, pass by Lawrence Road merging in from your left—continue onward, turning to the right. Continue on Hoffman Road and in a quarter mile you will reach a relatively smooth road heading to Bacona. Turn left at this intersection to follow Bacona Road east. About 5.4 miles from the starting point at Tophill, several driveways and a solitary house are set on the edge of a small clearing. This is Bacona, one of Oregon's more remote communities.

Beyond Bacona the road degrades again into lengthy stretches of bouncing and jolting. Several side roads appear on the right; stay on the main track that roughly follows the crest of the hills. At 10.2 miles into this bumpy road a road comes in from the left. This tributary road originates at the summit of the Scappoose–Vernonia Highway and connects with Bacona Road by climbing over a small peak known as Tater Mountain. Pass by this northern detour and proceed straight through the clearing (where Tater Mountain Road enters) to reach the Buck Mountain Crossing 11.45 miles from the starting point in Tophill. At the Buck Mountain Crossing (described in Chapter 6) turn left and continue east on Pisgah Home Road.

The entire journey is about 16 miles long. Several of the roads in this area have been washed out, so use this map or any detailed map showing the major logging roads to locate the correct route through this maze of dusty roads. It's easy to get lost and drive around in scenic, but bumpy, circles. Believe me, pavement never felt so good as after this journey!

Despite my pejorative descriptions of the road conditions, this hilltop road affords a unique glimpse into an isolated mountain range stretching across our otherwise well-populated region. Once a formidable barrier for pioneers wishing to penetrate into the Nehalem Valley, this ridgeline track is still difficult to navigate and remains nearly as remote as ever.

Kanakas and Klickitats

Settlers were crossing the Tualatin Mountains to reach the Willamette Valley as early as the 1820s. Mostly they used the Logie Trail to reach the long narrow valleys of northeastern Washington County. Thomas McKay, the famed pioneer and scout, was known to operate a horse farm on the western slopes of the Tualatin Mountains, and the Hudson's Bay Company had its largest dairy operations at the base of this trail, where it emerged into the Dairy Creek valley. The well-known Presbyterian circuit rider Jason Lee, accompanied by Thomas McKay, was reported to have established a horse trail from Scappoose to Hillsboro as early as 1834.

But these trails were often the remnants of earlier trails that served Native American travelers and raiders trying to enter the northern parts of the Willamette Valley. Following the epidemics of the late eighteenth and early nineteenth centuries, there was much upheaval in native society, with many tribes vanishing completely and the remnants merging. Powerful tribes such as the Chinook, the Clackamas, and the Multnomah atrophied under the withering onslaught of pestilence and pox. But several tribes managed to shrug off the debilitating effects of European epidemics, mainly because they had developed increasing resistance to the virulent pathogens laying waste to the peoples of the Lower Columbia.

The story of the Klickitats' ascendency during this period is one of the most vivid examples of how outsiders took advantage of the social turmoil among the Native Americans and turned it to their advantage. It is said the Klickitats originated in the southern or western slopes of the Rockies, but were pushed out by the encroaching Cayuse. Eventually they resettled in the vicinity of Mount Adams and along the White Salmon and Klickitat Rivers. We know these peoples by their Chinook name, meaning "those that came from beyond the Cascades." Hailing from the sparse eastern slopes of the Cascades, they were known for their agile horses and their deadly weaponry. It was this bellicose heritage that gave them a fearsome reputation among the canoe Indians of the Lower Columbia River.

The canoe Indians, including the Chinook, the Clackamas, the Clatskanie, and the Clatsop residents of the Lower Columbia, were unaccustomed to equestrian warfare. They were expert boatmen, whose skill at navigating the winds and currents of the wide Columbia River astounded Lewis and Clark. Their experience handling canoes was said to have influenced their physical stature. Many of the early explorers noted their relative short stature and wide stance.

Over the ages, as travelers journeyed south from Puget Sound they would inevitably congregate at the big bend in the river, where a midstream island spread the river out and made it easier to cross. For eons weary feet had polished a well-trodden route to the most advantageous crossing points. And it was along this wide expanse of river frontage that the Chinooks settled and carved out a niche serving as the portal between the inland trade and the coastal goods that were brought from as far away as Vancouver Island, the Queen Charlotte Islands, and southern Alaska. By the 1780s, these ocean encounters began to introduce increasing varieties of British- and American-made trade goods as "coasters" traded for sea-otter pelts up and down the Pacific Northwest coast.

All this trade flowed up and down the Northwest's mighty rivers, but it also penetrated deep into the hinterlands on polished footpaths radiating out from the Columbia to the open slopes of eastern Washington and eastern Oregon. This hint of wealth and the mystery of goods from Europe attracted traders from the interior. But it also brought the Klickitats, the horse-mounted raiders, off the slopes of Mount Adams.

The Klickitats frequently crossed the Columbia River to hunt in the Willamette Valley, and after the epidemics of the 1820s and 1830s they were able to overwhelm the remaining populations and strengthen their control over the northern Willamette Valley. During the early nineteenth century they extended their control south to the Umpqua Valley, as far north as Puget Sound, and west into Oregon's Coast Range. Among the local tribes and the early settlers the Klickitats acquired a reputation for being robbers and plunderers. Using guns acquired from the Hudson's Bay Company, the Klickitats attacked the Umpqua tribe in the Rogue Valley. A decade later, they were serving as scouts and auxiliaries to the US Army during the Rogue Wars. In 1855, the Klickitats took up arms under the chieftain Kamaikin to protect their homelands from white miners and settlers. A campaign of extensive fort building eventually convinced the Klickitat leaders that resistance was futile, but their abortive rebellion badly scared many of the early settlers.

Even so, it came as quite a shock when, in 1860, a party of Klickitat raiders swam the Columbia and ascended Logie Trail to raid the Calapuyan villages of Chakontweiftei, Chapanakhtin, and Chatakwin, located at the base of present-day Pumpkin Ridge. Descending swiftly from the top of the Tualatin Mountains, the Klickitat marauders swept through the hapless Calapuyan villages to snatch whatever booty, food, and slaves they could. These raids panicked the defenseless Calapuyans. They had no way to protect themselves, until help arrived from an unexpected neighbor.

Hearing about the incursion, the Hawaiian chieftain Cowaniah quickly rallied his tribe and several settlers to pursue the mounted Klickitats across the Tualatin Mountains. Cowaniah caught up with the fleeing Klickitats in a hollow west of present-day Upper Bishop Road.

Facing determined opposition for the first time, the Klickitats fled amid a hail of gunfire. As the escaping raiders crested the ridgeline, their final warrior paused to take one last shot before slipping from view and disappearing into history. And in so doing, this nameless Klickitat managed to shoot Cowaniah's horse out from under him, ending the pursuit in a tangle of tumbling bodies.

But this incident raises an interesting question: how did a Hawaiian come to be leading a local tribe? The answer lies in the long and deep ties between the Hudson's Bay Company and the hundreds of Hawaiians that they hired to carve a civilization out of these dank forests.

Eventually, some of the Owyhees, as they were called, became disenchanted with the Hudson's Bay Company's disciplined approach to empire building and established hybrid tribes at the fringes of the growing white-population areas. Thus it was not surprising that the uncharted hills just west of the Tualatin Mountains were the home stomping grounds of a hybrid clan led by Cowaniah.

From the very beginning of the European penetration into the Columbia River, Hawaiians had been involved. Curious about the outside world, many Hawaiians had readily agreed to accompany the early explorers as they probed the vast shores of the Pacific. In 1792, when Captain Gray first entered the Columbia River, it was none other than Crown Prince Attoo who stood at his side, resplendent in his helmet of feathers and cloak of yellow and scarlet plumage.

Less than twenty years after Lewis and Clark, the British in Vancouver and the Americans in Astoria were discovering the huge potential of trade across the Pacific. Under the direction of its chief factor, John McLoughlin, the Hudson's Bay Company began to harvest, process, and export smoked fish, butter, and lumber to the Russian settlements in Nootka. In 1827, McLoughlin shipped the first load of long, tall Pacific Northwest timber to Honolulu. The wood was desperately needed to service the Pacific whaling fleet, which was getting chewed up by big Pacific storms. By the late 1820s it was clear that Fort Vancouver had gone beyond being self-subsistent. It was now engaged in vibrant trade relationships—based on agricultural products—with Alaska, Hawaii, China, and the settlements in California. Even as the sun was setting on the company's beaver-fueled empire, Fort Vancouver was thriving by selling butter, fish, and enormous logs.

But the Hudson's Bay Company had a problem. The local Native American tribes were content to fish and hunt as usual, and they really couldn't see the sense in eradicating the friendly sea otters or the industrious beavers. Although the Hudson's Bay traders had brought with them some Algonquians from the Great Lakes, Cree from the northern Plains, and Chipewyans from the eastern slopes of the Rockies, few of them could speak more than a few phrases of Chinook Wawa, as the trade lingo was called. And fewer yet were able to persuade the Chinookans to give up their fishing nets for the disagreeable work of tromping up devil's club–infested streams to trap the ever-diminishing beavers and otters.

That's when John McLoughlin came up with the idea of importing labor from Hawaii. As early as 1818, Astoria had about fifty inhabitants—half of them Hawaiians. Soon the Hudson's Bay Company was recruiting laborers from the Hawaiian Islands in droves. These Owhyees would sign on for several years and then return to the islands. But some of them stayed and continued to work for the Hudson's Bay Company and the North West Company; they were known as the *Kanakas*. By 1845, there were more than three hundred Kanakas working in and around Fort Vancouver. The London-based management of the Hudson's Bay Company tried to curtail this practice of importing labor, but John McLoughlin intervened. Even as the original voyageurs and explorers who helped establish the fort were retiring, McLoughlin recognized that he needed to grow the operation and the best contract laborers were from the islands. They often accompanied the various expeditions that the company dispatched around the region. It was found that having a contingent of large Polynesians along discouraged conflict with the local tribes. On one such excursion into southern Idaho, the expedition encountered hostile Paiutes operating from a desert mountain range. Two Hawaiians were sent to parlay with the Paiutes, but they were never seen again. As a consolation, it was decided to name the mountains after the ill-fated messengers. To this day these arid peaks are known as the Owyhees, the western transliteration of Hawaii. Back at Fort Vancouver the increase in the Hawaiian population had led to the construction of a village dedicated to the Hawaiian workforce. This so-called Kanaka village soon grew to house more than six hundred Hawaiians.

The Hawaiians became intermediaries between the Europeans and the local Native Americans, often taking local wives and establishing their own villages. It is thought that Chief Cowaniah, whose band lived in the Tualatin Mountains near Logie Trail, was such a transplant. Thus it was that he was the first to respond to the Klickitat incursions.

Upon reflection, the skirmish at the crest of the Tualatin Mountains was quite remarkable, coming almost five years after the last significant Indian resistance along the Columbia River. Even more unusual is the fact that the defense was mounted not by the victimized Calapuyans, or even by the local white settlers, but instead the resistance by transplanted Hawaiians.

Notes

1. Ralph Friedman, *Tracking Down Oregon* (Caldwell, ID: Caxton Printers Ltd., 1951), 43.

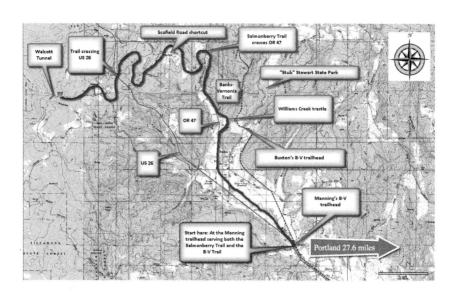

Walcott Tunnel

Trail crossing US 26

Scofield Road shortcut

Salmonberry Trail crosses OR 47

"Stub" Stewart State Park

Banks-Vernonia Trail

Williams Creek trestle

OR 47

Buxton's B-V trailhead

US 26

Manning's B-V trailhead

Start here: At the Manning trailhead serving both the Salmonberry Trail and the B-V Trail

Portland 27.6 miles

11. Salmonberry Trail—From Manning Trailhead to the Walcott Tunnel

BRIEF DESCRIPTION: We begin our journey along the Salmonberry Trail at Manning, one of the last hamlets before ascending into the mountains. Just beyond it is the small community of Buxton. The intersection with OR 47, which heads north to Vernonia, is just beyond Buxton. The first segment of the Salmonberry Trail parallels US 26 and then climbs up past Buxton. At Buxton there is another trailhead, but I've been told that this trailhead attracts car prowlers. From the Buxton trailhead, the route winds north up West Fork Dairy Creek before it crosses OR 47. From there it twists and turns in a southerly direction until it crosses US 26 and continues on to the Walcott Tunnel.

DISTANCE: 10.55 miles one way. This is much longer than the direct distance, but the winding of the railroad adds appreciably to the length of this segment. This old railroad grade will eventually become part of the Salmonberry Trail. For those interested in a more direct or more scenic route to the Walcott Tunnel, I recommend one of the other three routes described in subsequent chapters.

ELEVATION CHANGE: 862 feet, from 240 feet at the Manning trailhead to 1,102 feet at the entrance to the Walcott Tunnel

TRAIL CONDITION: This portion of the Salmonberry Trail exists by virtue of the railbed and tracks that ascend the slope. In some places the alders have encroached upon the railbed, but the route is still clearly visible and accessible. I often carry rose clippers to deal with the stray blackberry vines that threaten to ensnare me.

APPROXIMATE DURATION: 4–5 hours

TRAVEL TIME FROM PORTLAND TO TRAILHEAD: 30 minutes

DRIVING DIRECTIONS: From the Sylvan exit (exit 71B), head 27.6 miles west on US 26 to Manning. You will recognize the trailhead by the cute little church alongside the railroad tracks. On the far side, a parking lot serves the Banks–Vernonia (B-V) Trail. The Salmonberry Trail will also commence at this location. Until that trail is constructed, follow the B-V Trail.

TRAIL LOG: The most prominent among the trails crisscrossing Cape Horn Mountain is the proposed Salmonberry Trail. According to the proposal, it will begin at the trailhead in Manning and parallel US 26. After crossing Mendenhall Creek it will pass by the hamlet of Buxton and continue north.

A little over 3 miles from the trailhead the Salmonberry Trail will cross the Williams Creek trestle. Planning documents propose the development of connector trails that will provide access to and from OR 47, and to the B-V Trail.

About 4.5 miles into the hike, the Salmonberry Trail begins to make the wide sweeping turn west to cross both the West Fork Dairy Creek and OR 47. Then the trail continues to ascend the slope, snaking back and forth in a series of wide loops. At 5.9 miles the Salmonberry Trail crosses Scofield Road for the first time. At 6.4 miles into the hike, cross Scofield Road again as the sweeping loops continue to carry you up and to the west. From here the trail enters a forested area and crosses Cummings Creek several times before it climbs the slope to US 26.

After 8.7 miles the route finally reaches the railroad bridge that crosses the highway.

Given the slope that the rail line is trying to overcome, it should not come as any surprise that this entire stretch from OR 47 across US 26 and nearly all the way to the Walcott Tunnel is one long series of winding curves. That is another reason why I have also provided several alternatives that are both shorter and in some cases much more scenic that the actual rail line. At 9.4 miles into the official Salmonberry Trail alignment, the trail runs close to Strassel Road, which could provide a hiker with another vehicular access point.

As of this writing, this is the proposed alignment for the Salmonberry Trail. Clocking in at over 10 miles, this is the longest option for reaching the Walcott Tunnel. The following three trails each represent alternatives that are shorter or more scenic.

Kamaikin and the Klickitat War of 1855

In the mid-1800s the first homesteads began to spring up on West Fork Dairy Creek. But the homesteaders' hold over the land was still tenuous, and there was general unease among the far-flung settlements about relations with the Native American tribes, especially those living in the eastern portions of Oregon and Washington.

Astoria had been sold to the British in 1813, and was ultimately abandoned in 1824. Twenty years later Astoria had only four white residents. But then gold was discovered in California and a massive building boom soon revived Astoria's fortunes. The new settlements in the northern Coast

The Walcott Tunnel.

Range remained sparse due to the lack of arable land and the unceasing rain. By the mid-1840s settlers began using Youngs Bay and the navigable channels leading inland, eventually penetrating the Nehalem Valley.

The isolation of these communities was extreme. At the time there was much anxiety over the threat that the Native Americans posed. And this was no idle worry, because in November of 1847 the Cayuse had attacked and killed all the residents of the Whitman Mission in eastern Washington.

A few years later, the Sioux lost patience with the endless stream of wagons crossing their hunting grounds. Thereafter they massacred almost every wagon train that they found.

In 1855, news of a Klickitat revolt against encroaching miners flashed across the Lower Columbia. Families from Cathlamet to the Clackamas and Kalama Rivers scurried to get inside the walls of the forts. After all, the Klickitats were horse people, and they had a habit of showing up anywhere without any warning, as happened five years later in what is now Washington County.

One of the more interesting characters from this period was the Klickitat leader Kamaikin, who resided with his bands in the proximity of Mount Rainier. Although their upland territory was not the target of Euro-American expansion, the huge influx of settlers was putting pressure on the Klickitat homelands, mostly in the form of miners and land speculators.

In a remarkable travelogue, *The Canoe and the Saddle*, written by a twenty-four-year-old New Englander, Theodore Winthrop, we get a first-hand report on the character of this Klickitat leader. Winthrop describes how they met by chance sometime during late August of 1853 in the highlands near the 4,800-foot-high Naches Pass. He writes about the quiet dignity of the Yakima chieftain who would go on to launch a war on the white settlers only two years later.

Winthrop had only recently graduated from Yale and was touring the Pacific Northwest. His book, although written through the eyes of a classically educated New England patrician, is one of the earliest narratives describing the raw beauty of the region and the natives that he encountered.

Winthrop writes this:

> Enter, then, upon this scene Kamaikin, the chiefest of the Yakimah chiefs. He was a tall, large man, very dark with a massive square face, and grave, reflective look . . . his manner was strikingly distinguished, quiet and dignified.
>
> Kamaikin, in order to be the chiefest chief of the Yakimah's must be clever enough to master the dodges of the salmon, and the will of the wayward mustang . . . he must know where the kamas bulbs are mining a passage for their sprouts, or he must be able to tramp farther and fare better than his fellows; or by a certain "tamanous" (magic) that is in him, he must have power to persuade or convince to win or overbear.[1]

At the meeting, Winthrop asks Kamaikin for a guide who will get him to The Dalles. Kamaikin indeed supplies a guide. Not surprisingly, Winthrop, in his adieu, extolls his Klickitat host as a "prudent and weighty" chief.

In retrospect, we can see how Theodore Winthrop is himself a symptom of the seismic shifts affecting the Pacific Northwest. Whites are "touring" all over the region, surveyors are planning railroad routes through the Cascades, miners are befouling the streams, the settlers' pigs are destroying the native tribes' camas fields, river navigation is wrecking the tribes' fisheries, and land speculators are selling the tribes' patrimony right out from under their feet. Simultaneously, the region is beset with new outbreaks of smallpox, measles, and malaria that reduce the native population of the Lower Columbia from fifteen thousand in 1830 to less than two thousand in the mid-1840s. Winthrop is a witness to this epic transformation, but he is unapologetic for its consequences to the indigenous cultures. After a brief encounter with a group of road builders, he boasts that he "could ride more boldly forward into savageness, knowing that the front ranks of my nation were following close behind."

Given the increasing inflow of settlers, it should come as no surprise that less than a year later this "prudent and weighty" chief would be at the center of Klickitat resistance to the white setters' encroachments. By 1855, deadly confrontations with miners and the murder of a Yakima leader had seriously degraded relations with the Klickitats on the Columbia Plateau. At the time, the settlers tried to buy their way out of the impending conflict, but the Klickitats would have none of it. Realizing the seriousness of this situation, A. J. Bolen, an Indian agent, confronted one of the Yakima bands and threatened to send soldiers to kill them if they misbehaved. This blunt approach was not well received. Bolen was subsequently killed by some of the more hostile warriors. They subsequently burned his body and that of his horse, dancing on his scalp as the carcasses were reduced to ashes.

This frightful act of revenge was reported back to the settlers, who immediately dispatched all the women and children in the area to the safety of The Dalles. There, Major Haller mobilized 107 mounted soldiers and set off in pursuit of the Yakimas. Two days later they made contact. One soldier was killed and seven wounded, but by nightfall seven hundred angry Yakimas had cornered Haller's party on a narrow ridge. The next day the Yakimas managed to kill two more soldiers and wounded another thirteen. The situation was on the verge of a disaster, but fortunately for Haller's group, one of their scouts managed to find a route down the steep bluff and overnight Haller and his troops fled back to The Dalles.

Kamaikin sued for peace, but the governor of the Washington territories, Isaac Stevens, wanted to use the conflict to force the Yakimas onto reservations. Responding to Kamaikin's offer, he wrote that

> The whites are as the stars in the heavens, or the leaves in the trees in the summer time. Our warriors in the field are many, as you must see; but if not enough, a thousand for every one more will be sent to hunt you and to kill you; and my advice to you, as you will see, is to scatter yourselves among the Indian tribes more peaceable and therefore forget you were ever Yakimahs.

The settlers began building forts throughout the region, reducing the potential danger posed by attacks. Like nails in the coffin of indigenous resistance, each of the new forts drove home the futility of militant resistance. In the end, the "prudent and weighty" chieftain Kamaikin was forced to flee into exile—just as Isaac Stevens had predicted.

Though lost in the footnotes of history, Kamaikin still stands tall as one of the "chiefest of chiefs." No doubt it was a tough time for men of wisdom and vision. Especially when wisdom was seldom reciprocated and the vision of what lay ahead appeared so apocalyptic for the Native American way of life.

Notes

1. Theodore Winthrop, *The Canoe and the Saddle: A Critical Edition*, ed. Paul J. Lindholdt (Lincoln and London: University of Nebraska Press, 2006), 165.

Springs along the North Fork.

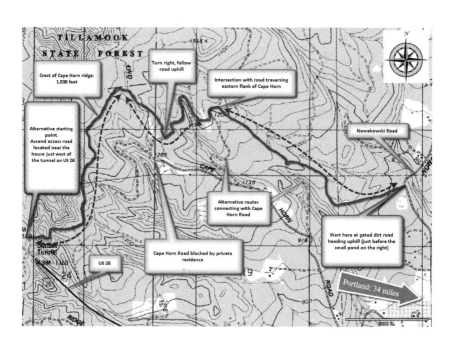

TILLAMOOK STATE FOREST

Crest of Cape Horn ridge:
1,536 feet

Turn right, follow
road uphill

Intersection with road traversing
eastern flank of Cape Horn

Nowakowski Road

Alternative starting
point.
Ascend access road
located near the
house just west of
the tunnel on US 26

Alternative routes
connecting with Cape
Horn Road

Start here at gated dirt road
heading uphill (just before the
small pond on the right)

Cape Horn Road blocked by private
residence

Sunset
Tunnel

US 26

Portland: 34 miles

12. Cape Horn Traverse

BRIEF DESCRIPTION: My favorite route to the Walcott Tunnel is also the most remote and the longest. But to make it more approachable, and less a feat of endurance, I have split the journey into two parts: Nowakowski Road to US 26 and US 26 to the Walcott Tunnel. Permit required on Weyerhaueser land. Visit www.wyrecreationnw.com.

DISTANCE: 3.5 miles one way

ELEVATION CHANGE: 788 feet. The base of the route lies at 742 feet in elevation at the blue gate entrance on Nowakowski Road. At its highest, this route reaches 1,530 feet, near the crest of the Cape Horn ridge. According to my calculations, the blue gate situated directly above the tunnel is located at an elevation of 1,453 feet.

TRAIL CONDITION: Mostly graveled logging roads

APPROXIMATE DURATION: 90 minutes going uphill; less than 3 hours round trip

TRAVEL TIME FROM PORTLAND TO TRAILHEAD: 45 minutes

DRIVING DIRECTIONS: I'll describe two approaches to this trailhead, one from Tophill and the other from US 26.

From Tophill, leave OR 47 and turn onto Nowakowski Road. Follow this dirt road through a scattering of farms and miscellaneous outbuildings. After a half mile, arrive at the intersection of Nowakowski Road and the Banks–Vernonia Trail.

Continue south on Nowakowski Road for another 0.9 miles to an unnamed logging road on your right that climbs up the slope of Cape Horn Mountain. The turnoff can also be identified by a shallow pond along the right side of Nowakowski Road just beyond the turnoff.

Alternatively, access Nowakowski Road from US 26 by ascending OR 47. The turnoff to Nowakowski Road comes right after you have passed under the railroad bridge that carries the official Salmonberry Trail over the highway. The intersection with Nowakowski Road is located immediately after a sharp turn to the left. From this lower end of Nowakowski Road, travel about 1.25 miles—just past a marshy pond on your left. The gated logging road heads up the hill directly after this marshy patch. This road is blocked to unauthorized motorized traffic by the typical blue gate, complete with its prescriptive sign defining the recreational user's rights and obligations.

Remember to reset your pedometer or GPS device, since the trail distances are all measured from this gate.

TRAIL LOG: The road climbs west for 0.4 miles, gaining about 100 feet in elevation before turning the corner and heading to the northwest. When I last surveyed this route it had been re-rocked and the going was tough on the soles and ankles, but eventually you will pass these "improvements" and be all the more thankful for the soft forest duff that covers most of this route. Keep following the road uphill, passing a spur on your left, until you reach a triangular intersection (1.3 miles from the blue gate). Turn left at this intersection and follow the dirt road as it twists and turns in and out of the ravines and ridges for another 0.6 miles. There you will pass another road leading down the slope. Ignore it and continue on the main route that traverses the slope, eventually emerging at the lower boundary of a clear-cut. A lesser-used road skirts the bottom of the cleared area; follow the main road as it turns right and ascends the northern edge of the clear-cut. This intersection is 1.9 miles from the blue gate.

Continue up this clearly visible roadway to a three-way intersection at the crest of the hill, at an approximate elevation of 1,470 feet, and 2.47 miles from the blue gate. The view east into the plains of Washington County is quite spectacular. Looking south, you can begin to discern the mountains clustered around the headwaters of the Salmonberry River. A smaller track heads northwest toward Cape Horn's summit; ignore this (0.2-mile) detour and follow the main track in a southwesterly direction along the crest of the ridge, heading toward the tunnel that funnels US 26 under this ridge. Three miles from the blue gate, the road passes by another substantial road heading down the slope; ignore this spur and stick with the main road heading south. A tenth of a mile further along, a road drops down to the left. Once again, ignore it and continue on the main track. At 3.47 miles from the beginning of this route you will arrive at the blue gate that defines the southern end of the route.

At that gate the route splits into two trails. The right-hand option is a short trail (0.45 miles) that leads down to US 26 and emerges just west of the tunnel next to the solitary residence located alongside the highway. Keep this access point in mind if you're seeking a quick way to reach the ridgetop route we just described. The left-hand option continues across the tunnel, bypassing two cellular towers and proceeding south along the ridgetop toward Ridge Road. This portion of the route is described in chapter 13, "Ridge Road to the Walcott Tunnel."

A shady portion of our route; dogs running ahead . . .

Contagion

EIGHTEENTH-CENTURY EPIDEMICS

There is plenty of evidence that substantial trade occurred between the Pacific Northwest tribes and the native cultures of the American Southwest. This was probably the first path of contagion that brought serious epidemics to the Pacific Northwest.

The epidemic that swept through the Pacific Northwest in the 1770s began two hundred years earlier, when Cortez first landed in Mexico. It has been documented that among Cortez's troops there was an African slave who had contracted smallpox. The disease spread to the native population as the invading soldiers traveled west toward the capital of the Aztec empire. From there the disease spread quickly to all parts of the Americas.

Eventually, the pandemic swept north, reaching the Navajo in New Mexico. From there it moved to the Comanches, who traded with their linguistic cousins the Shoshones and the Crows. The Shoshones traded with the Kootenai and Piegan peoples on the western slopes of the Rockies. Following that line of transmission, smallpox soon devastated the Salish tribe in Idaho and Montana, then the Nez Perce perished as it spread down the Columbia to the Chinooks and the coastal tribes. By the late 1770s the

Pacific Northwest was engulfed in one of the most calamitous pandemics ever known. Before the multiple waves of disease had played themselves out, smallpox, diphtheria, influenza, and malaria had killed more than nine out of ten people in the Lower Columbia River region.

What's significant about this is that most of the die-offs occurred prior to the arrival of Europeans in the Pacific Northwest. Even before Captain Robert Gray crossed the Columbia River bar, the region had been devastated by at least two smallpox scourges that killed almost 20 percent of the population. There is also some evidence that a second infection path originated in Nootka, at the north end of Vancouver Island. When Captain Cook visited this trading community he had among his crew at least one sailor who was infected by smallpox. Thus, it is possible that the Pacific Northwest coast may have sustained penetration by multiple disease vectors coming from two directions. Lewis and Clark also noted evidence that an epidemic had passed through the area about thirty years before their arrival. Early travelers on the Columbia mention many deserted villages, as well as widespread illness and death among the native peoples. Regardless of where the diseases originated, the worst was still to come.

NINETEENTH-CENTURY EPIDEMICS

The contemporary accounts by fur trappers during the periodic outbreaks of contagion are haunting. As traders made their rounds and collected packets of pelts from local indigenous trappers, fewer and fewer Native Americans turned up with pelts to trade. Soon the fur traders began to venture into the mountains to see what had happened—only to find whole encampments filled with the dead or dying.[1] Native Americans lay in their lodges too weak to fend for themselves. The mountains that had once been wild and beautiful had suddenly become a landscape of death that even the wolves avoided.[2]

In one haunting incident, a fur trader asked about a village he had previously visited. He was told that not only had the village perished, but everyone else who had known of the place had also died. It was said of that village that "there remained not even a name."[3]

It was during this turmoil and catastrophe that the Europeans began to arrive. Gray's successful crossing of the Columbia River bar in 1792 came just a decade after the most deadly contagion hit the Northwest coast. Another epidemic hit in 1801, just before Lewis and Clark arrived. Increasing contacts with British and American coastal traders, often referred to as "coasters," brought more frequent incidents of contagion to the Lower Columbia.

Jared Diamond, in his seminal anthropological work *Guns, Germs, and Steel*, explains that the indigenous peoples of North America were especially vulnerable to European diseases because they had no inherited immunities with which to withstand these pathogens.[4]

The diseases that originated in North America were adapted to a society of hunter-gatherers who often lived in widely dispersed groups and typically only mingled annually at trading centers or ceremonial gatherings. Among such a diffuse population, diseases had to have a gestation period that exceeded a year. Otherwise, the disease might kill its host population before it could be transmitted to new populations. Diseases originating among hunter-gatherer societies shared this characteristic of slow development. Such diseases included gonorrhea and syphilis—both examples of New World diseases.

The European diseases that attacked Native Americans had adapted to sweep through a crowded populace, killing some but not all of those who contracted the disease. The survivors developed immunities that protected them from subsequent exposures. Europe was crowded enough to survive such periodic waves of disease, but since the ind\igenous peoples were all susceptible to these pathogens, they were doomed to annihilation.

The final phase of this disease-ridden invasion came in the 1820s with the introduction of measles and malaria. By that time Native American society had already been severely disrupted, with tribes merging, villages being abandoned, and the collective wisdom of the society fading as the elders died before they could pass on their rich cultural heritage. Into this fragile environment, ships now routinely sailed up the Columbia River to trade at the newly established Fort Vancouver. Unfortunately, these ships brought with them an influx of unwelcome passengers: malarial mosquitos that lived in the filthy bilge water sloshing around in the bottoms of the visiting ships. At night, the sailors would open the scuppers to permit ventilation under the decks, and in so doing would release swarms of mosquitos that would descend on the natives living along the river. Since much of tribal society was based along the shores of the Lower Columbia, the impact was devastating, and proved to be the death knell for the Chinooks, the Clatsops, the Cowlitz, the Clatskanies, the Multnomahs, and others. In less than a single lifetime, the peoples of the Lower Columbia vanished, taking with them all the vestiges of their rich history and culture. These powerful tribes all but disappeared overnight, and by 1859 the few survivors were marched off to the Grande Ronde Reservation.

The impact along the Columbia River was much worse than in Puget Sound because the sound was typically about two degrees colder than the Columbia River basin, and that temperature difference was enough to kill the mosquitos. This is why Washington has so many more places that still retain their Native American names. In Oregon the names of so many villages were simply lost as their inhabitants perished or fled. Had it been otherwise, Beaverton might still be called Chapeki, and our mountains would still bear their ancestral names.

By the time settlers began to arrive in the 1840s, the local tribes had all but vanished. Many of the bands fell apart, leaving their ancestral lands and sometimes moving in with the remnants of other tattered tribes. Trade and transportation routes collapsed. Local languages began to disappear as Chinook trade jargon and English began to replace the older languages.

The renowned scholar Henry Dobyens is credited with having done the greatest amount of work on establishing the actual population levels prior to contact.[5] He has estimated that in the first 130 years after contact more than 95 percent of the native peoples in the Americas perished.

DEMISE OF THE MULTNOMAHS

Perhaps the most tragic story was that of the Multnomah tribe, who lived in six villages along Sauvie Island and the banks of the Lower Willamette River. They lived in large, sturdy lodges colorfully decorated with carved totemic images and painted upright roof posts. Rows of brightly colored canoes with carved figures on the prow lined the channel. On the shore, women worked on curing meat and fish over fires, or weaving garments from rushes and cedar bark. The very old and young bustled along the shores tending to the fish traps, while the men of the village flung seining nets into the river. Life was good for the Multnomahs, blessed as they were with a plethora of food sources, including salmon, sturgeon, seals, elk, deer, wapato, and camas lilies. But when white men began navigating the Columbia River, that good life came to a sudden and tragic end.

Due to their proximity to Fort Vancouver, the Multnomahs were frequent visitors at the fort, but one day they ceased coming. When people were sent to investigate they found the villages littered with hundreds of dead bodies. Only one woman was still alive, and she told of a great sickness that had literally extinguished the Multnomahs. She too died hours later. It is now theorized that the *Convoy*, a recently arrived American brig out of Boston, had anchored offshore after signaling the fort of its arrival. Thereafter the sailors had opened the hatches and released clouds of malarial mosquitos that swarmed out of the ship's bilge and infected the Native Americans who lined the shore watching the billowing white sails of the square-rigger as she rode the gentle swell of the river's currents.[6]

In their legends the Multnomahs had foretold of a great canoe with white wings that would ascend the Columbia River. When it came to rest in the evening it was said to issue a great roar that struck terror into the heart of all that heard it. From the sides of the vessel would come black clouds that brought death and destruction. And thus indeed, it came to pass.

Notes

1. William G. Robbins, *Landscapes of Promise: The Oregon Story 1800–1840* (Seattle and London: University of Washington Press, 1997), 60.
2. Robert Clark, *River of the West* (New York: Harper Collins, 1995), 43.
3. Gray H. Whaley, *Oregon and the Collapse of Illahee*. (Chapel Hill: University of North Carolina Press, 2010), 91–3.
4. Jared Diamond, *Guns, Germs, and Steel* (New York: W. W. Norton, 1997).
5. Henry F. Dobyens, *Their Number Became Thinned: Native American Population Dynamics in Eastern North America* (Knoxville: University of Tennessee Press, 1983).
6. American Association of University Women, *Land of the Multnomahs*, compiled by Margaret Watt Edwards (Portland, OR: Binford & Mort, 1973), 60.

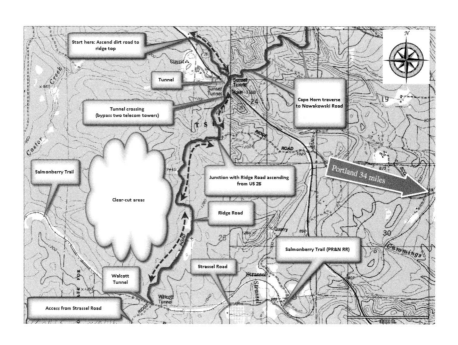

Start here: Ascend dirt road to ridge top

Tunnel

Tunnel crossing (bypass two telecom towers)

Cape Horn traverse to Nowakowski Road

Salmonberry Trail

Junction with Ridge Road ascending from US 26

Clear-cut areas

Portland 34 miles

Ridge Road

Salmonberry Trail (PR&N RR)

Walcott Tunnel

Strassel Road

Access from Strassel Road

13. Ridge Road to the Walcott Tunnel

BRIEF DESCRIPTION: This trail begins on a narrow strip of land directly over the Dennis L. Edwards Tunnel and ends above the Walcott Tunnel. Various access routes for the Salmonberry Trail are being considered, but for now bushwhack down the north side of the tunnel. This trail segment can be reached using several routes, including approaching the top of the Dennis L. Edwards Tunnel via the access road located on the western side of the tunnel, by walking up Cape Horn Mountain from Nowakowski Road, or by accessing Ridge Road from Strassel Road. Permit required on Weyerhaeuser land. Visit www.wyrecreationnw.com.

DISTANCE: 2.26 miles one way

ELEVATION CHANGE: 170 feet

TRAIL CONDITION: Mostly logging roads

APPROXIMATE DURATION: 1 hour for one-way transit from the Dennis L. Edwards Tunnel to Walcott Tunnel

TRAVEL TIME FROM PORTLAND TO TRAILHEAD: 35 minutes

DRIVING DIRECTIONS: If using the access road, travel 34 miles along US 26 from the Sylvan exit (exit 71B) and go through the Dennis L. Edwards Tunnel. Park near the roadside residence located on the north side of US 26. From there a dirt road leads up over the tunnel to a blue-gated intersection that marks the end of Cape Horn Mountain Road and the beginning of Ridge Road.

For the route that takes you up Cape Horn Mountain from Nowakowski Road, walk up a logging road to the top of the ridge and south along the crest of the hill to the blue gates situated directly above the Dennis L. Edwards Tunnel (see Chapter 12).

Caution: From the blue gate situated above the Dennis L. Edwards Tunnel, this route heads directly south and follows the descending ridgeline all the way to the Walcott Tunnel. It does, however, have one distinct disadvantage. Two telecommunications towers located directly over the tunnel are posted with No Trespassing signs. The ridge trail passes about 50 feet from the towers before exiting the private property. For obvious reasons I cannot recommend this convenient over-the-top route and have thus given hikers at least two alternative approaches: the Scofield Road route (chapter 14) and the Salmonberry Trail (chapter 11), which follows the rail alignment.

TRAIL LOG: After following the dirt road up to the ridgeline above the Dennis L. Edwards Tunnel, reset your GPS or pedometer. All subsequent distance calculations are based on the distance from this three-way intersection. The left-hand trail leads north to the Cape Horn Traverse and ultimately to Nowakowski Road. The middle road leads up to a cell tower located directly above the tunnel. The right-hand trail leads across the tunnel and ultimately connects to a network of trails proceeding south along the ridge toward the Walcott Tunnel. On the far side of the tunnel, a yellow gate is posted with No Trespassing signs. Unfortunately, the Western Oregon Electric Cooperative, which owns these facilities, has erected these signs, making a legal transit over the tunnel impossible. To avoid violating this trespassing advisory, the Scofield Road route (Chapter 14) allows you to reach this ridgetop trail without breaching any posted areas.

On the south end of the road that straddles the ridgetop above the tunnel, a neat graveled road leads up to a building and attached radio tower. Just before the driveway veers to the right, an older road disappears into the trees. Follow this overgrown trail even though it appears to have had little traffic in the past few years. A little farther (0.57 miles), pass through another yellow gate. Just beyond the gate (0.61 miles) the road splits again.

The left-hand track heads down the hill in an easterly direction, ultimately to intersect with US 26 at the Scofield Road junction. But in order to get to the Walcott Tunnel, ignore this left-hand option. Instead continue along the top of the ridge (right-hand option), which proceeds south to the Walcott Tunnel.

About 0.7 miles from the start of this hike, reach a wide clearing where the road splits once again. Stick to the right and follow the ridgeline. A bit farther (0.9 miles from the start), a path leads down off the ridge heading to the southwest. Ignore that spur and follow the path that continues to wend its way along the ridgeline through the mature stands of Douglas fir trees.

Not much farther (1.05 miles from the start), emerge from the trees to gaze over a large clear-cut that wraps over the top of the ridge. Cross the clear-cut using the gravel road that runs along the spine of the hill. At the southern end of the clear-cut (1.4 miles from the start), arrive at a green gate. Turn right and follow an old road uphill toward a tall stand of timber that crowns the next high point of the ridge. (Remember that tall trees have a way of disappearing in these commercial forests, so the ridgeline may be a more reliable landmark to follow.) At the crown of this ridge you will have reached the highest point of the hike, at about 1,470 feet in elevation.

Looking west toward Cochran Pond.

Another 0.1 mile farther, the road dips down and emerges into a clear-cut that covers the southern end of this ridge. At the end of the ridge a gate bars vehicular traffic from Strassel Road. At this point you will be standing directly above the Walcott Tunnel.

Reaching the train tracks from the ridge road is best accomplished by bushwhacking down the northeasterly facing slope on your left. There are plans to build trails down to the tracks in the future. By the time you read this, the future may have already arrived. In the meantime, take some time to gaze out into the welter of mountains that constitute the Coast Range. The town of Timber is just a short distance to the southwest and Cochran Pond is just over the next rise.

The Brazil Roll

In the pioneer days tobacco was sold in pretzel-like twists weighing about an ounce, referred to as "carrots." These carrots were ubiquitous throughout the West, part of every story and the focal point of every important meeting. Regardless of what was being negotiated it all had to be "sealed and agreed to" under a wreath of swirling smoke to make it official.

Chief Three Eagles was cautiously observing the group. They clearly weren't Shoshones, Blackfeet, or Piegans. And besides, they moved too methodically, without taking defensive measures. There was a woman with them and a child. And there was a man painted entirely in black—possibly a powerful shaman. This was clearly not a raiding party. Much of their route had led them through heavily timbered hillsides, and at times across steep slopes that ran along the top of precipitous heights. Several of their horses fell; one rolled several hundred feet before becoming wedged into a tree. Miraculously the horse shook himself off and walked away uninjured.

Three Eagles sent a boy to lead them into the village. It was the first meeting between these western Native Americans and the visitors, who apparently were of two distinctly different races: the bearded white people and a huge man with black skin! None too soon for the travelers, they were led into the chieftain's tent to introduce themselves and make clear their purpose for crossing these snowbound heights in the dead of winter.

This meeting has come to symbolize an epic encounter when the lucrative trade in furs crossed the Rockies. The resulting distribution network would eventually reach from the shores of the Pacific Ocean all the way to the London hatmakers whose products were sold across Europe.

Translation at that first meeting was tough. Lewis conveyed his questions in English to fellow expeditionary Francois LaBiche, who passed it on to Toussaint Charbonneau in French. Charbonneau then asked his wife, Sacajawea, in the Hidatsa language, and she in turn conveyed the message in Shoshone, which the Salish could understand. Needless to say, much was lost in the translation.

But one matter was not misunderstood by the travelers. Their hosts were low on smokes! The visitors were quick to oblige and proffered their best Virginia tobacco. But the Salish coughed violently as they smoked the Virginia tobacco. The captains quickly mixed in some kinnikinnick, a ground-covering shrub whose leaves were smoked across much of the Pacific Northwest. The resulting herbal mixture was less harsh. This was important since the natives were in the habit of "swallowing" their smoke—that is, they never permitted any smoke to be exhaled. The coughing fits produced by the Virginia tobacco deeply embarrassed the Salish. Typically among the Salish, the only way for the smoke to be dispelled was to politely lift a cheek and let loose with a fulsome fart. I can only imagine the sidelong glances that Lewis and Clark exchanged as their hosts proudly broke wind to signify their satisfaction with the kinnikinnick-infused smokes.

Tobacco cultivation and ritual usage was deeply rooted in Native American culture. Traded tobacco began to filter across the north as the fur traders of the Hudson's Bay Company and the North West Company began to send brigades deeper into the interior. The fact that tobacco was one of the most important trade goods should come as no surprise. But what is really astonishing is the story of how this tobacco was produced and how it came to be the preferred smoke all across Indian country.

The origins of the native peoples' preferred smoke came from a most unlikely source—the Amazon. Beginning in the 1670s, when the Hudson's Bay Company's first outposts were established, they realized the great potential for using tobacco as a trade good. Different strains of tobacco were tried, but what the Native Americans preferred was a special blend found only in the Amazon. One trader described it as the most "bewitching weed amongst all the natives." Purchased by Portuguese traders in Trinidad, it was shipped to Lisbon and sold to British traders there. From Lisbon it was imported to England and promptly shipped to North America, where the sweet moist flavor of the so-called Brazil roll was exactly what the natives prized.

For years the development of the canoe routes across Canada have been touted as one of the free enterprise system's most impressive achievements. Eric Morse's book *Fur Trade Canoe Routes of Canada/Then and Now* epitomizes this perspective when he describes how

> a transport and supply system spanning 4,000 miles had to be developed. Overcoming the formidable physical difficulties in moving the furs through a million square miles of the northern wilderness out to the sea at Montreal or York Factory and carrying back the trade goods—these essentially comprise the story of the fur trade in Canada.

This perspective often leads to images of the fur traders smoking with Native Americans as they trade for furs that are destined to move down this four-thousand-mile supply chain. But the reality was that the Amazonian tobacco that the natives were smoking had traveled more than five times as far to get to that fabled campfire. Altogether the Brazil roll would travel more than twenty thousand miles from its origin in the Amazonian jungles to reach the chilly slopes of the Rockies.

Regardless of which goods traveled farther, it is true that a vast flow of animal pelts was siphoned out of the northern wilds in exchange for a steady supply of mirrors, nails, combs, knives, printed fabrics, buttons, and other European utensils. But chief among these trade items were the numerous bundles of Brazil rolls. Tobacco was more than an incidental part of the Hudson's Bay Company's inventory; it constituted a major part of their trading goods.

Given the popularity of tobacco with the Native Americans, the inclusion of large quantities of tobacco might appear to reflect good business acumen. But there is another perspective on this trade that has more sinister undertones. One need only look at British trade practices in China to see that addictive substances were an essential mechanism for opening new markets. Consider the fact that in 1780, Warren Hastings, the governor of India, began exporting opium to China in a bid to increase demand for foreign imports. Within a few years this stratagem proved so successful that nearly a fifth of India's trade revenues were derived from opium. And this lesson was not lost on the Hudson's Bay Company. In response, they began to import tobacco in larger quantities.

Within a reasonably short time, the demand for tobacco among the Pacific Northwest tribes increased so much that a quarter of all the trade goods stored in Fort Vancouver was tobacco! By the summer of 1844 they had ninety-six thousand pounds of tobacco on hand. That's about five pounds for every Native American residing between the mouth of the Columbia River all the way up to Celilo Falls. But there was just one problem . . .

The Hudson's Bay Company's strategy was to leverage the addictive powers of tobacco as a way to motivate the Native Americans to gather animal pelts for them. Throughout the company's expansion into the West this approach had delivered a steady supply of skins to the fur traders. But in the early 1800s the unthinkable happened. The Native Americans stopped coming to the rendezvous points. It wasn't that they brought fewer furs; they simply didn't show up! The fur traders soon learned why when they discovered whole swathes of villages filled with dead natives. We now know that a devastating series of epidemics, including smallpox, diphtheria, influenza, and even malaria, was sweeping across the region, killing more than 90 percent of the population.

Red Racer hanging out.

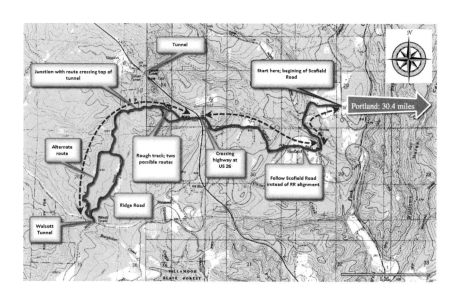

Tunnel

Junction with route crossing top of tunnel

Start here; begining of Scofield Road

Portland: 30.4 miles

Alternate route

Rough track; two possible routes

Crossing highway at US 26

Follow Scofield Road instead of RR alignment

Ridge Road

Walcott Tunnel

14. Scofield Road to the Walcott Tunnel via Ridge Road

BRIEF DESCRIPTION: This route is a shortcut that diverges from the old railroad alignment (soon to be the Salmonberry Trail) and takes you to the top of the ridge just south of US 26. From there it follows the Ridge Road route (chapter 13) down to the Walcott Tunnel. The advantages of this route are threefold: First, it's the shortest route to US 26 and thence up the slope to Ridge Road. Second, it's less curvy and shorter than the railroad alignment. Finally, it doesn't entail climbing to the top of Cape Horn Mountain. This route (as well as the Salmonberry Trail) avoids crossing private property located above the tunnel.

DISTANCE: 3.5 miles. It's about 2.75 miles from a parking spot on Nowakowski Road to US 26. From US 26 (up Ridge Road) to the top of the ridge (south of the highway) is another 0.75 miles.

ELEVATION CHANGE: 462 feet. The Scofield intersection with US 26 is at an elevation of 962 feet; the Scofield Road intersection with Nowakowski Road is at 500 feet—which is a noticeable slope. The railroad grade through this area was also considered relatively steep, achieving a 2 percent grade on the steeper stretches.

TRAIL CONDITION: Mostly graveled logging roads, with one highway crossing and one rough stretch

APPROXIMATE DURATION: 2 hours

TRAVEL TIME FROM PORTLAND TO TRAILHEAD: 40 minutes

DRIVING DIRECTIONS: From the Sylvan exit (exit 71B), drive 30.4 miles west on US 26 to the intersection with Scofield Road. (The intersection with Scofield Road is located 3.7 miles past the intersection with OR 47.) Scofield Road enters US 26 on your right, from the north.

My suggestion is to park near this intersection (take care not to obstruct other cars) and walk the 2.75 miles of Scofield Road until you reach Nowakowski Road; then return by the same route. One can approach the hike from Ridge Road on the south side of US 26 the same way—hike up as far as you want and backtrack to the intersection of US 26 and Scofield Road.

Breaking these routes into shorter bite-sized portions will help the hiker by providing some trips that are not overly taxing. It splits the hike into two segments, both directly accessible from US 26.

SPECIAL ATTRIBUTES: This Scofield area has the feeling of being a dispersed village stretched along the looping rail lines. Along this relatively steep grade (2 percent), the westbound trains would have been straining as they rumbled noisily around the tight curves. Today you'll run into friendly and engaging folks as they trundle by in old pickups with dogs in the back. You never know who you're going to run into up here. One time it's a timber cruiser, another time a cavalcade of ATVs, a cyclist or two—even an elderly neurophysicist from Reed College.

TRAIL LOG: These descriptions are based on a north-to-south travel direction, crossing US 26 in the middle. Start at Nowakowski Road and walk along Scofield Road to US 26. Then climb up the old Ridge Road (on the other side of the highway) to the summit of the ridge and travel south along the ridge to the Walcott Tunnel.

Start at the eastern end of Scofield Road, heading in a southwesterly direction toward US 26. Scofield Road branches off from Nowakowski Road about a half mile from the lower entrance to Nowakowski Road. From there proceed another mile to the first railroad crossing. Following Scofield Road you can now take a shortcut across the big loops made by the train tracks and reach US 26 in a mere 1.6 miles instead of the 4.5 miles it takes when following the tracks.

At US 26 take care in crossing the highway since cars go whizzing by this intersection at high speeds. On the opposite side, walk around a concrete barrier and follow the trail that leads up into the forest on the south side of the road. This rough track is actually part of what was called Ridge Road.

Just beyond the concrete barrier, Ridge Road climbs rapidly up the slope. About a quarter of a mile up the slope, the trail splits; the two routes rejoin a little more than a quarter of a mile later. Either route will get you to the top, but I recommend the left-hand option. After 0.9 miles the trail intersects with another little-used logging road that cuts across the top of the ridgeline. This is the extension of the road that leads past the cell phone towers (see chapter 13) above the tunnel and links up with the Cape Horn Traverse.

Follow this ridge-hugging road to the left, in a southeasterly direction. This track is actually the continuation of the original Ridge Road that you just ascended. In less than a mile, reach a wide clearing where the road splits once again. Stick to the right and follow the ridgeline along the height of land. A bit farther along (0.9 miles from the start of the tunnel-crossing route) a path leads down off the ridge to the southwest. Ignore that spur and follow the path that continues to wend its way along the ridgeline

"Two Rocks"—logger art located near Ridge Road where it crosses the Walcott Tunnel.

through fairly mature stands of Douglas fir trees. When I last walked this section I saw a long-necked blue grouse who thought she could fool me by not moving.

After a bit more than a mile, emerge from the trees to gaze over a large clear-cut that wraps over the top of the ridge. Cross the clear-cut using the gravel road that runs along the spine of the hill. At the southern end of the clear-cut, arrive at a green gate. Turn right and follow an old road uphill toward a tall stand of timber that crowns the next high point of the ridge. Here you've reached the highest point of the hike at about 1,470 feet in elevation and are surrounded by trees about 2–3 feet in diameter and about 120–150 feet high. It's likely that these stands too, will come thumping down as Oregon goes about harvesting its patrimony.

Another 0.1 mile farther the road dips down and emerges on the clear-cut that covers the southern end of this ridge and affords a wide vantage point from which to examine the mountains that cluster around the headwaters of the Salmonberry River. Cochran Pond is just over the next rise and all around a massive carpet of mountains bars the way west.

At the end of the ridge is the gate that bars vehicular access to this area. The gate is located immediately above the Walcott Tunnel. As of this writing there is debate about repairing the tunnel, said to be rotten under the shot concrete. This is the longest tunnel on the entire Pacific Railway & Navigation line, measuring 1,435 feet in length. It was built entirely by hand labor, extracting 24,150 cubic feet of rock.

Be Careful What You Ask For

Life on the edge of civilization was undoubtedly difficult in the early part of the twentieth century. Trying to scratch out a living near the headwaters of the Nehalem and Salmonberry Rivers must have presented unique challenges in 1911. One can hardly imagine the challenges faced by Mary Strassel or Alva Scofield, both of whom managed rowdy little villages that sprang up along the planned route of the Pacific Railway & Navigation line. Over the hill in Timber, a new railroad was snaking its way down the Salmonberry River and Charles Lindgren was just setting up business as the proprietor of the Timber Saloon. A hotel and restaurant soon followed, and Timber was in business![1] Farther to the north more settlers were staking their homestead claims. By 1910, Mist had a big store, a hotel, a blacksmith's shop, and a cheese factory.[2]

On the Lower Columbia both logging and fishing were fueling the growth of several communities, such as Clatskanie and Rainier. The first settlers arrived in Rainier in 1853, and by 1878 the town launched its own steamboat, *The Novelty*, designed to meet the big river steamers that raced up and down the Columbia River between Portland and

My dog, Loki, enjoys the sunset bathing the west slope of the Tualatin Range.

Astoria. It was here in Rainier that I found one of the more curious tales of frontier love.

It all started because Eunice Huntington was trying to encourage her beau to propose marriage to her. But it seemed as if he could never summon up the courage to pitch the question. Then she learned that her friend Charles Fox was getting married in Rainier. So when the invitation arrived, she asked her beau to escort her to the wedding. He may have been a bit nervous at the prospect, but nonetheless he agreed.

In 1853 Rainier and many of the other towns along the Lower Columbia were too small to support a church or engage a priest on a permanent basis. If they needed one, they hired someone to come downriver from Portland. And while they were at it, they hired the band, and soon a Portland steamer was fully loaded with friends and strangers all intent on putting on one hell of a hullabaloo.

In those days it was the river that connected people, and the paddlewheelers would churn their way back and forth across the river tying together the communities on opposite sides of the river like the laces of a boot. Zigzagging down the river, the steamer stopped at Scappoose,

Kalama, St. Helens, Goble, and Cowlitz, loading up with scores of eager celebrants.

As the wedding-bound steamer approached Rainier, she let loose a piercing whistle that set off instant pandemonium in town. Soon the steamer's sailors were cinching their hawsers to the wharf, the band was scurrying about collecting their instruments, and a dozen horses stamped about the wooden decks, impatient to be led ashore. Rainier seemed to swell as the passengers spilled onto the streets. River folk came up the channels in their skiffs. And even the homesteaders who had gotten wind of the coming nuptials were soon tramping down from the heights above town. Excitement rippled all through the waterways of the Lower Columbia. The prospect of a festive marriage was always welcome news.

It was this celebratory atmosphere that Eunice Huntington had in mind when she invited her hesitant beau to attend the Charles Fox wedding. By all accounts it was a tremendous wedding party, but it's for what followed next that people still remember it.

At the end of the ceremonies and just before the celebrating got irreversibly out of hand, the preacher rose before the would-be revelers and asked if anyone else would like to take advantage of his presence, since he did not plan to return to Rainier for another half year. He gestured around him. "The table is decked, the party has been laid on, the band is tuned to within a hair's breadth of a whistle, and I'm here. If you were thinking of hitching up soon, now would be the time to act."

At this point Eunice stepped forth and announced that she was ready to be wed. Turning around to face her beau, she was thunderstruck as he hesitated and then fled from the hall. Eunice was mortified and stood all alone in the middle of the dance floor. Everyone stood in an awkward silence until Henry Windsor, the local stage driver, stepped out and declared that if her beau wasn't convinced, he was ready to marry Eunice on the spot!

In less time than it takes to read these words Eunice looked her unexpected suitor up and down and declared herself ready as well. And so the two were married, on the heels of the Fox wedding. In spite of his in-laws' initial doubts, Henry Windsor turned out to be the best freight agent on the Lower Columbia, and Eunice soon presided over an extended and boisterous clan.

I first came across this curious tale of frontier love while perusing a 1903 newspaper announcement in the *Astorian* celebrating Eunice and Henry's golden wedding anniversary!

Notes

1. *Oregon Coast Crawler* #1, July 15, 2006 (from collected documents at the Tillamook State Forest Heritage Trust).
2. Edna Carl Johnson, "Early Nehalem Valley," interview with Bill and Lee Logue (Vesper, OR), April 13, 1968.

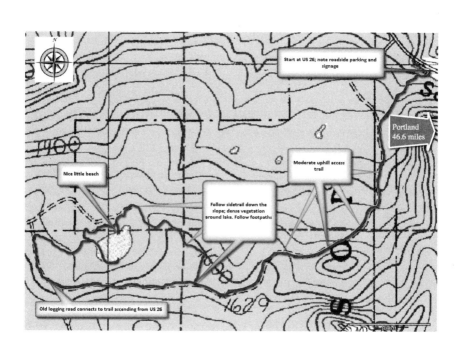

Start at US 26; note roadside parking and signage

Portland 46.6 miles

Moderate uphill access trail

Nice little beach

Follow sidetrail down the slope; dense vegetation around lake. Follow footpaths

Old logging road connects to trail ascending from US 26

15. Bloom Lake

BRIEF DESCRIPTION: Bloom Lake is one of the easiest hikes in this book and is perfectly suited for family outings with small children in tow. It is best enjoyed on a hot summer day since the trail is nicely shaded and cool.

DISTANCE: 3 miles round trip

ELEVATION CHANGE: 470 feet

TRAIL CONDITION: Mostly it's a footpath. The quality of the trail construction is a bit rough, but that could have been the effect of a hard winter that had worn away at the trail. The upper portions of the trail are located partially on logging roads.

APPROXIMATE DURATION: 1.5 hours, with time to dangle your toes in the lake

TRAVEL TIME FROM PORTLAND TO TRAILHEAD: 1 hour, 20 minutes

DRIVING DIRECTIONS: From the Sylvan exit (exit 71B), take US 26 west about 46 miles to a wide pull-off past milepost 25. The trailhead is easy to find and requires no dirt-road driving.

SPECIAL ATTRIBUTES: Easily accessible from US 26. This short family-friendly hike has access to a lake with its own tiny beach.

TRAIL LOG: From the roadside parking area, cross a footbridge and immediately begin to ascend the hillside. The climb is moderate, rising 470 feet from the parking area to the highest point at 1,688 feet in less than a mile.

Just short of a mile up this trail, a secondary trail heads off to the right and leads to the lake. Follow this trail around the lake in a counterclockwise direction. Right after rounding the northern end of the lake, the trail meets an older logging road (at 1.22 miles) that completes the circuit. Also at this juncture, a small trail leads to the water's edge and several scenic spots. Bring a picnic and sit back to relax in the warm afternoon sunlight.

When you're ready, double back to the road and continue to follow it around the northwestern edge of the lake. The trail is actually a bit removed from the edge of the water; several informal trails allow you to approach the lake itself. But for simplicity and ease of navigation, the map simply routes you back to the road that encircles the lake.

At 1.5 miles into the hike, the road intersects another path that skirts the southwestern vicinity of the lake. Turn left to follow this trail. It eventually

Bloom Lake.

leads back to the trail that brought you up to the lake (and past the northerly side spur you took when entering the area).

When Bullwhackers Ruled the Forest

If you drive out of Portland headed north toward Scappoose and the Oregon side of the Lower Columbia, you are likely to travel along NW Yeon Avenue. There is some confusion about how to pronounce this name. Newcomers are tempted to omit the *y* and pronounce it as *eon*. But old-timers omit the *e* and refer to this industrial thoroughfare as *yon*. Regardless of how you pronounce it, few Oregonians know that this industrial avenue is a tribute to one of Oregon's most successful bullwhackers, Jean Baptiste Yeon (1865–1928). Indeed, most have no idea what a bullwhacker was. So let us digress briefly into the early logging practices of the Pacific Northwest.

When the first loggers arrived in the Northwest they learned that the size of the trees, the rough terrain, and the sodden conditions made it impossible to log with horses. They realized that they needed enormous strength and a strong, steady pull. Consequently, they soon traded their horses for teams of oxen. For half a century these "bulls," as the loggers referred to them, did most of the heavy lifting in the Pacific Northwest. Often they would hitch five, six, and even ten yokes of bulls together to pull the massive old-growth trunks down the skid roads to the river's edge. The skid roads were made from felled tree trunks laid side by side to form a track that would prevent logs from getting hung up on rocks or buried in the mud.

A memorable passage in *Holy Old MacKinaw*, by Stewart Holbrook, that noted chronicler of Pacific Northwest history, recounts the following scene from a bull-powered logging operation:

> First, you heard the loud, clear call of the bullwhacker's voice echoing down the forest road that was more like a deep green canyon so tall and thick stood the fir; and the clank of chains and the wailing of oxen as the heavy animals got into the pull and "leaned on her." And then the powerful line of red and black and spotted white would swing by with measured tread, the teamster, sacred goadstick over his shoulder, walking beside the team, petting and cursing them to high heaven by turns, the huge logs coming along behind with a dignified roll.[1]

The bullwhacker reigned supreme during the bull-team era; he was the rock star of the woods crew. Paid three times as much as an axman, he was the unquestioned authority figure, handing down judgment on everything from women to the mysteries of the universe. The bullwhacker presided over the skid road with a firm and practiced hand, but his explosive profanity could lash his beasts into unearthly exertion. When profane persuasion failed to arouse the necessary effort, his goad stick, a slim piece of wood with a steel point on one end, served as an added encouragement. When neither goad stick nor profanity roused the brutish charges to their utmost, bullwhackers were known to leap up on the backs of the bulls. There they would stomp down the entire length of the team, piercing their backs with their nail-studded calk boots and "yelling like all the devils in hell."

Such a man was "Johnnie" Yeon. Having arrived penniless from Quebec, he borrowed enough money to purchase land and a team of bulls and proceeded to cut his way into the hills above Cathlamet. In winter he kept warm by bunking alongside his bulls in their oxen hovel. Up at 4:00 to feed his huge companions, he worked as a bullwhacker, an axman, a cook, a timekeeper, and a foreman. He liked to keep in shape and was known to fell a two-hundred-foot fir tree just for the exercise. After twenty years he became one of Portland's most successful timber barons. In 1911 he built Portland's first high-rise building. The Yeon Building was fifteen stories high and clad in glazed terra-cotta. At the time it was Portland's tallest building.

Like his oxen, Johnnie was a giant, and he helped carve this state out of the primeval forests. His legacy survives through the roads he constructed and the buildings he erected.

Notes

1. Stewart H. Holbrook, *Holy Old Mackinaw: A Natural History of the American Lumberjack* (New York: MacMillan, 1938), 164.

Zoe, my partner, staring off the peak of Kings Mountain.

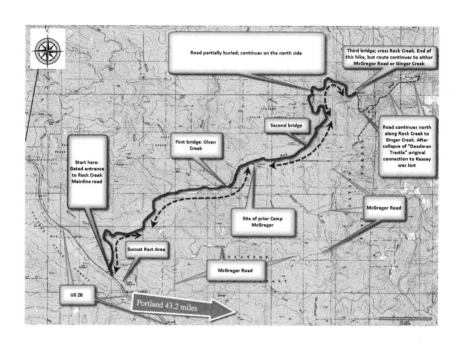

Road partially buried; continues on the north side

Third bridge; cross Rock Creek. End of this hike, but route continues to either McGregor Road or Ginger Creek

Second bridge

First bridge: Olsen Creek

Road continues north along Rock Creek to Ginger Creek. After collapse of "Deadman Trestle" original connection to Keasey was lost

Start here: Gated entrance to Rock Creek Mainline road

Site of prior Camp McGregor

McGregor Road

Sunset Rest Area

McGregor Road

US 26

Portland 43.2 miles

16. Rock Creek

BRIEF DESCRIPTION: This trail is about halfway to the coast. You can access it on a dirt road about a quarter mile west of the Sunset Rest Area. A leisurely walk along a mostly deserted logging road, this hike runs along one of the area's prettiest streams. It is an ideal trail to bicycle with youngsters, because the route is pretty flat from beginning to end. Permit required on Weyerhaueser land. Visit www.wyrecreationnw.com.

DISTANCE: 10.6 miles one way

ELEVATION CHANGE: 400 feet

TRAIL CONDITION: Graveled logging roads, with a short distance of washed-out area between Martin Creek and Sunset Spring where the road has been reclaimed by earth movement, encroachment by the forest, and several exposed streams. This wild section is only about a half mile long; then the road reappears and the trail quality improves significantly.

APPROXIMATE DURATION: 7 hours on foot, 3 hours on a modest street bike with sturdy tires

TRAVEL TIME FROM PORTLAND TO TRAILHEAD: 45 minutes

DRIVING DIRECTIONS: From the Sylvan exit (exit 71B), continue west on US 26 for 43.2 miles. The entry is a small dirt road located just west of the Sunset Rest Area, on the north side of the highway.

TRAIL LOG: This hike begins where the Rock Creek Mainline heads north from the US 26, about 100 yards west of the Sunset Rest Area. The Rock Creek Mainline follows the idyllic Rock Creek all the way to the Columbia/Clatsop County divide more than 10 miles north of US 26.

From the gate near the highway, it's about 5.75 miles to the first bridge. The next bridge is 3.47 miles farther along. Our destination is the third bridge. On foot the long straight stretches (typical of a logging "mainline" route) can get tedious. I prefer to tour this trail by bicycle. For those on foot I recommend exploring any of the side roads, such as Olson Road, that climb up to the scenic ridges.

The third bridge, about 10.6 miles north of US 26, crosses the dappled waters of Rock Creek at the border of Columbia County and Clatsop County. I recommend using this as your destination, even though the road continues farther into Columbia County.

If you were to continue along the road ahead, you would eventually re-cross Rock Creek 3.2 miles onward near the base of a logging road that ascends Ginger Creek. This approach permits determined hikers to connect with the Vernonia-area logging roads. For the solo hiker, I would caution that these are remote landscapes and daunting distances to cover while traveling alone, so be sure to have safety resources at hand. I carry a satellite beacon that can send three distinct messages in escalating tones of urgency. A GPS lets me know how to retrace my steps, but is not completely reliable when trying to locate more recent roads. Water, emergency food, moisture-wicking clothing, and a bivy sack are included in my kit in the event I can't proceed.

A Million Board Feet a Day

Today, long lines of cars whisk along US 26 passing what were once impenetrable forests, impassable mountains, and untamed rivers. The contemporary traveler rarely glimpses past the "green curtain"—the fringe of forests that parallels the highway. Hopefully this guide will help give that hurried traveler some insight into the network of railroad lines, old logging roads, and forgotten timber towns that existed in this area before the advent of automobiles.

The Rock Creek Trail is perhaps the best example of this hidden history, and happily it is also one of the most accessible trails into the surrounding hills. As with most of the history associated with the North Coast, time and nature have overgrown much of the evidence. Today, one can walk through the center of Camp McGregor and not realize that once, not so long ago, the town boasted a school that taught through the eighth grade. It had more than forty family homes and enough bunkhouses to house two hundred loggers.[1] The camp burned down in 1933, but it was so important that it was completely rebuilt in 1936.[2]

In its heyday, Camp McGregor was the nerve center for an extended rail network that reached way up to the windy ridges above the Salmonberry and Nehalem Rivers. Looking at the dusty road that marks the entrance to the Rock Creek Mainline you would never guess that this humble portal played a crucial role in the history of the northern Coast Range. More than a million board feet of logs flowed down this road every day for more than seventeen years.[3] That's almost enough to frame a half million homes. From 1922 through 1957 the Oregon-American Lumber Company extracted most of the twenty million board feet of lumber growing in the twenty-two-thousand-acre Dubois logging tract. It was a Herculean feat

Rock Creek as it flows from Clatsop County into Columbia County.

any way you calculate it. Today we know that these gains came with a calculable cost to our environment. Hopefully, someday we will arrive at a valuation process that also considers standing timber as an active contributor to our clean atmosphere, and the equation that sets our priorities will shift gradually from harvesting timber to managing it for optimal carbon retention.

Wildfires in 1932 and 1933 burned large areas, releasing untold tons of carbon into the atmosphere. Those losses to wildfires, along with the timber extracted by the Oregon-American Lumber Company, reduced our forests' annual absorption of carbon dioxide. This loss is equivalent to adding the annual carbon footprint of another fifty thousand people to the Portland area. Like the Amazon, the wide swath of forests along our West Coast acts like an enormous scrubber that transforms harmful carbon into productive and beautiful landscapes. Recent studies have shown that the ancient conifer forests of the Pacific Northwest can sequester an average of one thousand metric tons of carbon per hectare. Perhaps someday this cleansing effect will be recognized, and forestry will refocus its efforts on maximizing not just the structural value of wood, but also the atmospheric cleansing value of big trees.

To the casual traveler on US 26 none of this is apparent. In fact, few drivers will even spot the dirt road that slices into the forest just past the Sunset Rest Area. It was the Oregon-American Lumber Company whose steam-driven logging operations in 1922 first laid down the roadbed that led up the Rock Creek valley. Their rail line ran west from Vernonia and crossed Rock Creek on a lofty trestle just beyond Keasey. From there the line followed Rock Creek all the way to the top of the watershed high above the Salmonberry River, south of US 26.

Well into modern times the rail line up Rock Creek was the only way to access this part of the Coast Range. It was not until a road was punched all the way through the mountains to the coast that another avenue of approach was developed along Wolf Creek, a stream that flowed west from the small community of Timber. It wasn't until 1933 that the federal government, through the efforts of its Works Progress Administration and the Civilian Conservation Corps, began the enormous task of building a major highway all the way through to the coastal community of Seaside. At that time the road was known as the Wolf Creek Highway, later renamed the Sunset Highway, or US 26.[4] It took sixteen years to build and was finally completed in 1949. Since then it has served Portlanders and their coastal neighbors as the most convenient way to connect the northern Oregon coast to the Portland area.

Notes

1. Edward Kamholz, Jim Blain, and Greg Kamholz, *The Oregon-American Lumber Company: Ain't No More* (Palo Alto, CA: Stanford University Press, 2003), 102.
2. Ibid.
3. Ibid., 296.
4. Ibid., 163–5.

Rock Creek, crossing from Clatsop County into Columbia County.

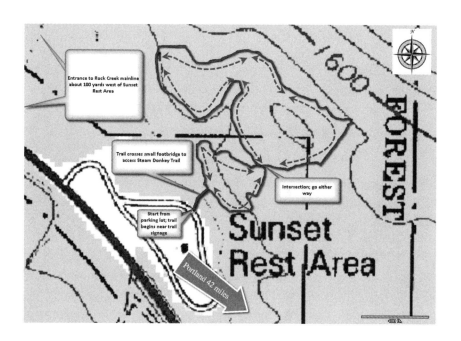

HIKING FROM PORTLAND TO THE COAST

17. Steam Donkey Trail

BRIEF DESCRIPTION: The Steam Donkey Trail is about halfway to the coast and is accessed from the Sunset Rest Area, situated alongside US 26 just west of mile marker 29.

DISTANCE: 0.8 miles

ELEVATION CHANGE: About 120 feet—minimal!

TRAIL CONDITION: Well maintained

APPROXIMATE DURATION: 20–30 minutes

TRAVEL TIME FROM PORTLAND TO TRAILHEAD: 45 minutes

DRIVING DIRECTIONS: From the Sylvan exit (exit 71B), head 42 miles west on US 26 to the Sunset Rest Area.

TRAIL LOG: Two short trails configured like a figure 8 form an interpretative trail that attempts to give you some idea of what it was like to log these hills in the early twentieth century. As an interpretive trail, I think the two trails—the Springboard Trail (0.3 miles) and the Upper Dooley Spur Loop Trail (0.5 miles)—fail to adequately convey the experience. However, these short trails do succeed in showing off the huge stumps of yesteryear and the charm of our deeply shaded forests.

Both trails are well maintained, and there is a nice bench near the interpretive sign at the midpoint of the figure 8 where the two trails join. The signage does give a good description of the logging rigging that was used. It's unfortunate that they could not leave an actual old steam donkey in situ to help bring this early logging technology to life. Also, the fact that the hills all around have now been obscured by new growth makes it more difficult to envision the scale of the operation when it was operating in the 1920s.

But the walk is certainly to be recommended. I've driven by this rest area for years and until recently had never stopped to consider this little trail. Now I will cheerfully recommend it as a very worthwhile diversion for the 20–30 minutes it takes to circumnavigate the two linked trails!

Muskets and Tall Tales

Among the Chinook, little children commenced to hunt and fish as soon as they could nock an arrow to a bowstring. Most made do with spears and arrows, but by the mid-1800s the infamously inaccurate and unreliable

"Queen Anne muskets" were filtering down into the Native American population. However, the powder and the balls were so expensive that this approach was only worthwhile if they could shoot more than one animal with each shot! Enterprising native kids would lie flat on their one-man canoes covering themselves with "green boughs so that it would appear to be a mere floating heap of brushwood, and lying in ambush under this the hunter would patiently wait for hours for the birds to come near or for favoring winds to float him into their midst." According to the earliest European chroniclers, Native American youths loved "the stealth and the ease of it, and because it meant many birds with one shot."[1]

One young fourteen-year-old is said to have observed a big cougar preparing to cross a creek on a log. Rather than shoot the cat as it passed broadside to him, the youth snuck up the side of the ravine and positioned himself at the other end of the log so that the cougar would walk right up to the end of his muzzle. Luckily, the musket didn't misfire, and afterward, the young hunter explained that he "blowed a hole in that cougar so big that a bull bat could a' flew through without 'tetching' his wings on either side."[2]

When his listener pointed out the notorious unreliability of the old Queen Anne muskets and asked why the youth would take such a huge risk, the boy replied that his own life was the cheapest of his possessions—he had paid nothing for it—but the cougar was of immeasurable value in honor, in reward, and in status.

By the late 1880s, the Native Americans had disappeared, but there were still lots of muskets in use. They kicked like a mule, spat out masses of smoke and powder, and blinded you to the consequences of your shot. But they were essential for augmenting the diets of the early settlers in the Nehalem Valley. Most of the hunting was done in early December after it snowed and they could track the game.

One old-timer had quite a tangle with an elk. Using his old muzzle-loader, he had wounded the great beast. But contrary to plan, the elk failed to accept his fate gracefully. Instead he chose to vent his ire on the quickly retreating hunter. As the elk charged at him, the settler quickly took refuge behind a tree, and for a while the two just kept circling. Each time the elk would pause, the settler would attempt to reload the gun. But the rattling of the ramrod would infuriate the elk, and he would spring into action, chasing the fleeing settler round and round again. Eventually, the settler got the musket loaded, and leaning around the tree he dispatched the beast once and for all. While the image of the circling foes does present a humorous tableau, it also goes to show what little margin for safety existed out in those woods.

Entrance to Steam Donkey Trail.

Then there's the tale attributed to Ed Jarvis, a known retailer of Western yarns.[3] According to this impeccable source, he was out hunting when he spotted a herd of elk. Unfortunately, he had already used up all his shot, so he looked for some alternatives. All around him were thick bushes of huckleberries, so it soon came into his mind that perhaps he might have some impact with the greener and harder specimens. After loading his gun with powder he now added in the huckleberries, aimed, and fired at the center of the herd. When the smoke finally cleared there was no trace of the elk herd to be seen.

The following year he was once again hunting up the same ravine when his attention was diverted by what looked like giant huckleberry bushes slowing moving across the opposing slope. When he finally got close enough to see what was afoot, he was amazed to see a herd of elk that had sprouted huckleberry branches right out of their thick pelts!

But then again, Ed Jarvis was known for being one of the best storytellers around, someone who could keep you on the edge of your seat until you fell right into the inevitable "gotcha" at the end of the yarn.

Notes

1. Thomas Nelson Strong, *Cathlamet on the Columbia* (Portland, OR: Binford & Mort, 1906), 22.

2. Ibid., 23.

3. Inez Stafford Hanson, *Life on Clatsop* (Eugene, OR: Central Printing and Reprographic Services, 2004), 72.

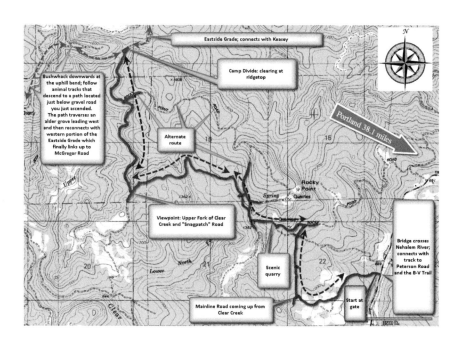

Eastside Grade; connects with Keasey

Camp Divide: clearing at ridgetop

Bushwhack downwards at the uphill bend; follow animal tracks that descend to a path located just below gravel road you just ascended. The path traverses an alder grove leading west and then reconnects with western portion of the Eastside Grade which finally links up to McGregor Road

Portland 38.1 miles

Alternate route

Viewpoint: Upper Fork of Clear Creek and "Snagpatch" Road

Scenic quarry

Bridge crosses Nehalem River; connects with track to Peterson Road and the B-V Trail

Mainline Road coming up from Clear Creek

Start at gate

18. Timber Road to Camp Divide

BRIEF DESCRIPTION: This trail begins north of US 26, on the road that leads to Vernonia from the so-called Timber junction. It traverses the southern face of Rocky Point (no relation to Rocky Point Road located near Scappoose) and eventually crests the ridgeline at the location of the long-forgotten Camp Divide (elevation 1,495 feet). The eastern end of this ridge features a precipitous slope known as Rocky Point, hence the road's name. Permit required on Weyerhaueser land. Visit www.wyrecreationnw.com.

DISTANCE: 10.4 miles round trip

ELEVATION CHANGE: Just under 800 feet

TRAIL CONDITION: Mostly graveled logging roads

APPROXIMATE DURATION: 5 hours

TRAVEL TIME FROM PORTLAND TO TRAILHEAD: 45 minutes

DRIVING DIRECTIONS: From the Sylvan exit (exit 71B), head 38.1 miles west on US 26. Turn right onto Timber Road. A short distance north of US 26, Timber Road crosses the Nehalem River. A few hundred yards farther, a paved and gated entrance on the left leads uphill from Timber Road. I recommend you park nearby, on the edge of Timber Road.

SPECIAL ATTRIBUTES: Camp Divide was once an important logging camp. All that is left today is a flat expanse next to an inactive quarry. Another road, known as the Eastside Grade, climbs up the northern face of Rocky Point to reach Camp Divide. This camp and the grade-level road that served it were owned by the Eastside Box Company, whose main business was manufacturing boxes in their factory on the lower east side of Portland. This approach to Camp Divide starts at the southern side, climbing a gentle ridgeline northward. Then the route turns and traverses the slope westward to the top of the Clear Creek drainage. Climb the track along the edge of this wide ravine to the site of Camp Divide, located on a flat expanse that straddles this ridge.

The area is quite secluded, except during hunting season, when the gates are opened and pickup trucks loaded with hunters are cruising through. These slopes are riddled with old logging roads, including the Eastside Grade and Snagpatch Road, which provide direct links to the Rock Creek drainage located one ridge farther west. This area is also heavily trafficked by deer, elk, and even bears at the higher elevations—when the hunters aren't present.

TRAIL LOG: After parking along Timber Road, walk past the blue gate and proceed into Weyerhaeuser country. Currently, access may be limited to permit holders who have secured their access rights by applying for a permit in May of every year. The permits, according to current rules, are good from June 1 through December 31. During the other half of the year access is open without a permit.

This road leads uphill for 0.9 miles before it intersects with a well-established logging road that ascends the slope in a northerly direction. At the intersection, turn right and follow this broad road uphill. The uphill slope on your left has recently been clear-cut and is beginning to show signs of reforestation. As you climb you will pass two side spurs. The first is just 0.2 miles up the road. The second is 0.3 miles from the gate. Just beyond that second spur the road enters a medium-aged forest. Continue until you're about 1.4 miles from the gate; here you will encounter a road on the left heading up the hill. This is Rocky Point Road; follow it as it ascends the slope for the next half mile.

At this point you will begin ascending a major north-south ridge; beyond it is a broad basin that drains south into Clear Creek. To the north, the road splits. Take the left-hand option; it leads along the side of the hill, descending gently as it goes. Follow this road 0.3 miles to the next intersection.

The next intersection provides two options: go straight or make a left-hand turn. Either way will work, but the straight option (the continuation of Rocky Point Road) will require you to climb higher before the road connects with the final ascent to Camp Divide. By dint of this added elevation, it's the prettier of the two routes. The lower option avoids any unnecessary elevation gain. For this initial excursion, opt for the lower road (turn left at the intersection). This route crosses a south-facing slope, and 1.1 miles later you'll reach the edge of a wide ravine that feeds into Clear Creek. This basin has been extensively clear-cut and affords a great view north up to the summit of this mountain ridge, which is where you're headed.

At the lip of the clear-cut basin, turn uphill and follow a track that ascends (north-south orientation) along the edge of the clear-cut. Going straight up the slope will require navigating a huge berm and trough that blocks any vehicular access. Walkers can easily scramble across this impediment and begin to climb up the valley following the old logging road that skirts the lip of the wide ravine to the left. The ascent continues for 0.9 miles, whereupon this route meets Rocky Point Road (discussed earlier) coming in from the right. At this point you're pretty close to the top of the ridge, but continue farther along a trail that heads northwest from this intersection.

This basalt quarry on Rocky Point Road is a rock hound's delight.

This short trail is a half mile long and it debouches into an open area bounded on the right by a stone quarry and on the left by an open gravel field. The stone quarry is notable because it is one of the sites mentioned in a 1957 Department of Geology and Mineral Industries report that lists the best locations for finding Oligocene fossil beds. Basalt is exposed at the base of the quarry, but overlying the basalt is about 15 feet of basal conglomerate of the Cowlitz formation, containing many Eocene marine fossils. These are said to contain numerous pelecypods and the occasional shark's tooth.

Rocky Point Road looking west toward the bushwhack connecting Camp Divide to the Eastside Grade in the far distance.

Facing north in the middle of the wide-open area where Camp Divide used to be located, you can see trails all around that terminate at this saddle. This memorable hilltop intersection will serve as the end of this trek, but it is also the start of a trail west along the Eastside Grade that will ultimately lead to Camp McGregor, located on the Rock Creek Mainline road. **Connecting with the western segment of the Eastside Grade.** Camp Divide is located at the eastern end of a long ridge. Using the Eastside Grade it is possible to walk west all the way to Camp McGregor, the next strategic point along a route that ultimately leads to Seaside. But finding the connection from Camp Divide to McGregor Road is somewhat challenging. Hopefully this description will succeed in guiding you through the short bushwhack required to connect with the western portion of the Eastside Grade.

Standing in the center of the wide saddle on which Camp Divide once stood, you have several options. To the north, the Eastside Grade descends the slope all the way to the tiny community of Keasey. To the left, and across the flat gravel expanse, you can see how the Eastside Grade bends and heads west as it reaches this saddle. Barely grazing what would have been the northern edge of Camp Divide, the Eastside Grade turns to climb the ridgeline westward. This road is important because it forms the backbone of a long east-west ridge from Camp Divide on the east to Camp McGregor on the western end. Both McGregor Road and the Eastside Grade straddle this ridge, constituting an effective bridge from the Upper Nehalem River (start of this hike) all the way to Rock Creek.

From Rock Creek another network of private logging roads provides connectivity all the way to the Lower Nehalem. Due to space constraints and some difficult access issues I have not provided a complete route description for the Portland-to-Seaside option. Rest assured that the best segments, such as Ridge-Runner's Delight, are included. So much for the big picture!

From the center of the large empty area that marks the location of Camp Divide, walk north nearly to the edge. There you will observe that a roadway skirts Camp Divide and heads west up the ridgeline. Climbing the ridgeline is an underused road. It eventually makes a U-turn to complete the ascent of this recently logged peak. This is where it gets tricky! About 100 feet *before* the U-turn, descend over the left edge of the road, down to a wide ledge overgrown with alders. Watch for snapped ends of alder branches—hunters often blaze their trails in this way. Below the road you'll soon find yourself in the midst of a young grove of alders growing on a wide ledge that parallels the road above. Proceed through the alders heading west. The ledge narrows, and elk trails lead through a gap and around deep trenches. Suddenly you emerge at the end of a long unused road. This is the western section of the Eastside Grade.

Once through the "secret" bushwhack you can follow the Eastside Grade along the ridgeline. Eventually it branches, with one route heading to the northern side of the ridge, and the right-hand option ascending the ridge directly to your west. Take the middle option; it continues west all the way to McGregor Road. A few miles farther, Olson Creek Road heads off to the right. That rough track will eventually take you down to the old Camp McGregor site. This western portion of the Eastside Grade is best accessed using McGregor Road and Rock Creek Road. I will leave the continuation of this northern route for those intrepid readers to explore on their own.

Wishing for a Wet Mattress on a Hot August Day

The great Tillamook Burn of 1933 has received a lot of attention, but it is often forgotten that during that same year another fire, the Wolf Creek Fire, burned a total of forty-seven-thousand acres of timber and reduced Camp McGregor to a heap of smoldering ashes. It is thought that the fire broke out in some unburned slash (logging debris) late in the afternoon of August 24, 1933. Men and equipment were rushed by train from Vernonia to the scene, but a rapid change of wind direction and intensity soon caused the fire to jump the firefighters' lines. The wind, rising to gale proportions, whipped the inferno into a frenzy. Late in the afternoon of August 26, the wind suddenly reversed direction and began to blow at near-hurricane strength—directly threatening Camp McGregor itself. The firefighters rallied and initially thought that they could save the community, but then a blazing tree broke the pipeline that supplied the community's water. At that point they realized that the firestorm was unstoppable and Camp McGregor had to be abandoned.

Judd Greenman, the general manager of the Oregon-American Lumber Company, recalled that

> this fire crowned whole sections of timber; it spotted ahead
> as much as two miles at one jump and it burned downhill and
> against the wind, so you know it did an enormous amount of
> damage. We never had a chance. Ten thousand of the best men
> that ever wore calks could never have done as we did—stood and
> watched her go.[1]

As the authorities realized that saving Camp McGregor was hopeless, they ordered the residents and the Civilian Conservation Crew (CCC) to evacuate by train. But the CCC boys, being mostly city kids from the eastern part of the country, panicked and started to push the loggers' families off the train until it was made clear that there was room enough for everyone.

Meanwhile, up in the woods above the camp two teenage boys were making the rounds of several hives that they had established along the slopes of Dogthief Mountain, just west of Camp McGregor. These previously logged areas were awash in fireweed (*Chamerion angustifolium*)— a colorful plant that thrives in the disturbed soils left behind by man's heavy-handed activities. And fireweed, as the boys knew, made the best honey! So this combination of native wood lore and entrepreneurship now placed them square in the path of the fast-approaching fire. But they weren't too worried. After all, Camp McGregor, with its hundreds of buildings, numerous loggers, and tracks to Vernonia, guaranteed an escape hatch out of the Rock Creek valley that would surely carry them away from the impending danger. Too bad about the bees, they thought as they scurried downhill to the camp.

Imagine their shock at finding Camp McGregor completely deserted. The usually bustling camp lay still as a graveyard, even as the crackling fire began to creep down the slopes toward them. Following the rail line north, they soon found that fire had already cut off that route of escape. They were surrounded, with no way to escape the inevitable inferno that would soon sweep through the camp.

Seeing a shallow pool of water near the center of the camp, the boys ran to the nearest bunkhouse, where they grabbed two of the thin mattresses that the loggers used on their crude bunks. They dragged these mattresses to the pool of water, soaked them until they were thoroughly wet, and then in desperation laid one mattress in the water and pulled the other soaking wet mattress over them. Within the hour the entire camp was engulfed in flames. The wooden walkways that connected the houses caught fire like a fuse leading the conflagration from one cabin to the next! But the boys escaped harm, lying sandwiched between the smoldering mattresses as the fire swept over the entire camp, burning it to the ground all around them. When the returning loggers finally reentered the smoking ruins of the camp, they were amazed to find the two boys awaiting them, clutching their scorched mattresses!

Notes

1. Edward Kamholz, Jim Blain, and Greg Kamholz, *The Oregon-American Lumber Company: Ain't No More.* (Palo Alto, CA: Stanford University Press, 2003), 134.

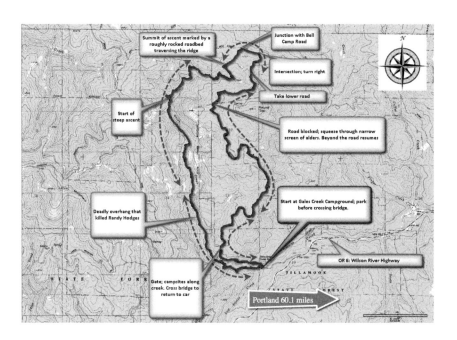

Summit of ascent marked by a roughly rocked roadbed traversing the ridge

Junction with Bell Camp Road

Intersection; turn right

Take lower road

Start of steep ascent

Road blocked; squeeze through narrow screen of alders. Beyond the road resumes

Deadly overhang that killed Randy Hodges

Start at Gales Creek Campground; park before crossing bridge.

OR 6: Wilson River Highway

Gate; campsites along creek. Cross bridge to return to car

Portland 60.1 miles

19. Gales Creek Loop via Round Top

BRIEF DESCRIPTION: From the Gales Creek Campground, accessible from OR 6, this trail follows Gales Creek to its headwaters and into the headwaters of the Nehalem River. The trail meets Bell Camp Road as it runs along the top of Round Top Mountain. This loop hike follows an old logging road along the top of the ridge, circling Round Top. The road seems to end at a thick screen of alders. Approach the grove and you'll see where the elk have carved a narrow path through the trees. Follow it for a few twists and turns and you will emerge at the end of a little-used logging road that will lead you back down to the Gales Creek Campground.

DISTANCE: About 14 miles round trip

ELEVATION CHANGE: 1,449 feet. The elevation at Gales Creek Campground is 914 feet. The summit ridge along which Bell Camp Road runs is at an elevation of 2,363 feet.

TRAIL CONDITION: The ascent from Gales Creek Campground to the summit is mostly a single-track hiking/biking trail. From mile 6 to mile 9 the route is quite steep. Along the ridgeline, Bell Camp Road has infrequent vehicular traffic. The descent along the east face of Round Top uses an existing logging road that is mostly clear enough to permit cycling.

APPROXIMATE DURATION: 6 hours

TRAVEL TIME FROM PORTLAND TO TRAILHEAD: 1 hour, 20 minutes

DRIVING DIRECTIONS: Gales Creek Campground is just off OR 6, 60.1 miles from the US 26 Sylvan exit (exit 71B). To reach it, drive out US 26 and take the turnoff to Tillamook. After passing through Gales Creek and Glenwood, the road gets steeper as it climbs the Coast Range. The turnoff to Gales Creek Campground is clearly marked on the right side of the road.

SPECIAL ATTRIBUTES: This is a lovely, though steep, trail. The first half, ascending the southern side of Gales Creek, is a single-track trail that gets steeper as it approaches the summit. The second half of the loop uses several linked logging roads to bring you back down on the north side of Gales Creek. Completing the loop and descending the eastern face of Round Top will reveal lovely views of western Washington County. In all, it's a good workout with rewarding views, especially on a nice summer day.

TRAIL LOG: Upon reaching Gales Creek Campground, park in the spaces on your left. Do not cross the bridge, but look for a clearly marked trailhead that begins right at the edge of this parking area. The trail heads up the south side of Gales Creek in a westerly direction. Remember to set your GPS device or pedometer, as subsequent points of interest will be noted using their distance from this trailhead.

Ascending to Bell Camp Road. The trail along the south shore of Gales Creek is quite windy and climbs 255 feet in just 0.6 miles. At 0.8 miles, the first bridge crosses a small stream. On your left, the Storey Burn Trail climbs upward from the intersection; however, you will turn right and continue to follow the river. At 2.2 miles into the hike, come around a left-leaning corner, which will guide you past a narrow section of the trail that passes below a substantial rock overhang. Unless you are aware of its significance, you're likely to miss this stony outcropping and never appreciate the dangerous energy that looms overhead.

I call this the Spirit Trail, or Memelose Trail, in the Chinookan language. The Chinookan people were strong believers in magic forces and feared supernatural powers (*tamanous*). Whole villages were often abandoned simply because the place was felt to be haunted.

James Swan, a prolific chronicler of Native American lore, reported that the tribespeople were afraid to go back to the site of an abandoned village "on account of the dead people; but if a white man went there they would go back too, because memelose tilicums (dead people) were afraid of whites."[1] On several occasions Swan tried to convince the natives that their fears were unfounded, but as he relates,

> it was no use for me to attempt to reason with them on the folly of their superstition; they would not reason or talk on the subject; but to any attempt to convince them of the absurdity of their fears they had but one reply, "You are a white man, and can't see or hear our memelose; but we Indians can, and we understand their talk, and you do not."[2]

Though I am not a Native American, this trail has always seemed to have a spiritual presence that permeates the place. Especially at this overhanging rock face one can sense nature's raw energy reasserting itself. Despite all that we know of geology and the instability of our Northwest geography, nature often exerts its awesome powers when we least expect it. It was under this outcropping that Randy Hodges, a professional trail builder, was killed; a massive chunk of the rock face slid down and crushed him while he was rebuilding this trail in February 2011.

As you pass below it, look up at that wall and you can almost feel an unruly willfulness anchored in the rock. Today we may blithely follow the smooth path under its looming weight, but someday it will once again shrug off its constraints to burst forth, guided by an ancient *tamanous* that will never rest.

But you have miles to cover before you're done, so with another pensive glance at the rock face above, hurry onward. At 2.6 miles into the hike, you'll cross another stream, and after 3 miles, yet another. By this time you've gained almost 500 feet in elevation, but the steepest is yet to come. At 5.5 miles the trail starts to climb up and out of the valley floor. It begins to gain steepness, graduating from a gradual grade of 4 percent up to a steep grade of 7–10 percent.

In this area you may spot several old tree trunks with charcoal-colored swirls spiraling up their cone-shaped remains. These too are spirits of a by-gone era, ghosts of the vanished forest giants that once towered overhead. These charred remains are all that remains of the behemoths that were among the first trees destroyed by the Tillamook fires that raged from 1933 into the mid-1950s. These cone-shaped stumps with their charcoal swirls are the *memelose* of the ancient trees that once towered over these slopes.

At 8.25 miles, the trail makes its final turn and doubles back up along a ridge, leaving the tiny streambed that carries the headwaters of Gales Creek. The path is really steep in this portion, achieving an upward pitch of more than 17 percent. Your only consolation is that the end is nigh—any way you figure it! Fortunately, the top of the ridge soon brings you to the first of two dirt roads that this trail crosses. At 9 miles you reach the first road, and if you choose to continue a bit farther you will find Bell Camp Road just beyond it. This is a good place for a rest. Drink some water, have some nourishment, and take some time to recover from the steep climb out of the Gales Creek valley.

At this point you have three choices:

1. Continue onward past Bell Camp Road and head 3.4 miles down the other side of the mountain until you cross the Salmonberry Railroad, and later reach the bridge over the Nehalem, just south of Reehers Camp. This might be a perfect place to park a second car.

2. Turn around and return back down the way you came in. That's officially only 6.8 miles, but according to my GPS device it was almost 9 miles of walking back to Gales Creek Campground.

3. Turn right and follow the road to the east (right). It quickly runs into Bell Camp Road. Head north; you will soon approach a three-way intersection.

Facing you are two roads; chose the right-hand option. This road circles around the summit of Round Top and delivers you to what appears to be a cul-de-sac. On more careful examination you will see that it actually leads though an alder thicket and from there down to the Gales Creek Campground.

From Bell Camp Road to Round Top and down to Gales Creek. This part of the trail log starts at the three-way intersection where Bell Camp Road, heading east along the ridgetop, splits into two distinct roads. The road on the left is called Round Top Road; it leads all the way down to the Upper Nehalem River. The right-hand option leads to an unnamed road that turns right and circles the top of the Gales Creek basin that you just ascended. On the eastern side of the Gales Creek basin is the peak of Round Top, a hillock that is visible all the way across Washington County. One road leads to the summit of Round Top; another circles the western side of the peak. Yet another road encircles Round Top's western face at a slightly lower elevation. Avoid this lower road—it's a dead end.

Choose the fairly flat road that encircles the summit of Round Top. In some of its curves, the beavers have been busy constructing ponds, which are a welcome diversion for any dog that might be accompanying you on a hot and sunny summer's day!

Another good idea for those who plan ahead would be to stash a bicycle along this stretch. From here all the way back to Gales Creek Campground the route will be mostly downhill. So a well-placed bicycle would be the icing on the cake for this lovely hike. I would leave the bike (even a street bike will do) stashed in the woods near the intersection of the Gales Creek Trail and Bell Camp Road; this portion of the ridge is accessible by cars coming up from Timber by way of Round Top Road.

As you head along the southern side of Round Top you will pass several less-used logging roads that partially climb the slope; ignore these and stay on the lower option that continues around the peak. After about 1.5 miles the road you are on begins to become less used, and it ends in a screen of alders, boulders, and berms intended to prevent ATVs from proceeding. But you are on foot (or astride a bike), and no berms or alders will hold you back. So get up close to the alder screen and notice where the elk have conveniently carved a path through the alder grove. Beyond that the road resumes, although it is much more overgrown and rough on the far side of the barrier. Do not be discouraged; the road (now called Rogers Road) continues along, circling the slope of Round Top until it reaches the southeastern exposure. At this point Rogers Road passes through a series of

Storey Burn Trail.

clear-cuts that provide panoramic views of Washington County. This slope is also easily visible from US 26 as you travel west—it's that big round hill just south of the highway that's been heavily logged on the east-facing side.

Follow this road downhill for about 4 miles. Along the way several tracks will lead off to the left, but stay on the main logging road. After approximately 4 miles, a metal gate marks the back end of the Gales Creek Campground. Pass around the gate; the road bends to the left, following the river for about 0.75 miles until it reaches the bridge over Gales Creek. Your car should be parked on the far side of this bridge. Congrats—you've now completed a 14-mile circuit of the Gales Creek headwaters!

Memelose

In the 1998 edition of *The Pacific Crest Trail Hiker's Handbook*, author Ray Jardine admonishes us that trail building should "try to hurt the earth as little as possible."[1] The overriding objective should be to keep the wilderness experience as natural as possible. Trail engineering should blend in so that it can be overlooked as we focus on the natural environment around us. Like so many things in life, the ultimate compliment that can

Memelose trees with charcoal-colored burns spiraling up their cone-shaped remains.

be accorded our work is that it blends so perfectly with the world around us that human intervention is all but invisible.

I have walked the trail from Gales Creek to Reehers Camp both before the restoration of the trail and after, and I can attest that building an alignment that blended into the rough walls of this canyon was no easy task. My appreciation goes out to the great trail engineers working in our region, including Randy Hodges, who tragically lost his life building this trail. At the time, he was carving the trail past an overhang of exposed, weathered, and fractured rock when it suddenly split off, hitting Randy and his equipment. Together they tumbled off the trail and down into a rocky ravine. The tractor landed on top of Randy. Because he always worked alone, he had no chance of rescue. For well over a year the trail was left unfinished, with Randy's equipment parked around the bend, but eventually the Tillamook State Forest managers found another contractor to finish the trail. Today, there is no trace of Randy's unfortunate demise, which is partly why I wanted to acknowledge his sacrifice and use his untimely death as a reminder to all of us that these trails don't just magically appear. They are the work of professional trail builders who spend great efforts to make their work as invisible as they can. So just for a moment, I want to pull the covers back and acknowledge the dedicated work of our trail-building community—those who build something that no one is ever supposed to notice.

I never knew Randy, but I think it's fitting to reflect on the spirit he imbued into his trail-building work. He had a reputation as an exceptional contributor to this solitary occupation. One of his customers offered this accolade: "There's a lot of guys who call themselves trail builders, but they're not like Randy. He's an artist."[4] His family insisted that he'd been a source of light and laughter for everyone he'd touched, and for every mile he'd walked. Randy opened some of Oregon's special places. When he left us this path to enjoy, he too became one of the *memelose* whose spirit imbues this place.

Notes

1. James G. Swan, *The Northwest Coast* (Seattle and London: University of Washington Press, 1857), 77.

2. Ibid., 148.

3. Ray Jardine, *The Pacific Crest Trail Hiker's Handbook* (Arizona City, AZ: AdventureLore Press, 1996).

4. Jim Thayer, "Hurting the Earth as Little as Possible—In Memory of Randy Hodges," *Forest Hiker* (blog), September 5, 2011, http://www.foresthiker.com/?p=2141.

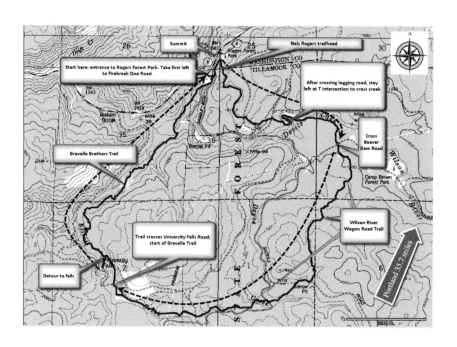

Summit

Nels Rogers trailhead

Start here: entrance to Rogers Forest Park. Take first left to Firebreak One Road

After crossing logging road, stay left at T intersection to cross creek

Cross Beaver Dam Road

Gravelle Brothers Trail

Wilson River Wagon Road Trail

Trail crosses University Falls Road; start of Gravelle Trail

Portland 35.7 miles

Detour to falls

20. Gravelle Brothers Trail and University Falls

BRIEF DESCRIPTION: This nice wooded trail is part of the Tillamook State Forest. It begins at Rogers Camp, heads southeast on the Nels Rogers Trail, crosses Beaver Dam Road, and eventually reaches the Wilson River Wagon Road Trail. It includes a short detour to University Falls. Thereafter it continues along Elliott Creek using the Gravelle Brothers Trail. Complete the loop to arrive back at Rogers Camp.

DISTANCE: 7.4 miles round trip

ELEVATION CHANGE: 387 feet. The trailhead is at about 1,600 feet. The highest point on the hike is at about 1,774 feet in elevation, which you reach at the very beginning of the Nels Rogers Trail. The lowest point comes near the end of the hike as you cruise along Elliott Creek.

TRAIL CONDITION: Nicely maintained trails, but also used by mountain bikers

APPROXIMATE DURATION: 4 hours at a steady amble

TRAVEL TIME FROM PORTLAND TO TRAILHEAD: About 40 minutes

DRIVING DIRECTIONS: From Portland, drive west on US 26, turn left on OR 6, and continue to just past milepost 33. Turn left into Browns Camp and take a left at the T intersection immediately ahead. Drive 0.1 mile to Firebreak One Road and park at the staging area near the entrance to the Nels Rogers Trail. Altogether the distance to the trailhead is 35.7 miles.

SPECIAL ATTRIBUTES: This is a well-maintained series of trails. The biggest challenge is transitioning from one trail to the next, but hopefully my directions will see you through to the end. This part of the forest is relatively close to Browns Camp, an active OHV area, so it can be noisy at times.

TRAIL LOG: From the trailhead near Rogers Camp, walk uphill on Firebreak One Road, which marks the beginning of the Nels Rogers Trail. This short (1.6-mile) trail segment wends its way through a forest that was planted in 1949. It's named for Nels Rogers, who served as state forester from 1940 to 1949. Along this section of the trail look for a flower that could easily be mistaken for a dogwood flower, except that it's a ground flower. This is the ubiquitous bunchberry. Native Americans throughout the Northwest enjoyed this flower for its pulpy fruit, which they ate raw.

After approximately a mile the trail crosses an unnamed forest road, and shortly thereafter it reaches a T intersection. Continue to follow the Nels

Rogers Trail by staying left. Eventually you will cross the Beaver Dam Road. From this juncture, follow the Wilson River Wagon Road Trail for 3 miles until it intersects with the University Falls Road. Immediately opposite is the entrance to the Gravelle Brothers Trail. According to the Tillamook State Forest literature, this trail was named after the Gravelle twins, Elroy and Edmund, devoted trail builders who helped to develop and maintain the Tillamook State Forest trail system.[1]

University Falls is accessible from the Gravelle Brothers Trail. It's a wonderful place to come during the hot summer months when the spray wafting off the steep falls fills the clearing with cool mist. While you're there, observe the lush, water-loving plants that flourish in that misty ravine, including the aptly named streambank spring beauty (*Montia parviflora*). Growing in wet habitats at low and middle elevations, it is not that common. Native American children used to play a game with this flower. Holding the flower by its stem, one player would try to hook his or her flower around the base of the opponent's flower and then pull. One of the two would "lose their head" to the other in this floral tug-of-war.

When you're done at University Falls, climb back to the Gravelle Brothers Trail. At the intersection turn left and proceed along Gravelle Brothers Trail in a northwesterly direction. Notice the scorched trunks that still remain from the great series of Tillamook fires that swept through this area in 1933 and several times thereafter.

As you approach Rogers Camp, stay right and follow the old road grade. Soon you will find yourself on a gravel road that skirts the bottom of the camp. Continue uphill until you reach an ODOT maintenance shed. Here cement barriers on either side demarcate the trail. At the entrance to the camp turn left and follow Beaver Dam Road north to the parking area at the Rogers Camp trailhead.

Salem-to-Astoria Military Road

Six years before Jefferson Davis was proclaimed president of the rebellious southern confederacy, he was the United States' secretary of war. In 1855 he was preparing to defend us against foreign invasions—not in the south but here on Oregon's distant beaches!

It may seem strange to us that this desolate and forbidding coastline was of great concern to the secretary of war, but for the growing number of Willamette Valley settlers the threat posed by the British Navy was no

University Falls, part of the Tillamook State Forest's excellent trail system.

fantasy. The memory of "losing" Astoria to the British in 1813 was still fresh in the minds of many American pioneers. The early settlers were quick to recall the bold assault by the British man-of-war HMS *Raccoon* as it sailed into the Columbia River to capture the wooden stockade that represented America's only West Coast outpost. To the chagrin of the proud British Navy, it turned out that the fort had been sold to representatives of the Hudson's Bay Company just a few weeks prior. Greatly annoyed, the captain of the *Raccoon* decided to underscore British supremacy by leading a "show" assault on the hapless fort anyway. Needless to say, the Hudson's Bay Company employees in the fort put up no resistance.

Despite the dominance of the Hudson's Bay Company on the Lower Columbia River, the Oregon country continued to be contested by the Americans and the British. Throughout the Willamette Valley, British spies actively mobilized loyal sympathizers.[2] And as late as 1845, the British positioned a fleet of no fewer than sixteen vessels along the Oregon coast as a show of force supporting British claims on the disputed lands.

But offsetting British influence in the Pacific Northwest was the rising tide of American emigrants flooding into the Willamette Valley. From their perspective, the best way to neutralize Britain's naval power was to deny the British access to the Columbia River. So it was not surprising that from 1843 on, numerous territorial petitions were dispatched from the American pioneers to the secretary of war, calling for authorization and funding to build a road from Salem to Astoria that would permit soldiers to reach the mouth of the Columbia River by the most direct route.

By 1858, Jefferson Davis had resumed his role as the senator from Mississippi and had become an ardent proponent of the Salem-to-Astoria road.

> This road is direct from one point to the other cutting off the great elbow made by the two rivers (Willamette and Columbia). It is deemed of great importance for military and territorial purposes, whether we look to defense against the Indians or a foreign foe on the exterior.[3]

His testimony was enough to secure passage of the $30,000 appropriations bill to build this road through the wilderness. Eventually, the federal government would contribute up to $70,000 to build this ambitious route to the coast. With Oregon's accession to statehood in 1859, the funding responsibilities shifted to the state, with support coming in the form of land allotments from the public domain.

As early as 1854, Joshua Elder had been engaged by Clatsop County to identify the most direct route from Astoria to the northern reaches of the Willamette Valley. In the following year Lieutenant George H. Derby was dispatched to complete an instrument survey of the sixty-eight-mile route proposed by Elder. Derby began recruiting men in Astoria, but soon realized that most of the local males had long since departed for Colville,

Washington, where a gold strike had recently been reported. Eventually, he was able to put together a team of ten men and six packhorses. A Cherokee also accompanied the group as a guide and messenger.

Derby's team followed the route indicated by Joshua Elder, and for the next twelve days they worked from dawn to dusk to reach the settlements along Gales Creek. Derby wrote that they were "laboring incessantly from daylight until almost dark, with six active axe men . . . seldom making more than five miles in a day."

This slow pace was due to the extremely congested vegetation and the rough terrain they found along the way. Derby described the "character of the country" as

> . . . mountainous and much cut up by gullies, heavily timbered with more or less brush on the hills while the bottoms (with a smaller amount of heavy timber) are covered with an almost impenetrable undergrowth, consisting of species of prickly brush [devil's club], wortleberry [huckleberry], vine maple and fern. This together with the fallen timber (in some instances as much as 30 ft. in circumference) renders any passage other than by trail cut through, impractical.[4]

Derby's assistant, Major H. Bache, had similar observations about the wild conditions through which they were attempting to plot a straight military road:

> It will be seen that the whole road from Astoria to the Nehalem River is over a mountainous and thickly timbered region abounding in almost impenetrable underbrush. It has the appearance of a grand primeval forest, which has never been disturbed since its creation.[5]

As if the terrain and vegetation were not enough, the crew Derby assembled did not make matters easier. Bache worked more directly with the local crew than Derby did, and toward the end of the surveying work, he vented his frustration in no uncertain terms:

> They do not seem to have the common sense to know that they receive wages to do what they are told, not what they choose. I cannot explain on paper what I have gone through with such a

set of the most disgusting subordinates as these Astoria men seem to be, banded together as they are, their chief end and aim is to prove that they are what they call independent. They seem to consider the whole amount of money expended is in a measure a gift to them. That the government provisions belong to them, etc.[6]

After they traversed the entire length of the proposed road to West Salem, the crew reversed course and began the actual instrument survey along the path that they had cleared on their way to Salem. The initial fifty-three miles from West Salem were relatively easy as they traveled along settler's roads to Harper's homestead on Gales Creek. But from there the going got much tougher. Their field book anticipates the coming struggle, noting that Gales Creek was the "Starting point in the Wilderness."

Following the route they had marked on their way eastward, the survey party under the command of Major Bache proceeded to ascend Beaver Creek, following the current road that connects present-day Glenwood with Timber. Near the top of Beaver Creek, the Military Road swings west and drops down to the Nehalem River, eventually crossing the creek and climbing a ridge to the north of Cochran Pond.

Descending the western end of that ridge, the road builders soon reached the upper reaches of the Salmonberry River, where they set up a camp in a clearing near a particularly spectacular logjam. Their maps refer to this site as Log Jam Camp and it later became a frequent stopping place for travelers along this route. From this location, the surveyors reported a clear view "down the valley for miles." This view along the Salmonberry River was reportedly unobstructed because the land was uncharacteristically bare of timber and underbrush. This may have been due to the Calapuyans' practice of setting fires during the cold months of the year to keep the landscape open and improve their hunting grounds. For Bache and the Astorians this was the only glimpse into the Salmonberry Gorge, because from here on their route led them inexorably northward toward Saddle Mountain.

Beyond this remote camp at the edge of the Salmonberry Gorge, the survey party continued north, crossing Bare Mountain and descending into the Rock Creek drainage. Here they ran into very dense undergrowth, swampy conditions, and a large amount of downed timber that forced the crew to traverse the east side of the valley until they could find a navigable passage across Rock Creek. As they ascended the hills to the west of Rock Creek, their surveyors' peregrinations led them over the summit of Green Mountain and west toward the present-day community of Elsie.

But by then the survey crew had tired of life on the trail; they were exhausted by the treacherous work and dispirited by the increasingly wet conditions. The mood turned ugly as several men were summarily fired, while others simply quit. A quarter mile short of reaching the Saddle Mountain Camp, the survey was officially abandoned and the entire crew hightailed it back to Astoria leaving a nine-and-a-half-mile stretch of the route from Saddle Mountain to Olney uncompleted.

In 1857, the actual road construction finally began in Astoria and Gales Creek, with the intent to meet in the middle. But the difficult terrain, the miserable weather, and the recalcitrance of the local laborers resurfaced almost immediately, and the road from Astoria was abandoned just short of the Nehalem River. On the southern end, the road builders made it as far as Log Jam Camp above the Salmonberry River before they too gave up the effort.

With the advent of the Civil War all meaningful work on the road ceased, but the road continued to be used as an important regional trail. In the 1870s the army used the southern portion of the road to march the last remaining Native Americans from the Nehalem Valley to the Grande Ronde Reservation in the Yamhill Valley. In the 1890s a number of Finnish families used the trail to transport all their worldly possessions to Elsie, and from there they were able to reach the newly established community of Hamlet in the Necanicum Valley. A year later the General Land Office published an accounting of the area that listed no less than eighty settlers in the vicinity, and affirmed that the military road was still a vital communications link serving the northwestern corner of Oregon.

Several other legends have been attributed to this abortive expedition, including the loss of a cannon as one of the packhorses tumbled off a steep slope and fell to his death deep in one of the treacherous ravines that lined the route around Saddle Mountain.

In another curious anecdote, we hear that in 1900 two travelers passed through Joe Lynch's homestead near Elsie, taking his shepherd dog when they departed. Lynch gave chase and found the couple camped out above the headwaters of Quartz Creek. Words were exchanged, but in the end Lynch returned home with his dog, and the mountain on which the acquisitive travelers were camped came to be known as Dogthief Mountain.

Over time, as is so often true in our wet and foggy environment, nature reclaimed the right-of-way and the military road slipped into obscurity like so many other forgotten trails in the Coast Range. By 1933, the

Olney-to-Elsie portion of the trail had been overgrown by underbrush and was no longer passable.

In 1987, George Martin and Lawrence Fick, two employees of the Oregon Department of Forestry, retraced a portion of this lost road. In 2002 they published their findings in a book entitled *A Road in the Wilderness*. Finally, in 2006, John Barnes, an employee of the Oregon Department of Forestry, retraced the portion of the trail explored by Martin and Fick and marked where this vestigial roadway crossed existing roads between Cochran Road and the summit of Giveout Mountain.

In 2015, I accompanied the recently retired Barnes on a tour of the blue carbonite markers that he had planted in the region to the west of Cochran Road. With luck and perseverance, I hope to reestablish and mark this long abandoned pioneer road so that this important historical route is not entirely lost in Oregon's infamous jungle.

Notes

1. *Tillamook State Forest Trail Guide: Historic Hiking Loop* (Forest Grove, OR: Oregon Department of Forestry), undated pamphlet.
2. George E. Martin and Lawrence R. Fick. *A Road in the : The Salem to Astoria Military Road* (Forest Grove, OR: Oregon Department of Forestry, 2002), xxii.
3. Ibid., 19.
4. Ibid., 47.
5. Ibid., 54.
6. Ibid., 42.

Salem-to-Astoria Military Road.

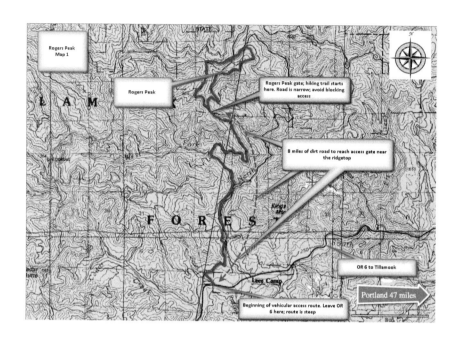

Rogers Peak
Map 1

Rogers Peak

L A M

F O R E S T

Rogers Peak gate; hiking trail starts here. Road is narrow; avoid blocking access

8 miles of dirt road to reach access gate near the ridgetop

Kings Mtn

OR 6 to Tillamook

Lees Camp

Portland 47 miles

Beginning of vehicular access route. Leave OR 6 here; route is steep

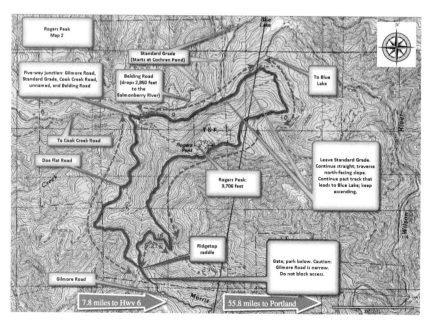

Rogers Peak
Map 2

Standard Grade
(Starts at Cochran Pond)

Five-way junction: Gilmore Road, Standard Grade, Cook Creek Road, unnamed, and Belding Road

Belding Road
(drops 2,850 feet to the Salmonberry River)

To Blue Lake

Blue Lake

River

To Cook Creek Road

Doe Flat Road

Rogers Peak

Leave Standard Grade. Continue straight; traverse north-facing slope. Continue past track that leads to Blue Lake; keep ascending.

Rogers Peak: 3,706 feet

Creek

Ridgetop saddle

Gate; park below. Caution: Gilmore Road is narrow. Do not block access.

Gilmore Road

Morris

7.8 miles to Hwy 6

55.8 miles to Portland

21. Rogers Peak

BRIEF DESCRIPTION: This higher-altitude hike has absolutely stellar views, rugged terrain, and exposure to coastal weather—it's well worth the effort. The approach road is daunting and requires a car with sufficient clearance and power to navigate the steeper slopes. That said, I have completed the climb several times in my Honda Odyssey.

DISTANCE: 7.15 miles

ELEVATION CHANGE: The biggest elevation change on this hike occurs during the approach. From the Jones Creek Campground to the crest of the Gilmore Road (2,740 feet), the elevation gain is 2,200 feet. But that's all accomplished in the comfort of your car! The hike itself, as it ascends Rogers Peak and returns to the gate on Gilmore Road, gains only 828 feet in elevation.

TRAIL CONDITION: Mostly logging roads; some are rutted, but most are smooth enough for cycling. Once over the crest the roads are fairly level, typically nothing more than a 4 percent grade. The actual ascent of Rogers Peak is a bit steeper, and the road conditions are rougher.

APPROXIMATE DURATION: 3.5 hours

TRAVEL TIME FROM PORTLAND TO TRAILHEAD: 55 minutes from the Sylvan exit (exit 71B) on US 26, via OR 6 to Jones Creek Campground

DRIVING DIRECTIONS: From Portland travel west on US 26. Take the turn-off (OR 6) for Tillamook, cruising past the towns of Banks and Gales Creek before crossing over the summit. About 46 miles from the Sylvan exit on US 26, just beyond the general store at Lee's Camp, you will approach a side road leading to Jones Creek Campground. Exit the highway to the right and cross the bridge to the campground. Continue straight for about 2,000 feet on North Fork Road, and then take the first major right-hand turn. This will put you on the North Fork Wilson River Road heading north. After about 1.6 miles you will reach the turnoff (on your right) to the Diamond Mill Park, but you will veer left and bypass the park.

Continue on up the North Fork Wilson River Road. At 2.3 miles from the highway, cross a small stream flowing down from the left. Continue on up the North Fork, even as the road gets rougher. A mile farther, cross the West Fork North Fork Wilson River. Turn left here and follow the aforementioned tributary up this valley for 1 mile, whereupon you will encounter a small concrete bridge leading off to the right. Cross that bridge and follow the road steeply uphill for the final 3.6 miles. This leg of the labyrinth will take you into the watershed of Morris Creek. The final stretch is on Gilmore Road, which leads up the ridge and is quite steep. I managed the steep grade in my Honda Odyssey, but this "flying toaster," as my wife refers to it, has climbed grades in excess of 30 percent! Nonetheless, my sense of automotive machismo was a bit dented when I found a Vespa parked at the final gate.

The trailhead on Gilmore Road is a narrow road that slants up along a recently clear-cut slope. At the top you will see a yellow gate. There is a small space to turn around next to the gate and another smaller widening of the road about 200 feet before the gate. Turn and park off the main track so as not to impede others on this narrow stretch of road.

If these instructions seem complicated, it's because they are. I urge anyone interested in this kind of backcountry exploration to invest in detailed maps that show the logging roads and permit you to trace your route up this maze of rocky roads. Better yet, use mapping software, such as Topofusion (Windows) or Base Camp (Apple OS) to map the route. Then you can transform it into a digital file and transfer it to your GPS device. In this manner you will have a clear route to follow. In a pinch, these roads are even marked on Google Maps.

SPECIAL ATTRIBUTES: This trail's remoteness and ruggedness are some of its greatest advantages, in my view. It is a beautiful landscape with vistas across the entire northern Coast Range! Because it runs parallel to the Salmonberry River to the north and the Wilson River to the south, it is a splendid alternative to descending into the Salmonberry Gorge—especially as efforts to rebuild a trail in the gorge will entail closures. This route gives you the eagle's-eye equivalent of the Salmonberry Trail and the Wilson River, all in one.

TRAIL LOG: The crest of the ridge is located about 600 feet above the gate. When you arrive at the crest take a few moments to absorb the panoramic view of the northern Coast Range. The Wilson River is 2,200 feet down behind you. Dwindling into obscurity in front of you is the Salmonberry River—way down below! To your right is a rocky hillock: Rogers Peak. The slope from the top of Rogers Peak down to the Salmonberry River is ten times steeper than the slope of Mount Hood between Sandy and Government Camp.

Immediately after crossing the summit, veer to the right and take Gilmore Road, which traverses the northern slope at a pretty level grade. Two and a quarter miles from the gate is a five-way road crossing that, aside from the route up from the trailhead, includes the following:

You can see all the way to the Pacific Ocean from the Standard Grade, and when the fog rolls in, even Saddle Mountain resembles an island in the clouds.

To the west: the extension of Gilmore Road heading toward Cook Creek and the coast;

To the northwest: a minor logging road that dead-ends farther on;

To the east: Belding Road, heading downhill to the Salmonberry River;

Also to the east: the Standard Grade, heading east to Cochran Pond and Storey Burn Road.

Follow the Standard Grade, the most level of all the ridges angling through the mountain's east-facing roads. In less than a mile, the Standard Grade turns left at a fork in the road; don't take this turn but continue on in a northeasterly direction for 0.2 miles where, at another split, a road leads down to Blue Lake. Again, bypass this option and take the right-hand option, which continues around the base of Rogers Peak.

As you begin to round the corner at the northern side of the mountain, leave the main trail that encircles the peak and take a steeper road that climbs up the shoulder of the north face. These slopes are mostly dirt and rock, but they are not precipitous. This steeper road splits after a few hundred feet. Take the left-hand option, which traverses the northern face. This road eventually circles around until it's facing south. Farther on it splits again; take the right option and climb uphill. As you climb, the

Looking west from the Standard Grade across the Salmonberry and into the final range abutting the coast.

grade gets progressively steeper and the rock underfoot chunkier. Along this route several vantage points provide a spectacular view of the northern Coast Range all the way to Saddle Mountain. Spread out below are the wide basins that empty into Ripple Creek and Bathtub Creek—both tributaries of the Salmonberry River. Far down, the deep Salmonberry Gorge with its massive escarpments may be glowing orange in the late afternoon sun.

The track exhibits much elk and deer traffic, but no evidence of bears, although on one of my trips, the berry bushes had been stripped bare.

From the first vantage point, at 3,415 feet in elevation, continue to climb another half mile, eventually reaching a narrow ridge that separates the southern flank from the northern flank at an elevation of 3,568 feet. Along the top of this mountain, the road dips a bit (to 3,517 feet), but quickly ascends again to about 3,553 feet before finally slipping down a south-facing ridge. Off the edge of the track the slope is very steep and falls away to Morris Creek about 1,000 feet below.

The descent continues over an overgrown route, eventually intersecting with a well-maintained road that traverses the southern slope. Turn right on this road and follow it back to the gate. The culmination of this

HIKING FROM PORTLAND TO THE COAST

hike is dramatic. It quickly transitions from a primitive scramble to a well-designed roadbed, and then you see the yellow gate and beyond that the car... Reentry is a jolt.

Gyppo Logging

In the summer I often get out into the woods during the workweek, which occasionally finds me having to contend with the loggers who make their living in these same forests. As you have probably realized by now, I have my own ideas about the quality of stewardship we should be applying to our resources. I will leave it to others to determine what are good forestry practices and what aren't—and I hope they make prudent choices that allow the forest to be valued for its many ecosystem services, not just its industrial value.

That disclaimer aside, let me also admit my fascination with the rough-hewn independence of our brawny Northwest logging culture. And nothing exemplifies that more than the quintessential Pacific Northwest tradition of the gyppo logger.[1]

In the Pacific Northwest, the tradition of assembling small bands of entrepreneurial woodsmen harks back as far as the adventures of the American Fur Company, and more recently the infamous "Wobblies" of the early twentieth century. The most current incarnation of this pioneering spirit can clearly be found within that small segment of the forest products industry colloquially known as the "gyppo loggers." "Gyppo logging" usually refers to a small, independent outfit of lumbermen who have contracted out the harvesting of timber. Typically, such a "gyppo show" will number no more than a dozen rugged woodsmen using battered skidders, loaders, caterpillars, a fire truck, a "crummie" to haul the crew in and out, and a portable yarding tower to pull massive amounts of lumber out of the most difficult terrain imaginable.

The term *gyppo* derives from the old railroad-building days, when groups of laborers would desert their employers and then form a small cooperative that competed for the work contracts, thus "gypping" their former employers of the work. The success of these entrepreneurial companies was due to working hard, keeping costs low, and undercutting the bigger operators by just enough to win the bid, but not by so much as to lose their profit—it took both experienced cost estimation and an efficient and determined crew.

Gyppo logging became a significant contributor to the logging industry beginning around 1946. With the war over, the government lifted restrictions on the purchase of heavy equipment and also began to sell surplus military vehicles, especially trucks, to independent operators. With the initial cost of entering the capital-intensive logging business dropping, many new operators emerged just in time to profit from the increasing demand for wood to build housing as soldiers returned to civilian life. It was during this period of increased demand that the major timber operators began to subcontract with the gyppos to harvest the more difficult tracts or those with smaller-diameter growth.

But gyppo logging had already existed for decades and was mainly used to access timber tracts that were either partially logged or difficult to access. One such special situation existed during the construction of the Pacific Railway & Navigation line alongside the Salmonberry River. All along the river, timber grew on the steep slopes that stretched up into the mist-enshrouded heights. All along the isolated benches that ran along these heights were valuable stands of virgin timber that had heretofore been inaccessible. The PR&N realized that contracting out the logging of these steep and narrow valleys to the gyppos could bring in much-needed capital since the railroad maintenance was proving more expensive than anticipated.

Perhaps one of the most famous of these operations was the West Oregon Logging Company. Located at the confluence of the North Fork and the main stem of the Salmonberry River, this logging operation began hauling logs off these steep northern slopes in 1929 and operated until 1932 when it was consumed by the Cochran Fire. To gain access to a large swath of older growth that clung to the upper slopes of this deep canyon, the crew built one of the steepest rail lines ever attempted. The so-called Edwards incline ran up the near-vertical canyon wall at an 80 percent grade! Just to be clear about what that means, a 100 percent grade equates to a forty-five-degree angle. A steeply pitched roof is typically slanted at less than a 75 percent grade. The Edwards incline exceeded that slope by another 5 percent. To prevent the log carriage from careening down the face of the mountain, the crew attached it to a railcar loaded with river rocks that served as ballast to balance the weight of the descending logs. Midway down the slope the tracks split, allowing the two heavily loaded cars to pass each other. As long as the cable held, this precarious arrangement permitted the West Oregon Logging crew to lower huge loads down the incline.[2]

However, the West Oregon Logging Company managed to make logging history when the cable did snap and a carriage loaded with huge old-growth logs came careening down the mountainside. Blasting past the ballast car, the fully loaded log carriage careened past the base of the incline and then jumped the entire Salmonberry River, taking out the main line of the PR&N before it came to rest in a spectacular mash-up against the face of the opposing slope. Amazingly, no one was hurt. But with this spectacular train wreck the West Oregon Logging Company ensured its place in Oregon's coastal logging annals.

This was not the only incline railroad to operate on the Salmonberry River. The Brix Lumber Company successfully ran an incline rail at Enright that had a 49 percent grade at its steepest point. A specially built steam donkey situated at the summit of the four-thousand-foot-long incline provided the hoisting power to safely lower the fully loaded cars and retrieve them once they had been unloaded down in Enright.[3] Farther up the Salmonberry River, the Gilmore Logging Company operated another incline that descended the steep slope at a 22 percent grade.[4] Recently, an abandoned steam donkey was recovered from the upper slopes across the river from Enright. This so-called Tunnel Creek donkey was apparently used to transport logs by high lead (cable line) across the valley to the Enright camp on the opposite side of the valley.[5]

But all this steam-driven audacity took the utmost discipline and a sizable army of loggers working in careful coordination. At the bottom of the logging show's hierarchy was, and still is, the choker setter, who spends his day dragging a thick choker cable across the steep slopes of fallen trees. This is exhausting and dangerous work, involving clambering up and down steep slopes through the devil's club and the dense tangle of vine maple branches. All around are newly bucked logs (stripped of branches) intertwined on the steep slope. Dragging the choker cables behind him, the setter scrambles underneath the precariously perched logs and wraps the heavy cables around one end of the fallen log. Once the cable is attached, the choker setter retreats from the collared trunk and issues two blasts on his radio instructing the yarder to tighten the "skyline." In response to the radio signal, the yarder fires up the winch and a massive cable lifts off the slope with the choker cables dangling like metal leashes from a laundry line. As the skyline tightens high above the slope, the tethered logs lurch off the debris-strewn slope. The choker setters watch this process warily as other logs shift and slide into new configurations. If too much strain is put on the choker cables they can snap, tossing these huge lengths of lumber onto the slope as if playing a giant's game of pick-up sticks.

Once the logs are deposited on the loading deck, the loader sorts the logs, strips off the remaining branches, and loads them onto the waiting log trucks. The loader resembles a huge battered crab from whose elevated arm dangles an enormous claw. The claw can be flung up to fifty feet to clutch at logs strewn across the loading deck, a large flat area resembling a helipad on which the logs are dumped. Like a beaver scrutinizes his trove of sticks, the loader operator hoists logs for inspection and sorting. Sliding the clamp deftly down the trunk, he strips off the remaining branches and then tosses the log aside for later loading or carefully lifts it onto the waiting log trucks. If the wood is not of sufficient quality, it will go to the plywood mill; otherwise, it will be milled into structural timber. Sorting the wood effectively can make or break a gyppo operator.

A single logging show can produce an average of a dozen or more log-truck loads per day—the equivalent of enough wood to complete five new homes. Truckers get paid by the load, averaging around $150 per load. Since they need more than $300 per day to cover their costs, they have to complete at least three loads per day. Usually the truckers work in rotation, so that hopefully they can achieve their desired quota every other day. But key to this regimen is getting the logs to the mill as quickly as possible, thus increasing the chances of snagging another load before shutting down for the night. This is why the loggers are known to race down the logging roads as if they owned them—which in fact they do!

If you're brave enough to navigate the logging roads during the weekdays, keep your head and give these barreling giants the biggest berth you can. Despite my years of experience driving these roads, I avoid active logging routes as much as I can, and when that's not possible I honk as I approach every blind corner and hug my side of the road to make as much room as possible for the trucks. Remember, that's more than forty tons of truck and logs coming at you!

Notes

1. Edward Kamholz, Jim Blain, and Greg Kamholz, *The Oregon-American Lumber Company: Ain't No More* (Palo Alto, CA: Stanford University Press, 2003), 250.
2. Ellis Lucia, *Tillamook Burn Country: A Pictorial History* (Caldwell, ID: Caxton Printers, 1984), 93.

3. Peter J. Brix and Byran Pentilla, *The Brix Logging Story: In the Woods of Washington and Oregon* (Portland, OR: BLM LLC, 2013), 110–11.

4. Lucia, *Tillamook Burn Country*, 94, 130.

5. Chris Friend, *The Lookout: What's New with Our Old Steam Donkey?* (Tillamook, OR: Tillamook Forest Heritage Center, 2011), 4.

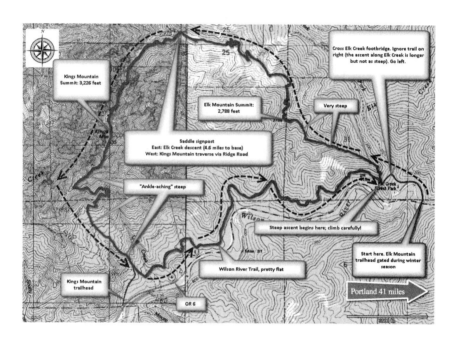

Kings Mountain
Summit: 3,226 feet

Elk Mountain Summit:
2,788 feet

Very steep

Cross Elk Creek footbridge. Ignore trail on
right (the ascent along Elk Creek is longer
but not as steep). Go left.

Saddle signpost
East: Elk Creek descent (4.6 miles to base)
West: Kings Mountain traverse via Ridge Road

"Ankle-aching" steep

Steep ascent begins here; climb carefully!

Wilson River Trail, pretty flat

Kings Mountain
trailhead

Start here. Elk Mountain
trailhead gated during winter
season

OR 6

Portland 41 miles

22. Elk Mountain and Kings Mountain Loop

BRIEF DESCRIPTION: A steep climb up Elk Mountain is followed by a rugged ridgeline traverse to Kings Mountain, culminating in a steep descent. The last 3.5 miles are along a roughly level trail paralleling the Wilson River and nearby highway. This trail is strenuous and best suited to the hiker in good condition. A good pair of boots is recommended for traction and ankle stability.

DISTANCE: 10 miles

ELEVATION CHANGE: 2,356 feet. The summit of Kings Mountain is at 3,226 feet. The Elk Creek Campground is at only 850 feet.

TRAIL CONDITION: The terrain is rugged, forcing a slower pace than the normal 3-mile-per-hour gait. In the winter, start early to get enough daylight with which to complete the circuit. The trail is well groomed and not particularly dangerous from the perspective of traversing open faces or being exposed to sheer drops. The Kings Mountain descent lacks adequate switchbacks, which makes it more difficult in wet, muddy conditions. The average uphill grade is 22.4 percent; the average downhill grade is 24 percent.

APPROXIMATE DURATION: 6 hours, unless you're in good enough shape to go sprinting up and down these peaks like a goat. I do not include myself in that category.

TRAVEL TIME FROM PORTLAND TO TRAILHEAD: At least 45 minutes

DRIVING DIRECTIONS: From the Sylvan exit (exit 71B) in Portland, head 41 miles west on US 26 and OR 6 to the Elk Creek Campground. (It is 28 miles from Tillamook.) The well-signed trailhead is located right off the highway. During the months that the park is open, drive into the parking area. Otherwise, park alongside OR 6 and walk in. No equestrian use is permitted; bikes are allowed only on the Elk Creek Trail.

SPECIAL ATTRIBUTES: This loop is one of the more vertically challenging hiking routes included in this guide, with dramatically steep rock formations and views over the crest of the Coast Range to Mount Hood, Mount Jefferson, and Mount Adams. Saddle Mountain is visible to the west.

TRAIL LOG: Starting at the Elk Creek Campground, follow the Wilson River Trail to the west. Don't go up the creek—that's the Elk Creek Trail, a scenic but much longer route. A quarter mile up the Wilson River Trail is the junction where the Elk Mountain Trail bends upward through the red alders and begins its serious ascent of the face of Elk Mountain. This climb is interspersed with open places offering fabulous views of the river and the forested slopes of the Coast Range. Given the steepness of the climb, you will not only enjoy the views, but also quietly give thanks for the excuse to pause during the grueling ascent. The Tillamook Burn devastated much of this area, and the tall snags that adorn these precipitous slopes are a lasting testament to the vast destruction that occurred during those fires.

The trail skirts the northern slope of Elk Mountain and ascends the ridge-line. A false summit about 1.5 miles up the trail affords fabulous views, but the main trail circles the base of this promontory and continues on to the real summit (elevation 2,788 feet) a half mile farther. From this vantage point it becomes clear how precipitous the coastal mountains can be underneath their usual camouflage of greenery, and how dangerous it can be to attempt unmarked descents in these areas. Summiting Elk Mountain is the hard part, but the trail continues to twist along the narrow ridgetop for another 2 miles. There you'll emerge at a saddle that marks the top of the Elk Creek Trail (4.8 miles back to the bottom), and also the beginning of the Kings Mountain connector trail heading off to the left.

Follow the Kings Mountain Trail to the left, as indicated on the signpost. It will guide you over to the next promontory. There a narrow ridgeline path leads out to a high point at 3,227 feet—Kings Mountain. The views across the Coast Range are spectacular, with Saddle Mountain off to the northwest. In that same direction you can spot the Standard Grade road, which traverses the entire backbone of the mountain system, from Buck Mountain over Rogers Peak, and past Larch Mountain back to Round Top, which overlooks Cochran Pond.

Directly below Kings Mountain is Lee's Camp, a popular spot for ATV enthusiasts. Unfortunately, it can sound like a hornet's nest on busy weekend days, as the ATVers snarl their way along the valley floors. Tarry awhile on the bare slope near the summit of Kings Mountain; it's all downhill from here.

But it would be disingenuous of me to suggest the remainder is easy. The descent is indeed a challenge; the first time I did it my thigh muscles screamed in agony. So take it easy, and take frequent rest stops to allow your leg muscles to recover. About 2 miles from the summit, or a half mile from the highway, the descent crosses the Wilson River Trail. Turn left and follow the signs for the Elk Creek Campground, another 3.5 miles to the east. This trail is relatively flat.

Elk Mountain summit, looking south into the Coffee Creek environs.

A half mile from the Elk Creek Campground you'll pass the Elk Mountain Trail, where you began this "walk in the woods" nearly 10 miles earlier. Continue a half mile to the camp. If the gate is closed you'll have to walk another half mile to the roadside parking. Collapsing into your car will feel glorious at this point, but be careful driving home on the Wilson River Highway; it's a winding journey that demands your full attention!

Tales from the Salmonberry River

A twenty-one-mile-long canyon cuts through the heart of the Oregon Coast Range from Washington County to Nehalem Bay. This is a wild and violent coastline where brutal storms, fresh off the North Pacific, hurl themselves at our coastal mountains with a momentum and determination born of the Pacific vastness from which they were spawned.

In 1911 the Pacific Railway & Navigation Company completed a rail connection from Washington County to Tillamook using the narrow passage carved out by the Salmonberry River. Tillamook lay in one of the most inaccessible locations on the northern Oregon coast. It was equally inaccessible from the mouth of the Columbia River and the Willamette Valley. This rail link was essential to sustain the vital arteries of Tillamook's industry, enabling resources to reach markets and people to travel reliably.

Yet the rail link came at a high cost. Storm damage and constant geological movement so plagued the PR&N that the locals took to calling it the "Punk, Rotten, and Nasty." A little more than a year after rail service was first launched, nature took its first swipe at the rails that snaked down the Salmonberry River. Early in January 1913, rough winter weather and snow triggered a host of landslides that cut rail service to Tillamook for more than thirty-five days.[1]

The break in rail service was dramatic, leaving people stranded away from home and resources. Toward the end of that first week in 1913, a group of eight stranded Tillamook residents assembled in Portland and decided to get back to Tillamook, regardless of what it took.

Leaving Portland early on Friday, the party of seven men and one woman reached Timber around midday. Their plan was to follow the railroad right-of-way all the way to the coast. But rail service had been discontinued several days earlier and no one knew how much of the railway line had been swept away by the raging storm. Nevertheless, after eating a meal in Timber, they set out on foot, determined to reach Tillamook. Nightfall found them still deep in the canyon, where they were forced to bivouac in a deserted cabin. With only two sandwiches between them, dinner did little to dent their appetites. A cold fog enveloped them, keeping them shivering most of the night.

The next morning they set off early and soon arrived at a railroad camp where they managed to secure some breakfast before resuming their long and arduous trek to the coast. In all, they reported crossing eight to ten slides. Of these, three were particularly difficult to traverse. In these three different places, the track, rails and all, had been swept into the river. In some places the fill that had been laid down to support the railbed had been washed away, leaving the rail line dangling in the air. About three miles above the tiny settlement of Enright, they encountered a slide that had obliterated the track for more than three hundred feet, covering the entire stretch with tons of dirt and rock. Below Enright the track was covered with loose dirt and mud, sometimes reaching more than eight feet deep. Eventually, the exhausted party reached the forward work party that was clearing the line from the coast. From there, the members of this bedraggled party were carried out to Tillamook in a special run.

While the ordeal was finally over for Mrs. Johnson and her seven male companions, the community was to suffer an extended ordeal as repeated storms kept creating new slides, destroying the repairs already made and burying the steam shovels under tons of rock and mud. In the end, it took them thirty-six days to restore the rail link. At one point the line was finally opened, but within three hours the next landslide took out another sixty-foot chunk of rails. A jubilant crowd welcomed the first Portland train to finally make it all the way through to Tillamook. By that time, the outgoing mail was piling up and Tillamook was running low on staples, fresh food, medicines, whiskey, and even the wood for the steam engines.

In those early days it was an epic struggle between the isolated township of Tillamook and the powerful forces that visited such violent weather upon them. The efforts by the rail crews to keep the line open were truly Herculean, but the Salmonberry Gorge was worthy of its awful reputation. No sooner had previous damage been removed then another section of the line would be washed away. The Salmonberry could be counted on to give as good as she got!

It happened in the steep confines of the Wolf Creek Canyon. There, on the level ground near the creek side, the railroad builders had erected their temporary quarters. On either side, the ravine's steep walls climbed almost a thousand feet to the rim of the forest above. Two ancient Douglas fir trees clung to the edge of the ravine. They leaned way out over the slope trying vainly to resist the increasing pull of gravity. But in the pre-dawn rainstorm their roots began to bend and the lip of the ravine curled downward as the firs began to topple. They fell in an arc, pitching over completely and smashing directly through the two houses cowering on the valley floor.

In the first lived the section foreman, William Conley, as well as the cook, his wife, and their seven-year-old girl. The crash occurred around 5:30 a.m. in the wet gray dawn. Both men had already risen and were sipping their coffee in the early morning. They must have heard the agonized creaking as the two massive trees slowly dropped end-over-end off the rim five hundred feet above. The foreman's house was hit in the middle. Louis Dudley, the cook, was killed immediately, but Conley lay mortally wounded, pinned down by the giant tree.

Unhurt by the crushed central portion of the house, Mrs. Dudley quickly went to the aid of the little girl, who had been sleeping at the far end of the house, beyond the fallen tree. Dressed only in their nightgowns, the woman and little girl climbed out of the wrecked house. A little way beyond lay the demolished shack occupied by several Japanese laborers, one of whom had also perished. With the wet coastal snow as deep as their waists, Mrs. Dudley let loose a bellow for help, hoping to attract the assistance of the Greek and Italian laborers camped just a short way down the line.

Eventually, they did arrive, but not to render aid. According to the newspaper reports, they quickly looted the foreman's house and rifled Mrs. Dudley's valise for her savings. But by now the bridge crew was arriving, and they soon bundled Mrs. Dudley and the surviving girl off to a local hostelry where they were helped to recuperate.

This was just the first of many violent incidents that the railroad builders had to contend with. After huge storms in 1996, scientists brought out pictures that showed Wolf Creek Canyon stripped to its roots. In 2007, the northern slope gave way, triggering a giant slide that caused more than $4 million in damages. The combined punches of the storm in 1996 and the storm in December 2007 were finally enough to change the math so that the Port of Tillamook agreed to abandon the rail service. After all, the repairs had risen in cost from $12 million in 1996 to $57 million in 1997!

One has to hope that our current plans to convert the rail line to a hiking trail will prove more resilient and sustainable, but we shouldn't ignore the legacy of wild storm damage in this gorge. No doubt this will remain a fearsome place during the more dramatic winter storms, and heavy stewardship costs may be a recurring reality.

Notes

1. "Tillamook People Have Rough Trip," *Tillamook Herald*, January 7, 1913, http://oregonnews.uoregon.edu/

The north face of Salmonberry canyon from Rogers Peak.

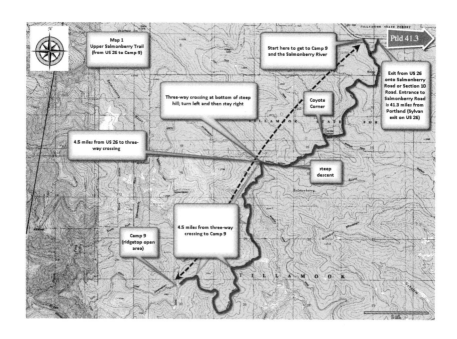

Map 1
Upper Salmonberry Trail
(from US 26 to Camp 9)

Start here to get to Camp 9
and the Salmonberry River

Ptld 41.3

Exit from US 26
onto Salmonberry
Road or Section 10
Road. Entrance to
Salmonberry Road
is 41.3 miles from
Portland (Sylvan
exit on US 26)

Three-way crossing at bottom of steep
hill; turn left and then stay right

Coyote
Corner

4.5 miles from US 26 to three-
way crossing

steep
descent

Camp 9
(ridgetop open
area)

4.5 miles from three-way
crossing to Camp 9

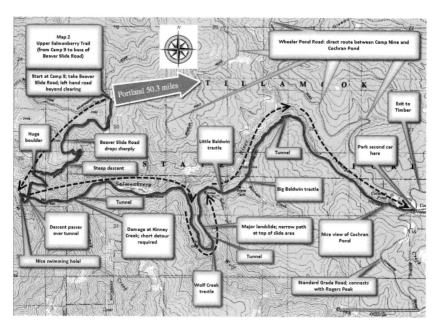

Map 2
Upper Salmonberry Trail
(from Camp 9 to base of
Beaver Slide Road)

Wheeler Pond Road: direct route between Camp Nine and
Cochran Pond

Start at Camp 9; take Beaver
Slide Road; left hand road
beyond clearing

Portland 50.3 miles

Exit to
Timber

Huge
boulder

Beaver Slide Road
drops sharply

Little Baldwin
trestle

Tunnel

Park second car
here

Steep descent

Big Baldwin trestle

Tunnel

Descent passes
over tunnel

Damage at Kinney
Creek; short detour
required

Major landslide; narrow path
at top of slide area

Nice view of Cochran
Pond

Nice swimming hole!

Tunnel

Wolf Creek
trestle

Standard Grade Road; connects
with Rogers Peak

23. Upper Salmonberry Trail (Beaver Slide Road to Cochran Pond)

Since 1911 the Salmonberry Trail has been Tillamook's only link to the Willamette Valley. When a series of severe storms caused irreparable damage to the railroad infrastructure, trail advocates (including the author) persuaded the state to convert this route into a unique eighty-four-mile recreational trail through the Oregon Coast Range. As the route is restored and made safe for the public, construction work may occasionally interrupt access. The descriptions of Salmonberry Trail that follow offer a historical view of the unimproved route as it existed in 2015.

This book also describes alternative approaches to the Salmonberry River that avoid the railroad right of way. The easiest is via the North Fork of the Salmonberry (chapter 25). A steeper approach utilizes Beaver Slide Road (chapter 23). The Salmonberry's confluence with the Nehalem River can be accessed via US 26 and Foss Road (chapter 24). Alternatively, chapter 21 describes a high altitude route along the Standard Grade that snakes its way along a narrow ridge two thousand feet above the Salmonberry River.

For information on the current status of Salmonberry Trail, visit: salmonberrytrail.org; salmonberrycorridor.wordpress.com/; foresthiker.com

BRIEF DESCRIPTION: The walk along the length of the Salmonberry River has got to be one of the most impressive hikes in Oregon, or even throughout the American West. In my opinion, the Salmonberry River is one of the most beautiful and awesome rivers in the state.

The upper portion of the Salmonberry Trail extends from Cochran Pond 6.25 miles down to where Beaver Slide Road meets this wild river. This section of the Salmonberry canyon features a number of impressive trestle bridges and several tunnels. There is only one moderate bushwhack to navigate. This hike has been oriented with the hiker starting at the "bottom" of the hike (at Beaver Slide Road) and ending at Cochran Pond. This arrangement may seem counterintuitive at first—until you realize that it makes more sense to walk down Beaver Slide Road than it does to walk up this very steep road. That's why I've oriented the hike to descend the Beaver Slide Road and ascend the rail alignment, which rises much more gradually. **DISTANCE:** 9 miles one way. I recommend leaving a shuttle car at Cochran Pond.

ELEVATION CHANGE: 1,459 feet. The biggest elevation change—almost 1,500 feet in 2.73 miles—occurs on Beaver Slide Road. The downhill grade at times exceeds 47 percent, so it's a struggle to keep from overbalancing downward and slipping on the rough gravel surface. No wonder it's called Beaver Slide Road!

TRAIL CONDITION: This section of the canyon comprises a railroad bed with plenty of alder and Scotch broom obstruction. Several tunnels make it advisable to bring a flashlight. Try not to step in between the ties, as the gaps are sometimes deeper than expected and full of water.

DURATION OF HIKE: At least 5 hours

TRAVEL TIME FROM PORTLAND TO TRAILHEAD: 2 hours, including time to drop off shuttle car

DRIVING DIRECTIONS TO DROP OFF CAR AT COCHRAN POND: From the Sylvan exit on US 26 (exit 71B) travel 33.6 miles on US 26 to the Timber junction and turn left (south). Travel 3 miles on Timber Road until you reach the hamlet of Timber. As you enter the town, turn right on Cochran Road (immediately after the bridge) and follow the Nehalem River upriver past small cottages and rustic dwellings lining the riverfront. This road is known as Cochran Pond Road, and after about a mile it turns into a gravel-surfaced road. Follow this road for 6.8 miles to the south. As you approach the upland plateau on which Cochran Pond is located, you will see a large area cleared of trees. Around 1910–1911 this clearing hosted a bustling village that supported all the railroad construction efforts on the eastern end of the track. Today it is a barren slope filled with Scotch broom.

As you enter this cleared slope, you will soon arrive at a three-way intersection. Straight ahead leads into a copse of trees where some local revelers like to party, drink, and practice target shooting. The right-hand turn is for Wheeler Pond Road, which goes to Beaver Slide Road. For now, veer off to the left and follow the Standard Grade (the more traveled track) until you get to the train tracks. Park nearby and transfer to the second car, which will take you to the top of Beaver Slide Road.

DRIVING DIRECTIONS TO THE TOP OF BEAVER SLIDE ROAD: With your second car, drive back about 750 feet from the railroad tracks to the three-way intersection just mentioned. Ignore the left-hand option that leads down to the pond, and also the option to the right that leads back out to Timber. Instead, cross the intersection (bearing slightly to the left), and proceed up Wheeler Pond Road as it heads west and climbs uphill from this junction. This road will follow the north side of the Salmonberry

Old water tank at Big Baldwin trestle.

canyon. After 5.2 miles you will arrive at the crest of a ridge where Wheeler Pond Road takes a sharp turn to the left. On your right is another road coming down a steep slope, Wheeler Cut-Off Road. Ignore the road to the right and turn left to follow Wheeler Pond Road for another 4.6 miles. The Salmonberry River actually runs at the base of the valley you are following. This road has some spectacular spots where it emerges from the woods and traverses large open slopes that provide impressive views of the Salmonberry River at the bottom of this steep gorge. This road always seems longer than its actual 4.6 miles. Eventually, you will emerge in a flat clearing that affords views both east toward the Salmonberry River valley and west toward the deep valley formed by the North Fork Salmonberry River. On maps this open plateau is marked as the location of Camp 9; however, today there is little left to suggest any prior camp.

At this junction, four roads join in a configuration resembling an H.

You entered the intersection from the north using Wheeler Pond Road.

As you enter the clearing, you'll see the North Fork Salmonberry Road entering the clearing on your right.

Forming the bottom half of the H are two forest roads.

The right-hand option is the extension of the North Fork Salmonberry Road and leads almost all the way down to the North Fork Salmonberry River (see chapter 25).

The left-hand option is Beaver Slide Road. Take this road.

The initial 0.7 miles of Beaver Slide Road are easily navigable. At that point the road splits, and a recently constructed logging road descends to your right. To your far left a short track leads into a cul-de-sac. But in the middle, a narrow passage allows cars to drive down a steep roadway. This drop-off marks the beginning of the more challenging portion of Beaver Slide Road. Large stumps sometimes block the two side roadways mentioned, especially when there is active logging in the vicinity, which was true at the time this book went to press.

Despite my sometimes casual approach to the inherent dangers of messing around in the "way outback," I have a healthy fear of getting my car stuck in steep canyons. Hence I chose to leave my non–four-wheel-drive vehicle parked on level ground located just before the drop-off. From there I walked the remaining 2.73 miles down to the Salmonberry River.

TRAIL LOG: Starting from the top of Beaver Slide Road it's a 2.7-mile steep descent to the riverside. From there it's another 6.25 miles walking east up the rail line to Cochran Pond.

Descent from Beaver Slide Road to the Salmonberry River. It's a steep descent right from the beginning, where Beaver Slide Road tips off the end of the ridge at about 2,400 feet in elevation. The first third of the descent winds about in a generally southeasterly direction, passing through a mixed alder and hemlock forest. After about 0.4 miles the trail turns to the southwest and traverses down the steep incline heading west. This traverse gets progressively steeper with a downhill slope in the 25–29 percent range and at places approaching a 48 percent slope!

Near the bottom you can glimpse the railroad tracks on your right among the trees, and to the left, the river lashing its way down the steep trench at the bottom. In midwinter the Salmonberry can become a gigantic washing machine, churning boulders and tree trunks and creating huge maelstroms between the steep embankments—crushing everything in its way!

But during the summer and early fall the river bottom is a place of solitary beauty, resplendent in the verdant shade of the overhanging fir trees. At the base of this road you will find a track leading down to one of the best swimming holes on the river. Take some time to rest here, and if the weather permits, dip your skinny butt in the blue-green waters of the Salmonberry!

From the base of Beaver Slide Road to Cochran Pond. After a rest and perhaps a swim in the Salmonberry, it's time to start following the railroad tracks up to Cochran Pond—a journey of about 6.5 miles with a rise in elevation of less than 1,000 feet. Start by going through Tunnel 27, over which Beaver Slide Road descends. This short tunnel has some debris piled outside the entrance, but is pretty clean walking throughout. On the other side, the railroad bed is soon covered with debris and you are left to follow a small trail that twists through the vegetation. ATV enthusiasts who have descended Beaver Slide Road have carved out a route for part of this way, and you should have no trouble following the route, even in the absence of rail lines, which are presumably buried beneath the slide materials.

According to the map, the original rail lines crossed the river along this stretch of water (a third of a mile from Tunnel 27), but apparently the bridges were destroyed. As a consequence the trail hugs the slope on the north side until it rejoins the rails farther along. A short distance on, the tracks cross to the southern side on a surviving bridge and the trail soon reaches a tributary, Kinney Creek. Here a bridge remains in place, but it's so mangled that you'll be forced to follow the creek uphill to find a way across. Once down in the creek bed, take a moment to identify the narrow track that leads up the opposite embankment. Set your course through the boulder-filled creek bed to reach the continuation of the track as it climbs the embankment. This bushwhack is narrow and steep, but also mercifully short. As you crest the top of the slope on the far side you'll arrive at the mouth of Tunnel 28.

Emerge from the tunnel and follow a relatively straight stretch that parallels the river in an easterly direction. After about 0.75 miles significant erosion has undercut the tracks and forces hikers to skirt the eroded embankment along the uphill side. Continue along another half mile of hiking the tracks on again, off again, depending on the erosion. At this point the tracks begin to curve to the right and enter Wolf Creek Canyon.

Wolf Creek is a major tributary to the Salmonberry, and the railroad tracks climb partially up the creek before crossing and doubling back to the main stem of the Salmonberry River. This canyon is one of the most landslide-prone areas in the watershed. A 2008 report by the Wild Salmon Center singled it out for the egregious erosion produced by the combination of violent storms and artificial railroad features that literally ripped

Engine number 2932 begins the hair-raising turn around the back of Wolf Creek. Courtesy of Paul Clock; originally published in *Punk, Rotten and Nasty* (Corbett Press, 2000).

the valley apart. The report also criticized forestry practices for contributing to railroad damage and affecting the unique steelhead habitat. Today, years after the frightful 2007 maelstrom that devoured this canyon, the awesome power of the water that destroyed these tree-laden slopes is evidenced by the enormous number of bleached logs littering Wolf Creek.

About 5.25 miles from the starting point, you will begin to approach the upper end of Wolf Creek; the tracks cross the creek on an impressive wooden trestle that looms high above the forest canopy below. Immediately thereafter, you enter another tunnel. On the far side of Tunnel 25, head north, doubling back along Wolf Creek before the tracks turn east again to parallel the main stem of the Salmonberry River. At this point you can witness the dramatic erosion that has stripped away the hillside on which the tracks used to run. In recent surveys it was estimated that the cost of repairing the damage caused by just this one landslide approached $5 million to $6 million.

Soon after the tracks turn east, they cross Little Baldwin Creek on another well-built trestle. This trestle was not always so reliable. In August 1935, while the Brix Logging Company was busy extracting timber from these slopes, a fully laden train collapsed the trestle, plunging the locomotive and all the cars over 100 feet down to the valley floor below. In all, two engineers, two brakemen, and a carpenter perished in the gruesome accident.

Moving right along, you'll soon arrive at the water tower (0.2 miles beyond the Little Baldwin trestle) and beyond that, the Big Baldwin Bridge. Completed in July 1911, this enormous trestle bridge looms hundreds of feet over the valley floor. Big Baldwin Bridge is the tallest structure on the line, measuring 167 feet in height and 520 feet in length. Remember that to build these huge structures, the Pacific Railway & Navigation Company had to excavate thousands of cubic feet of rock without the aid of machinery. Using picks and shovels, the mostly immigrant laborers loosened the rock and carried it away with donkey carts.

At this point the landscape seems to flatten out a bit as the trail approaches the top of the watershed. The embankments are farther away from the river and washouts are rare. As the railbed climbs the slope, you'll lose sight of the river itself, which splits into two final tributaries. The Upper Salmonberry comes in from the northeast, where it passes under Wheeler Pond Road. The train track runs parallel to Pennoyer Creek, which seeps out of the ground near the west end of Cochran Pond.

In all, it's a great hike that contrasts impressive feats of human engineering with the awesome forces of nature that twisted the rails into spaghetti-like tangles.

Between the Impenetrable and the Immeasurable

The Tillamooks inhabited a coastal territory extending north to the Nehalem River, south to the Siletz River, and as far east into the almost impenetrable Coast Range as they felt necessary. They were divided into three distinct bands: those living on the Nehalem River, those living around Tillamook Bay, and the southern branch living at the mouth of the Nestucca River. Linguistically, they were a Salish people, related to the tribes on Willapa Bay and in Grays Harbor.

Physically, the Tillamooks were short in stature with broad fat feet, thick ankles, and bandy legs. Their leading families flattened their foreheads much like the Chinooks, who lived on the Columbia. One reason why head flattening was practiced in this region was to distinguish social classes. Only the upper classes were permitted to undergo skull flattening as infants. This practice effectively protected the privileged families from being enslaved in the event of raids by opposing tribes. In fact, it was the duty of "flatheads" to rescue or ransom any enslaved flathead they encountered. Anyone without a flattened head was fair game for the slavers, who captured and sold them to native buyers as far north as Alaska.

In a curious twist of linguistic fate, the very term *flathead* appears to have been completely reversed from its original meaning. Originally, the term was used by the Columbia River tribes to describe their Salish neighbors in northern Idaho, Montana, and Alberta, who didn't practice skull shaping. To the Columbia River peoples, who considered their artificially shaped skulls as "pointed," the appearance of their northern neighbors' heads was relatively flat. Hence their designation as flatheads by the Columbia River tribes. But when the Europeans initially heard the Northern Salish being described as flatheads, they immediately associated them with the practice of flattening an infant's forehead. Due to this misinterpretation the meaning was entirely reversed as Europeans routinely used the term flathead to describe the practice of artificial cranial deformation, practiced by the Chinooks and the Tillamooks. Ironically, the

Northern Salish people, who did not practice head flattening at all, came to be known as the Flathead Indians. It's enough to give you a headache!

Despite their fierce reputation, the Tillamooks lived in relative harmony with the Clatsops, who occupied the Clatsop Plains to the north of Neahkahnie Mountain. Near the mouth of the Necanicum River both tribes lived together in a village that straddled the territorial divide. However, the Tillamooks' relations with many of their southern neighbors were not so cordial. Slaving was a major part of Tillamook culture. For the Tillamook, Oregon's coastal communities and villages, stretching as far south as the Cape of Mendocino, were "happy hunting grounds" from whence they could wrest able-bodied captives to sell as far north as Vancouver Island and Alaska.

THE CASTAWAYS

Both the Tillamooks and the Clatsops experienced random encounters with Asian and European visitors much earlier than the Columbia River tribes, who were shielded from external contacts by the nearly impenetrable Columbia River Bar.

Oregon's coastal communities may well have been receiving unbidden guests since the dawn of navigation. Indeed, one theory of how the Native Americans themselves arrived here involves the notion that they island-hopped from Asia using rudimentary boats swept along our coasts like flotsam. In prehistoric days, when more of the planet's water was trapped in gigantic glaciers, the ocean's water levels were almost a hundred feet lower—exposing a coastal shelf that now lies hidden under the frigid waters of the North Pacific. It is thought that this is where we might find evidence of a long-suspected coastal migration route. Seen over the long expanse of history and prehistory, the castaway phenomenon is not simply about individual sailors; it's the story of human migration, the absorption of human diversity, and the inevitable dispersion of knowledge.

Indeed, if you examine the history of the castaways it becomes clear that it was their knowledge and skills that saved them from being killed by the natives. The native tribes harbored a deep antipathy to outsiders. Unless they could demonstrate their value to the indigenous peoples, castaways were usually killed. Indeed, we have evidence that prior to the arrival of the Europeans at least seventy-five Asian junks may have been swept to their doom on the inhospitable Oregon coast. There is little evidence that any of these Asian sailors found a welcome amongst the coastal tribes.

Beginning in the late 1700s, Native American tales record a rising number of encounters with Europeans, such as the wreck of the Spanish ship *San Jose*, which was lost in 1789 while sailing north, supposedly carrying mission supplies, including beeswax. Some claim it was a Spanish galleon bound from Manila to Acapulco, but whichever it was, there's plenty of recovered beeswax to support the notion that some Spanish vessel found its untimely end at the base of Neahkahnie Mountain.

Another story recalls that a pirate ship was wrecked just south of Neahkahnie Mountain and the crew buried their treasure hoard deep under the mountain. The pirate crew killed one of their own and flung his body across the chests before they buried the cache. Some tales have the crew dispersing, but other versions claim the Tillamooks massacred them all except for an African who had fashioned a knife from some sort of metal and presented it to the chief. Treasure was of no value to the Tillamooks, but knowledge of how to make metal weapons was enough to spare the black pirate's life. And that may not have been his only legacy. Those who knew the Tillamook's last chieftain, Kilchis, insist that the genes of that black survivor were greatly evident in his appearance and temperament.

Then there was the freckled and red-haired sailor who was pulled from a wreck around 1780. To prevent his murder at the hands of the xenophobic Tillamooks, he escaped to Seaside where he came to be known among the Clatsops as Konapee, the iron-maker. With his knowledge of firearms and ironworking, Konapee brought invaluable innovation to his coastal community. His son George, known among the tribespeople by his Indian name, Lamasy, was an interpreter on several ships and also served as a river pilot on the Columbia. Later he was the sole survivor of the *Tonquin* massacre, when John Jacob Astor's ship was captured off Vancouver Island and subsequently blown up by the besieged crew.

By reputation, the Tillamooks were a tough crowd. When Captain Gray and his crew first entered Tillamook Bay in 1792, seemingly friendly natives greeted them and offered them food and berries. Given that Gray saw little potential for violence, he launched a foraging party to gather fresh vegetable materials with which to combat the scurvy that was afflicting the crew. However, during the foraging activities a Tillamook snatched a cutlass from Marcus Lopius, a black crew member, and in the ensuing mayhem Lopius was killed and the rest of the party barely escaped into the waiting boats. Frantically, they rowed for the distant ship with a swarm of Tillamook canoes in swift pursuit. By the time the crews reached the ship, the natives had vanished. The shipboard guns were fired but their impact was hollow as they resounded across an empty bay.

The next encounter with Europeans, in January 1806, was almost as disastrous. Hearing that a whale had been found beached in the territory of the Tillamooks, Lewis and Clark decided to make the arduous trip over Neahkahnie Mountain. At first the Tillamooks welcomed them cordially, but then the temptation to profit from the apparent wealth of the visitors proved too much. One of the Americans was soon invited into a plank house, where the Tillamooks planned to rob him of his weapons and garments. Quickly, other Tillamook sounded the alarm and the attempt on his life was averted with the would-be attacker fleeing into the woods. The Corps of Discovery immediately recognized the peril in which they found themselves—isolated, and deep in the territory of the unpredictable Tillamooks. They fled the village, fearful of an attack as they retreated over Neahkahnie Mountain.

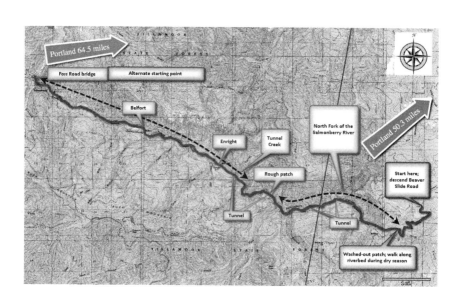

Portland 64.5 miles

Foss Road bridge   Alternate starting point

Belfort

Enright   Tunnel Creek

North Fork of the Salmonberry River

Portland 50.3 miles

Rough patch

Start here; descend Beaver Slide Road

Tunnel

Tunnel

Washed-out patch; walk along riverbed during dry season

1 mi.

24. Lower Salmonberry River

BRIEF DESCRIPTION: The Lower Salmonberry Trail begins at the bottom of the Beaver Slide Road and heads west along the Salmonberry River until it empties into the Nehalem River. Given the time required to reach the Salmonberry, one should plan on 2 days to access and hike this segment of the Salmonberry River. This portion of the river is reputed to be among the best steelhead fishing streams in the country. The gorge itself is ruggedly beautiful, and its innumerable stretches of deep blue-green pools interspersed by tumbling cataracts are stunning.

As of this writing, the Oregon Parks and Recreation Department and the Oregon Department of Forestry have agreed to collaborate on converting the existing Pacific Railway & Navigation line into an official trail for hikers, bikers, and equestrians. No doubt it will take some decades for the route to be completed, so these trail descriptions will remain relevant for some time. Even after the trail is completed, much of what is recorded in these pages will still hold true.

DISTANCE: 16 miles; 2.7-mile descent down to the river and 13.6 miles along the river

ELEVATION CHANGE: The biggest elevation change—a loss of 1,600 feet over 2.7 miles—occurs on Beaver Slide Road. The downhill grade at times exceeds 30 percent, so it's a struggle to keep from overbalancing downward and slipping on the rough gravel surface. The rest of the hike only loses about 500 feet in elevation over the remaining 13.6 miles along the Salmonberry River.

TRAIL CONDITION: Much broken terrain. The tracks are suspended in the air in some places, and several bushwhacks require strenuous climbing up the steep slopes on either side of the river.

APPROXIMATE DURATION: 10–12 hours. I planned an overnight stay along the way.

TRAVEL TIME FROM PORTLAND TO TRAILHEAD: Total setup time for this hike is just short of 3 hours: 1.5 hours to Foss Road Bridge; an additional 1.25 hours to Beaver Slide Road.

DRIVING DIRECTIONS: These directions assume that you will leave a car at the junction of the Salmonberry River and the Nehalem River, near the Foss Road Bridge. It also assumes that you will leave a second car at the top of Beaver Slide Road where the hike begins.

From the Sylvan exit on US 26 (exit 71B), travel 51.5 miles west on US 26 to the junction with Foss Road. Turn left and follow the signs for Spruce Run Campground. Continue on Foss Road past the Spruce Run Campground until you reach the bridge that crosses the Salmonberry, 13 miles from the turnoff from US 26. Total travel distance to the Foss Road Bridge is 64.5 miles.

At this point let me digress briefly on the direction of travel and timing of your hike. It is highly recommended that you leave a car at each end of the hike. After leaving a car at the Foss Road Bridge (where it crosses the mouth of the Salmonberry River), you will need to travel back to Beaver Slide Road. The drive between the put-in point on Beaver Slide Road and the take-out point at the Foss Bridge is 33.5 miles and requires about 1 hour and 15 minutes. It involves retracing your way back to US 26 and traveling 10.8 miles east until you reach the Section 10 Road (aka Wheeler Road). Take a sharp right to enter this dirt road and proceed into the wooded heights. After 1.6 miles you will encounter two dirt roads that split off to the left. Drive past these side roads and continue to travel generally uphill on what is known as Wheeler Road, but following signs that say Salmonberry Road. Yes, it's confusing, but I can only surmise they're indicating that the road will lead you to Salmonberry Road, which it does, eventually...

Another 0.7 miles onward you will pass Lousignant Road on your left; continue straight, following the more heavily used Wheeler Road. A half mile farther, another road ascends on your left. Ignore this side road and proceed straight to Wheeler Cut-Off Road. This road carries you downhill another 1.6 miles heading south, and passes Shields Road (on your right) about halfway down. At the end of Wheeler Cut-Off Road you will encounter an intersection at the bottom of a steep grade.

Turn left and pass through a gap in the ridge. Facing you is Wheeler Pond Road. Turn right to follow this road for another 4.6 miles. This road has some spectacular spots where it emerges from the woods and traverses large open slopes that provide impressive views of the entire region, including Rogers Peak and the Standard Grade running along the top of the mountains on the far side of the Salmonberry River. Eventually, you will emerge into a flat clearing that affords views both east toward the Salmonberry River valley and west toward the deep valley formed by the North Fork Salmonberry River. On maps this clearing is marked as the location of Camp 9; however, today there is little left to suggest any prior camp.

The open area just described serves as the junction for four roads that meet in a configuration resembling an H.

The Lower Salmonberry Trail was heavily damaged by the storms of 1997 and 2006. Note the fiber optic cable to the right of the dangling rails.

You entered the intersection from the north using Wheeler Pond Road.

As you enter the clearing, you'll see the North Fork Salmonberry Road entering the clearing on your right.

Forming the bottom half of the H are two forest roads.

The right-hand option is the extension of the North Fork Salmonberry Road and leads almost all the way down to the North Fork Salmonberry River (see chapter 25).

The left-hand option is Beaver Slide Road, which you will follow.

The initial 0.7 miles of Beaver Slide Road are easily navigable. At that point the road splits, and a recently constructed logging road descends to your right. To your far left a short track leads into a cul-de-sac. But in the middle a narrow passage allows cars to drive down a steep roadway. This drop-off marks the beginning of Beaver Slide Road. Unless you have a powerful vehicle with good clearance, I would suggest parking on this flat portion of Beaver Slide Road and walking the remaining 2.7 miles down to the Salmonberry River.

TRAIL LOG: For purposes of better organizing the trail description, I have segmented the hike into six segments:

- Descent from Beaver Slide Road to the Salmonberry River

- From the base of Beaver Slide Road west to Tunnel 29
- From Tunnel 29 to Tunnel 31
- Enright segment, including Tunnel 32
- Belfort segment
- Nehalem confluence

Descent from Beaver Slide Road to the Salmonberry River. Right from the beginning, where Beaver Slide Road drops off the end of the ridge at an elevation of 2,400 feet, it's a very steep descent. For 2.7 miles this very steep road winds down the side of the Salmonberry Gorge at a grade that at times exceeds 45 percent. At a major switchback, a huge boulder sits by the side of the road. For several years the rock was daubed with an exhortation to "F*** this road!" Despite the crude language, its sentiment brought sympathetic smiles to the hikers who came stumbling past it.

At the aforementioned boulder you reach the only relatively level area on the road. As you turn the corner the road tilts precipitously downhill. On your right side you can glimpse the railroad tracks that actually pass under Beaver Slide Road.

During the stormy months this canyon can descend into unfathomable violence as the whole 21-mile Salmonberry corridor turns into one vast washing machine. A 100-yard-wide torrent of malevolent brown water churns boulders, massive trees, and railroad parts as it blasts its way down the canyon. But during Oregon's mild summers this hard-to-reach riverside refuge is a place of unequaled beauty.

From the base of Beaver Slide Road to Tunnel 29. It always seems like there's just not enough time to sit quietly by this river, appreciating the untouched world that thrives in this green chasm. I sometimes feel as if I could almost merge with nature's rhythms if only I might be allowed to sit and contemplate the river flowing by for just little longer…

But to quote Robert Frost,

> The woods are lovely, dark and deep,
> But I have promises to keep,
> And miles to go before I sleep,
> And miles to go before I sleep.

And these next miles are the toughest on this hike.

Head west on the railroad tracks. Almost immediately the route is blocked by mangled tracks and a ruined railroad grade. On the left side of the track you will see a signboard (devoid of any postings). Immediately behind it a rough trail descends down to the riverbed. Follow that informal route if the water is not too high. At the far end of the washout you will find a ladder that ascends back up to the remaining railroad grade. If you're accompanied by a dog and can't climb the ladder, continue along the riverbed and eventually you will find a switchback trail that climbs up to the train tracks.

Trekking through the woods above the track is impossible! On that slope I encountered a many-layered logjam of tree trunks, enormous rocks, impenetrable vine maple, and moss covering everything. It was often hard to determine where the ground was located as we clambered from one rotten tree trunk to a boulder and through the vine maple to another slanting log. Like caterpillars we tried to navigate through this decaying shoal of forest debris plastered against the walls of this steep defile. This tangled detour above the river is probably not much longer than several hundred feet. But it took more than 30 minutes to cross. The summertime option of walking along the river itself is obviously much easier.

Immediately after this initial scramble, the tracks cross the Salmonberry River and pass through a tunnel (Tunnel 28)—the first tunnel west of Beaver Slide Road. Beyond that tunnel, the tracks cross the river twice, spanning a loop in the river's course and ending up on the south shore of the river. Two creeks flow into the Salmonberry along this relatively straight stretch, and as a consequence it is clogged with damaged track and grades that have been washed away, requiring frequent detours through the large debris strewn across the slopes of the steep canyon.

The first of these creeks is Belding Creek. Here and at Jones Creek (a quarter mile west of Belding Creek) you will encounter severe washouts requiring scrambles to circumvent the formidable logjams. For the next mile the route bends to the north and traverses several more washouts. It is mostly impossible to gauge where the trail goes beyond the next few yards, as washouts occur in almost every bend along the river.

Almost a mile beyond Belding Creek the river turns and resumes a northwesterly course, albeit constantly swerving back and forth across the narrow canyon. There are two more significant washouts in this section as you approach the second tunnel (Tunnel 29).

Tunnel 29 bores under a ridge that blocks the river's course. At the point where the river flows around the toe of this ridge, the North Fork of the Salmonberry spills in from the right. Amid the huge rounded boulders there is a small beach just upstream of the actual confluence. It has a lovely pool that is my dog's absolute favorite swimming hole. To get down to the water, proceed toward the tunnel. Just before the tunnel a set of tracks leads around the end of the ridge. If you follow these tracks you can climb down to the riverside at the point where the spur line bends around the end of the ridge.

Until 1967 a big log bridge spanned the Salmonberry at this point, but the railroad dynamited it to prevent vehicular access. In the years when these valleys were being harvested for timber, a rail spur crossed the river here and continued up the North Fork. All that remains today is a rough track that parallels the North Fork Salmonberry River. This approach to the Salmonberry River is described in chapter 25.

From Tunnel 29 to Tunnel 31. Once through Tunnel 29 you will emerge into a continuation of this narrow valley. About 0.3 miles from the tunnel, a major logjam has eroded the southern embankment. Three-quarters of mile from Tunnel 29, pass through Tunnel 30. About a half mile beyond that tunnel, cross Bathtub Creek, which has formed a kind of rock-strewn delta, covered by shoulder-high alders. Needless to say, the entire railroad embankment was swept into the river at this point.

Just past Bathtub Creek the narrow defile turns to the northwest. At this point you will encounter yet another massive detour. This requires a substantial scramble up the hillside and a tricky traverse about 30 feet above the prior embankment. At one point a rope dangles from a log, presumably to help hikers descend. (On our hike, we continued to ascend and surmounted the blockage by climbing over it.)

A quarter mile farther is the mouth of Ripple Creek, another major tributary flowing in from the south. The next mile, between Ripple Creek and Tunnel 31, is full of detours, bushwhacks, and strenuous hiking.

Enright segment, including Tunnel 32. On the far side of Tunnel 31 the terrain continues to be broken and will require at least one significant detour. Thereafter the river seems to have depleted its ferocious violence and the railroad embankment survives mostly intact. The occasional stream or creek entering the river has washed away the rail infrastructure, but at least the detours are not as long and treacherous as in previous stretches. It's about a mile from Tunnel 31 to Tunnel 32.

Near Tunnel 32, across from Tunnel Creek, the boulder-strewn waterway widens and even develops sandy stretches of riverside beaches. Go through Tunnel 32; on the far side it is possible to double back toward the point of the ridge, where a nice flat plateau overlooks a beautiful set of rapids with small pools interspersed. This would be a good place to stay overnight, but be careful not to trespass. Some of this land belongs to the folks who live in the cabins at Enright.

Night can fall quickly in these narrow valleys, so don't delay setting up camp or you might find yourself cooking in the dark. Be careful with your foodstuffs. Remember that you're deep in the Coast Range, which is home to a considerable population of black bears, who might be tempted to feast on your provisions if they're left casually strewn about.

During the storm of 2007, Tunnel Creek, which enters the Salmonberry River at the end of this ridge, was clogged by an enormous surge of debris that burst down the steep slope, carrying with it massive tree trunks and boulders the size of cars. All this debris rolled into the Salmonberry's main channel, creating a huge logjam that blocked the passage of the river. The obstruction formed a dam and caused the river to rise, flooding the valley as the roiling waters backed far up the river. Despite the mounting waters, the logjam held firm and the Salmonberry River continued to rise inexorably. At 50 feet above the normal water level, the river began flooding through the tunnel. At 75 feet above the normal water level, the river filled the tunnel to the ceiling. The howling river rose more than 125 feet above its normal stage, scouring all the vegetation off the rock face high above the tunnel entrance and shoving massive boulders through the tunnel. When the logjam finally did burst, the river surged downstream, dumping massive amounts of mud and detritus along the riverbed and raising the level of the river by almost 3 feet.

Today, one can still see the scouring effects of the river, but during the languid summer months it's hard to imagine the mayhem that befell Tunnel 32. From the hiker's perspective, the valley seems to open up a bit on the western side of Tunnel 32, and the river bends and flows in a northwesterly direction. About 0.1 mile after emerging from the tunnel, small cabins are nestled into the hillside above the railroad tracks. The first of these cabins belongs to Don Hennig, whose father acquired it in 1965. Probably built in the 1930s during the heyday of the logging activity in this area, it served as a bunkhouse for the loggers and railroad hands that operated out of the isolated hamlet of Enright. Today the community comprises a handful of remote cabins. Prior to the Tillamook Burn, which burned off most the timber, Enright had a population of nearly 400 people.

At Enright one can still see the original water tower. In 1915 there were seven such water tanks along the way, to provide ample water for the steam engines to exert sufficient power to navigate the 3 percent grade that began just beyond Enright.

Belfort segment. One mile beyond the water tank, the railroad crosses the river and begins to follow the north bank. About a half mile beyond the bridge, in the area known as Belfort, you'll encounter the last major detour where a fast-flowing tributary has swept away part of the roadway. Beyond, the river flows steadily toward the confluence with the Nehalem River. As the route progresses, tall pinnacles and bare cliffs loom above the valley. But the river at this stage becomes wider, and a long series of tree-shaded pools invite the tired hiker to shed his or her clothes and jump in.

Nehalem confluence. The final stage of the hike goes from Belfort all the way to the confluence of the Salmonberry and Nehalem Rivers. A curve in the river marks the location of Belfort on the north side of the Salmonberry; about 1 mile from Belfort is the quarry that supplied all the rock used to build this railroad. About a half mile farther, cross the river once again and begin to trek along the south side of the river.

Proceed downstream alongside an increasingly wide river. Keep a sharp eye peeled for a steel cable strung between two trees about a quarter mile east of the Foss Road Bridge. When you spot it, look carefully among the trees on the opposite shore for a nearly invisible house built into the forest. I would not recommend making a visit, since the last time I checked, there was a rifle leaning ominously next to the front door. I interpreted that tableau as a not-so-subtle request for privacy…

And anyway, just around the corner is one of the best swimming holes on the river—and it's close enough to the terminus of the trail to provide lasting refreshment for the drive out. As you turn the corner (the track bends to the left), follow the tracks along until you almost reach the narrow portion that bends to the right again. Just prior to that narrow area you will come across a small ravine that drops down the embankment toward the river. This is probably the best way to reach the shore. Once you've reached the river level, follow the shore a bit upstream to some nice pools interspersed by large rocks. A large boulder on the shore sits over a small patch of sand and offers a handy windbreak if the afternoon breezes are too cool for your liking. Now, shed your clothes and enter the water. This experience is heavenly, in my humble estimation!

Return to the railroad tracks and keep traveling west. After about 0.6 miles, cross the last bridge. Just past the bridge you'll come across two homes set along the north bank of the river. Shortly after that, a track angles away from the tracks on the right side. Take this route to a parking area alongside Foss Road.

At Foss Road, be sure to look at the bridge that crosses the Salmonberry River. The bridge that stood there in 2007 was destroyed, cutting this back-road connection to Nehalem Bay. During the summer of 2012 the bridge was replaced. Subsequently the Oregon Coast Scenic Railroad extended its rails up to the bridge. Eventually, they want to restore the rail traffic all the way to Enright, but there is much uncertainty about whether this is feasible.

This hike ends at the confluence with the Lower Nehalem River, but the Salmonberry master plan envisions the trail continuing along the railroad right-of-way all the way to Wheeler, situated on Nehalem Bay. From there the planned Salmonberry Trail parallels the railroad right-of-way through the coastal communities all the way down to Tillamook. All these plans are now under the purview of the Salmonberry Trail intergovernmental agency.

The Bushwhack from Hell

For weeks I had been itching to explore an old logging road that descends from the promontory just south of the Four Seven Ridge, a narrow shoulder that squeezes itself down into the North Fork Cronin Creek. According to my older maps there was once a road that twisted down the steep slopes of the ridge all the way to the upper reaches of the North Fork Cronin Creek. On bicycles my friend Andrew and I followed these tracks down into the depths of this remote valley, warily following the logging roads as they went from a gradual downhill slope, to precipitously steep, to nearly impossible to ride without toppling over one's handlebars. And all the while the road led ever downward.

At lunch we lurched to a halt on one particularly steep section. The slope had been so consistently downhill that we were having trouble gripping the hand brakes any longer. As we descended I was mentally logging the distance and slope we would have to climb if we decided to backtrack. And it was getting to the point that any retreat would take so long, it would be totally dark before we got back to the car. I was getting concerned, but the map clearly showed that the old road looped down the steep slope and then doubled back to follow the North Fork Cronin Creek down to Foss Road.

Down we rolled, brakes squeaking and one leg stretched out at the side in case the bicycle slipped away on the steep slope. A series of drops finally brought us to a level patch, where the dwindling road now rounded the corner, only to disappear down into the wildly overgrown creek below.

I was apprehensive as we neared the bend, because I could clearly see that the portion beyond the bend was rarely used and much overgrown. "Hold on," I urged, before Andrew and my dog Zoe lurched down the overgrown pathway. This was not looking good. To have the trail disintegrate this early in the descent did not bode well, as we had miles to cover before we could reach Foss Road.

It became obvious to me that this was one of those wilderness decisions you have to make that will really test your mettle, and if you're unlucky it'll turn you into a statistic. I peered down into the valley floor, trying the find that smooth dirt track that I had hoped would whisk me out of there. But all I saw were tightly packed alders and huge stumps that dated back to an earlier harvest. In front of me the opposing hillsides loomed, thickly forested and interspersed with small cliffs. Behind me was the incredibly steep descent that dropped over two thousand vertical feet in less than five miles. This would be a grueling and punishing climb if we had to retreat and push our bikes back up to the summit. We were in that treacherous situation where we'd already overextended ourselves so much that we were willing to take on even more risk simply because the alternative was too grueling to contemplate.

Before committing to any further descent we decided to exhaust all other options. We returned to a side road we had just passed. The map described this road as running all the way out to the farthest point of the ridge, to where the loggers had pulled the trees up to the waiting trucks. Unfortunately, there was no path or road that led beyond this promontory. Nearby, a short skidder road led down to an old hunters' camp overlooking a massive clear-cut. A thick alder jutted out from the embankment, presumably to hang the carcasses they had hoped to bag. But today the empty nooses simply signified the end of the road for us. This was a remote part of the Coast Range and apparently a lot farther from Foss Road than we had expected.

In Oregon, it is usually dangerous to descend into the riverbeds, due to the risk of hypothermia from all the wet and cold. And the rivers themselves can be astonishingly difficult to navigate, even on foot. But this was a hot day in early September, and the dark green jungle below me looked inviting—and besides there was that old road indicated on the map—so on we went, rolling down the ever-steeper slope. Down we went on this overgrown trail and finally into a narrow animal track that brought us to the river. Here we stopped amid the green canopy of alders, big-leaf maples, and immense tangles of blackberries, thimbleberries, salmonberries, salal, nettles, and devil's club. In the middle a small stream of water trickled amid the giant tree trunks and huge logjams that blocked much of the valley floor. There was no sign of any road. The valley had reverted so completely to its native jumble of rocks and roots that the very concept of road was unimaginable. But we had cast our dice upon the brow of the hill and there was no turning back at this point.

From here, we carried our bikes, using them to shield ourselves from fields of nettles and the clinging tangle of blackberries. Resolutely, we tromped through the tangled vine maple roots and up and over the towering logjams. Down the streambed we marched, rolling the bicycles over the boulders and over countless logs. We stopped repeatedly as I scouted the best way to proceed. About a half mile farther down the streambed, amid the wild clutter of branches and rocky embankments, I first saw what was identifiable as the remnants of the original road. It proceeded for ten feet before being swallowed up by the landscape and its wild vegetation. We retreated with our bikes to wade along the streambed that slipped under the thick curtain of branches, roots, and fallen alders. At every turn of the stream I feared the worst—an insurmountable logjam over which it would be impossible to clamber—so that we'd have to abandon the bikes to make it out by darkness.

I cannot recall how long we struggled through this rocky defile, fighting off the constant attack of vicious vegetation. At first I winced and yelped as my bare legs repeatedly swished through the stinging nettles, but eventually everything below my thighs reverberated with a constant stinging throb, interspersed with bramble tears and frequent lashing branches as I forced myself through the thickets that blocked our way. The "best parts" were when we had to cross the big muddy bogs that covered the abandoned trail, and the swamp sucked at our shoes and filled our socks with mud.

In all we descended several miles in such impossible conditions before the erstwhile road became more prominent. Back and forth we went, trying to follow the elusive trail, but eventually we arrived at the back end of a piece of private property that extended completely across the lower part of Cronin Creek. I have never been so glad to see a "Posted" sign, because it meant that civilization was right around the corner. Fording the creek one last time, we scrambled up onto a vast lawn that stretched across a majestic valley graced by tall Douglas fir groves, several ponds, and a gaily painted Huey helicopter!

The route we had taken marched us right through the middle of this idyllic scene, passing just below several homes tucked along the valley's length. No one seemed to be home, so we pedaled as quickly as we could for the exit. As we approached Foss Road undetected, we thought we were home free. But as we sailed through the open gate we triggered a resounding cacophony of alarms that reverberated through the narrow valley. Yikes! Just minutes ago the forest had been peaceful, but we were soon surrounded by several carloads of angry people inquiring why we felt entitled to breach the landowner's privacy.

While we didn't exactly endear ourselves to the local residents, an abbreviated version of our tale of poor decision-making in the wilds soon brought our accusers to understand that we were not bowhunters with illegal entry on our minds, but rather two "damned fools" who had gotten themselves trapped up the creek without a paddle or an exit strategy. Shaking his head at the idea of descending the slope of the North Fork Cronin Creek by bicycle, Jack Erikson, the landowner, just exclaimed, "That's a first!" I quickly agreed, suggesting it might also be the last.

Bridge on the Lower Salmonberry.

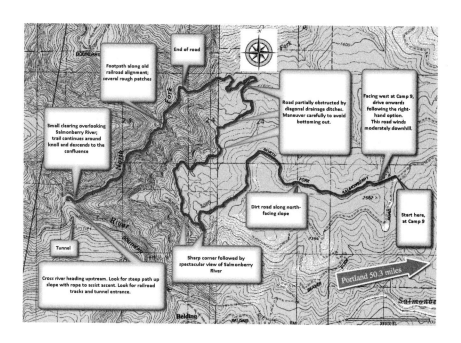

End of road

Footpath along old railroad alignment; several rough patches

Road partially obstructed by diagonal drainage ditches. Maneuver carefully to avoid bottoming out.

Facing west at Camp 9, drive onwards following the right-hand option. This road winds moderately downhill.

Small clearing overlooking Salmonberry River; trail continues around knoll and descends to the confluence

Dirt road along north-facing slope

Start here, at Camp 9

Tunnel

Sharp corner followed by spectacular view of Salmonberry River

Cross river heading upstream. Look for steep path up slope with rope to assist ascent. Look for railroad tracks and tunnel entrance.

Portland 50.3 miles

25. North Fork of the Salmonberry Trail

BRIEF DESCRIPTION: This trail really goes to the heart of what led me to write this guide: the desire to find the truly beautiful places that exist way out beyond where most people will venture. This hike begins with a bone-jarring but awe-inspiring drive that creeps along the edges of steep cliffs and reveals panoramic views into the fortress of mountains surrounding the Salmonberry River. It is a landscape that conjures up the presence of natural forces that are far from pastoral and quiescent. For me, this back way down to the Salmonberry River is a very special experience. If you really want to get out there, this trail will take you there (and get you home, as well).

DISTANCE: 1.4 miles one way

ELEVATION CHANGE: A negligible 240 feet. The toughest descent is accomplished in your car.

TRAIL CONDITION: The trail is fairly rugged with lots of fallen trees to cross, and several areas where the path has been buried by fallen rocks—you have to pick your way through the rocky slope. At other places the river has eaten away the supports for the railbed and you're left clutching at branches as you try to cross the slippery slopes overlooking the river. The trail also crosses a number of streams that can be quite active in the winter and spring.

APPROXIMATE DURATION: 2 hours for hike itself. Remember to add rest stops to your travel time, as well as time to enjoy the river.

TRAVEL TIME FROM PORTLAND TO TRAILHEAD: About 3.5 hours

DRIVING DIRECTIONS: From the Sylvan exit (exit 71B), take US 26 west 41.3 miles to the Section 10 Road. (Be sure to reset your odometer as you pass the Sylvan exit.) Turn left (south) onto Section 10 Road. (Should you miss this exit you can turn onto Salmonberry Road, 0.2 miles farther west. The Section 10 Road is easier to spot since it emerges alongside Highway 26 and debouches into a wide gravel area on your left. The Salmonberry Road junction is harder to spot since it's in a corner and the side road is not visible until you're nearly through the curve—so go slowly if you miss the Section 10 Road.)

TRAIL LOG: Because getting there is half the fun of this hike, I've included the back-road directions in the trail log.

"Loki's pool" at the confluence of the Salmonberry River and the North Fork of the Salmonberry River. This was the closest place to heaven that a husky could imagine, and I'll always remember the grin that spread across his face as he settled into the cold flowing stream.

Driving. Reset your odometer as you leave US 26; subsequent distance measurements are given in terms of distance traveled after departing the highway. At US 26, Section 10 Road has an elevation of 1,585 feet. Getting all the way down to the Salmonberry River will require navigating past two mountain ranges, each approaching 2,500 feet, and then descending down to the confluence at an elevation of 760 feet.

The route starts by following Section 10 Road, but this quickly merges with another access road (Salmonberry Road) coming in from the right. From here on the road is designated as Wheeler Road. Keep following Wheeler Road as it ascends the first heights. Many smaller roads connect to Wheeler Road; stay on the central road (which shows the most use). After 2.68 miles, pass another road coming in from the right: Shields Road. Immediately thereafter the main road begins to descend, and at 2.87 odometer miles you will enter an intersection referred to as Coyote Corner. On your left is a well-traveled road, which is the continuation of Wheeler Road. It heads east to Reehers Camp, located behind Timber. Bypass this road and continue straight—now traveling along Wheeler Cut-Off Road. At 3.66 odometer miles, pass another connecting road (Shields Road—yes, this is the other

HIKING FROM PORTLAND TO THE COAST

end of the Shields Road that you passed a mile back) coming in from the right. Immediately thereafter, Wheeler Cut-Off Road starts to drop dramatically. Near the bottom of this steep hill the road begins to sweep around to the left. On the right side is a small forest road veering gently to your right. (This is the continuation of the North Fork Salmonberry Road and can serve as an alternate route.) But continue to sweep around the corner to a three-way split.

On the extreme right a short skidder road peters out almost immediately as it ascends the clear-cut slope to your right. The left-hand option, Wheeler Pond Road, is also well used since it comes in from Cochran Pond. Choose the middle road; it turns slightly to the right and is the continuation of Wheeler Pond Road. Slightly more than 4.5 miles later, you will reach the summit of the final ridge—the site of a long-abandoned logging camp (Camp 9) at an elevation of 2,400 feet. If you need further information about how to navigate these labyrinthine roads, chapters 23 and 24 include descriptions of how to reach Camp 9.

Using the aforementioned route, you will enter the ridgetop clearing at Camp 9 from the northeast. I recommend stopping here to take in the impressive views and to scope out the various roads leading out of this clearing.

On your right is another road (Salmonberry Road) coming in from the north. Straight across the clearing (looking south) you will see three roads. The middle one is just a short trail into the woods, long enough to accommodate a pickup and trailer. Just to the right of this camping driveway is another road heading to the southwest. This is the North Fork Salmonberry Road, the route you will follow. The final choice, on the left, is the top of Beaver Slide Road, described in a previous chapter.

Follow the North Fork Salmonberry Road from this clearing. For 2 miles it traverses the south face of this ridge, then it makes a sharp U-turn and heads along the top of a south-facing ridge with stupendous views. Check your odometer at the U-turn. Soon the road turns north and begins the long descent into the basin carved by the North Fork of the Salmonberry River. The road continues in this northerly direction for about 1.7 miles (from the U-turn). During this stretch you will encounter the first water bars or runoff gutters; these will take patience to navigate (take them at an angle). At the 1.7-mile point (from the U-turn) the road swings around and begins to traverse the slope heading south. This last portion of the road can be challenging, so parking the car at this turn is not unreasonable. The final part of this descent is steep and rocky and drops precipitously as it winds its way 0.7 miles down to the base of the slope, just above the North Fork of the Salmonberry. In all, the trip from the highway to the bottom of the North Fork Salmonberry Road will take you about 1 hour and 25 minutes.

I have successfully traversed this descent in my Honda Odyssey during the dry months of the year, but nonetheless it's very difficult to navigate, with frequent rocks and branches that need removing, and diagonal gutters carved into the road that require careful maneuvering to avoid damaging the car's underside, not to mention retaining enough traction to climb the hill on the way out. The road gets rockier and the grade increases to more than 15 percent as you descend. It is quite sensible to park your car anywhere next to this road and complete the descent on foot if you are not comfortable driving in the steep and rough conditions. Such precautions are especially appropriate if conditions are wet or if you have passengers.

Hiking. The trailhead itself is a bit anticlimactic, especially after crawling your way down the steep and rocky approach road. Yes, now that you've reached the trailhead you can unclench your hands from their death grip on the steering wheel! During hunting season it's not unusual to find one or more hunters camped in this remote location, but at other times of the year it's quite deserted. The easily visible footpath leaves the open area on the left side (to the southwest) and heads south along the North Fork Salmonberry River.

The footpath down to the main stem of the Salmonberry River actually follows a rail spur that climbed the North Fork Salmonberry River. The original spur line terminated at the trailhead. The road that leads down to that point was added much later. Years ago, the southern end of this rail spur crossed the Salmonberry on a high wooden bridge that connected the spur to the main line of the Pacific Railway & Navigation line, which ran along the entire length of the Salmonberry River.

As you follow the old railbed down and around a corner you'll soon be confronted with the damage wrought by a vengeful nature. At some places the railbed has been buried by rockslides. At others it has been eroded to a whisper of a footpath. But in between you will find wide, level stretches of trail. And all along the way you'll love the charming waterfalls on the North Fork of the Salmonberry River that gurgle and leap their way down the valley.

The hike down this valley always seems longer than the return. It's probably due to the fact that I tend to forget the many different types of terrain. Eventually, you turn the final corner and begin a gentle descent into a

North Fork of the Salmonberry River.

cozy sunlight clearing. This is a favorite stopping place for the hunters and anglers who seasonally frequent this area. Indeed, it was through reading an angler's guide to Oregon's rivers that I first learned of this provisional trail and the "easy" access it provided to the river.

As you enter the clearing, I recommend that you walk to the southern edge where the lush grass ends abruptly above a cliff overlooking the river. It was from this elevated clearing that the original bridgehead crossed the river. To get down to the river, turn around and walk to the northern edge of the clearing. From there you will see that a small path leads west and wraps around a small knoll before descending to the riverside.

To cross the main stem of the river (during the warmer seasons of the year), I recommend turning left immediately after descending the final drop to the riverbank. To the left you will find a pool big enough to soak in, but also shallow enough at its lower end to cross on foot. On the other side, climb the shelf of river rocks and head upstream, while at the same time getting closer to the heavily vegetated slope that separates the riverbank from the forest growing above. There among the ferns and tree roots you will notice a track that leads up the steep slope. Look closer and you should find a rope dangling down the slick slope; use it to haul yourself up and into the forest above.

Once up the slope, head to your right, toward an area that seems relatively open—this is where the rail spurs that went around the end of the ridge are located. Once you've found them, follow them upstream through the dense underbrush until you emerge on the main rails near the mouth of the tunnel. Now you've found the PR&N, or as the old-timers called it, the "Punk, Rotten, and Nasty."

Next on your agenda is a walk through the tunnel. This tunnel is relatively short, so you can stumble your way through without a flashlight, but you would do well to come equipped with one. On the other side of the tunnel, note the sign that says "808." Its significance is that the Southern Pacific, which owned this difficult stretch of railroad, numbered all the tunnels to reflect their distance from the heart of the Union Pacific rail system—on Market Street in downtown San Francisco. So you are now standing 808 miles from downtown San Francisco!

This is also where the Edwards incline incident occurred. Had you been standing here on that fateful day in 1928, you'd have been mangled beyond recognition. But luckily for all, no one was hurt, even though the valley echoed with the impact of the fully loaded rail cars as they flew across the river and were obliterated when they struck the main line of the PR&N and the cliff face beyond the tracks. Read the anecdote about gyppo logging in chapter 21 for the full story of this dramatic incident.

If you have time before the light fades, hike along the rail line. There are many more spectacular examples of what an angry river can do to massive rails and iron bridges along the way.

Walking all the way down to the Foss Bridge from the 808 tunnel will take you another 5 or 6 hours. To walk the 2.5 miles upstream to the junction with Beaver Slide Road will take several hours because of the unusually heavy damage in this stretch of the river. As you plan your excursions along the main stem of the Salmonberry River, remember to leave enough time to climb out of the canyon before nightfall! There is *no way* to call home from the bottom of this gorge unless you carry a satellite beacon.

The Lidgerwood

Olson Road diverges from US 26 about forty-six miles from Portland, immediately across from the Sunset Rest Area. This gated road heads south from the highway and up into the watershed of the North Fork Salmonberry River. Stimson Lumber Company actively manages the area. Significantly, they do not permit private vehicles on their land. Most people go flying by this dirt road without a second glance. The potholed road provides no clue to the vast amounts of wood that were harvested off these hills and hauled down this road, starting long before the highway was built. Today the cars come zipping down the long downhill slope with nary a glance at the rugged slopes laid bare by successive generations of loggers.

In today's well-tempered existence it is nearly impossible to conceive of the sheer brawn, stubbornness, and outright stupid cussedness that it took to operate a massive steam-driven logging operation in these coastal hinterlands. The story behind these remote slopes is really the tale of how the last steam-driven loggers managed to survive and prosper for nearly thirty-five years, carving out an enterprise from the heart of this primeval forest.

The yellow gate at the entrance to the Stimson timberlands prevents most of us from penetrating too deeply into this terrain. Only during hunting season is it feasible to explore the endless labyrinth of logging roads, skidder tracks, and elk trails that dominate these uplands, and even then you'd best watch out they don't lock the gates before you return. Some of the gates are more than eight miles into the forest—a long way to walk in the dark. I can tell you that from experience.

Here on the headwaters of Rock Creek, civilization first arrived when the Oregon-American Lumber Company laid down tracks from its mill in Vernonia to access the Dubois tract that lay at the heart of the northern Coast Range. Starting in 1922, the company built a logger's empire that produced two trains per day, each hauling twenty-six cars full of virgin timber, nonstop for nearly thirty-five years! And it was all done—the logging, the yarding, the hauling, and the milling—using only steam power.

Until the Wolf Creek Highway finally penetrated into the Upper Rock Creek watershed, the only way into this remote region was to ride the rails out of Vernonia, past the little switching yard in Keasey, across Deadman's Trestle, and up all the way to the headwaters of Rock Creek. This was the route that the Oregon-American Lumber Company used to access the huge stands of trees secluded in the coastal mountains overlooking the Salmonberry River.

The Dubois tract was shaped like a huge bowl that drained a vast network of streams down into the Salmonberry and Nehalem Rivers. It was this rich timber that the Oregon-American Lumber Company had in its sights when it extended the railroad spur south across what would later become the Wolf Creek Highway, and then even later was improved and renamed the Sunset Highway, or US 26.

By the late 1940s, the Oregon-American Lumber Company was operating at the top of the Coast Range along a narrow rim of forested peaks looming over the Salmonberry and Nehalem Rivers. Located at the farthest extremity of a narrow ridge jutting over the precipitous slopes of Cronin Creek was a desolate ridge known to the loggers as Windy Gap. It was one of the most remote logging sites in the Pacific Northwest. From this isolated perch the loggers could look over the tops of the last coastal range and see ships plying their way along the Oregon coast. The site was also utterly at the mercy of the violent storms that came barreling down from the icy waters off Alaska. During one particularly gargantuan storm, the watchman's cabin at Windy Gap was ripped right off its foundations and flung headlong over the cliffs and into the depths below.

Logging the precipitous slopes this high in the Coast Range was of the utmost difficulty. So it was not surprising that the Oregon-American Lumber Company, one of the last of the big-time logging outfits that ran a 100 percent steam-operated logging operation, brought in a Lidgerwood Tower to do the job.

Not many people are familiar with these massive über-yarders. That's because there were only a few of them ever produced. Built on an oversized rail carriage, they were powered by three massive steam donkeys and supported a 150-foot-tall tower from which to deploy their skyline. On June 3, 1948, the Oregon-American Lumber Company finally wrestled this monstrous rail carriage to the top of the Coast Range. It took four locomotives pushing and pulling to coax the three-hundred-ton Lidgerwood Tower skidder into position on the edge of the Windy Gap plateau, from where it overlooked all three forks of Cronin Creek.

Ed Kamholz, one of the authors of *The Oregon-American Lumber Company: Ain't No More*, recalls how the Lidgerwood was used to haul the last of the timber out of the Cronin Creek watershed in November 1957.[1] With its 150-foot tower they could now log a 360-degree arc, extracting huge old-growth logs from a mile away and pulling them up three thousand feet to the waiting railcars on the ridge above. Despite the Lidgerwood Tower's size, the effort was well worth it, because it allowed them to deploy the skyline to an anchor situated nearly a mile away on a ridge above the rugged Middle Fork of Cronin Creek. Ed Kamholz writes, "the canyon walls were so steep that the skyline angled down as much as 45 degrees."[2] The only things that the crane operator could see of the choker setters working on the slopes below were their helmets, which looked like little specks of gray metal lost in a jungle of old-growth stumps.

The Lidgerwood was eventually scrapped in place, since it was uneconomical to move it—and there were no more trees left to cut. The gargantuan Lidgerwood was the last gasp of steam-powered logging. It was a mechanical monster whose destruction was the inevitable outcome of its success.

The shelf on which the Lidgerwood stood has long since acquired a thick carpet of moss. Small trees are scattered along the inside wall and the view into the Cronin Creek watershed is nearly vertical. The trees on the slopes below have grown back and are past the half-century mark. It is hard to imagine the din and racket that must have presided on this shelf when the Lidgerwood was in full operation. Today this outcropping is a very remote place, requiring many hours to reach on foot and bicycle. But it remains one of my favorite places, not only for its remoteness, but also for its echoes of a bygone era.

Notes

1. Kamholz, Blain, and Kamholz, *The Oregon-American Lumber Company,* 258 (see chap. 21, n. 1).

2. Ibid., 295.

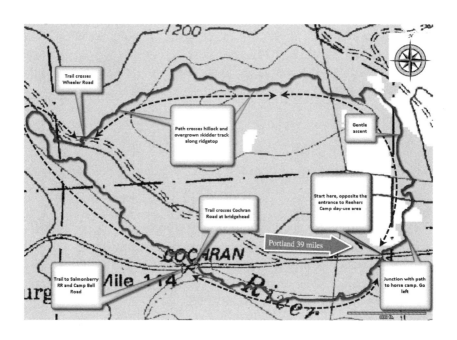

Trail crosses
Wheeler Road

Path crosses hillock and
overgrown skidder track
along ridgetop

Gentle
ascent

Start here, opposite the
entrance to Reehers
Camp day-use area

Trail crosses Cochran
Road at bridgehead

Portland 39 miles

COCHRAN

Mile 114

River.

Trail to Salmonberry
RR and Camp Bell
Road

Junction with path
to horse camp. Go
left

26. Triple C Trail

BRIEF DESCRIPTION: After climbing a small hill, the trail follows the Upper Nehalem River for about 2 miles through older forests to return to Reehers Camp and the associated horse camp on Cochran Road. The trail combines various kinds of scenic treats, including views of the high-country ridges, the heavier stands of timber along the Nehalem River, and the pleasant upland meadows in between. The area is full of typical Oregon woodland flowers, a wide variety of birds, and lots of deer and other mammals. The trail itself is well maintained and clearly marked. It's a thoroughly delightful mixture in a small package.

DISTANCE: 2.5 miles round trip

ELEVATION CHANGE: 320 feet

TRAIL CONDITION: The trail was recently built and it was constructed specifically to accommodate horses as well as foot traffic. As a result the surface is broad and flat, all the low spots prone to accumulating water have been paved with river rock, and the overhanging branches have been pruned to a height of 10 feet. The trail is broad and clearly marked throughout its length. I can imagine that the trail might be a bit muddy if you were to follow a string of horses in wet weather.

APPROXIMATE DURATION: 1 hour

TRAVEL TIME FROM PORTLAND TO TRAILHEAD: 50 minutes

DRIVING DIRECTIONS: Drive west from the Sylvan exit (exit 71B) on US 26 for 33.6 miles. Turn left on Timber Road. Follow this road 3 miles to the small community of Timber. As you approach Timber the road bends left and crosses a bridge over the Nehalem. Immediately after the bridge, turn right onto Cochran Road. (The main road, Timber Road, also turns right shortly after the bridge. Be sure to turn onto Cochran Road.) Cochran Road turns into a dirt road less than a mile from this intersection.

Follow Cochran Road for about 2.2 miles to Reehers Camp, and continue another 0.2 miles to the day-use area/horse camp. I recommend that you park in this section of the camp. The trail begins opposite the entrance to this camp.

TRAIL LOG: You can walk the trail by beginning at the entrance to the Reehers Camp day-use area. Directly opposite the entry to the parking lot a wooden signpost marks the beginning of the trail. Proceed up this trail, crossing a lovely meadow before you enter the woods. Shortly after entering the trees you will encounter a T fork in the road; the path on the right heads off to the main part of Reehers horse camp.

Take the left-hand trail, which leads up the hill. This well-maintained path weaves through the trees and eventually crests the ridge above Wheeler Road at an altitude of 1,362 feet. Off to your right you may spot the original road that served the logging operation that removed the trees. Eventually the trail crosses this ridgetop road and begins to descend the south face. Shortly thereafter you will cross Wheeler Road.

This trail offers a bounty of familiar Pacific Northwest plants. One of the common plants to be seen on this trail is *Trientalis latifolia,* commonly known as starflower, because of its symmetrical six-petal flower. The Cowlitz people who lived in this region used an infusion of this plant's juice as an eyewash.

Another lovely plant to be found along the higher portions of the Triple C Trail is the dwarf rose (*Rosa gymnocarpa*). Generally it grows in forests and shrub lands from sea level to higher altitudes. Native children loved this plant and used the colorful rose hips as beads strung into necklaces. Hunters used a wash from its branches to get rid of the human scent.

Also to be found is the American vetch (*Vicia americana*). This vine grows at the edges of forests, on coastal bluffs, and along stream banks near the coast. Just up the coast, the Makah revered this plant as potent love medicine: "If you want your girlfriend to love you, take the plant and rub down with it after bathing, and she will love you forever." The Quinault women would put it under their pillows to bring back their husbands.

As the trail reaches the higher elevations along the top of the ridge, you emerge onto an old logging road that once ran along the crest of the ridge. This old road continues down the ridge and terminates in a clear-cut area. It was here that I spotted a western tanager flitting across the brush piles. I took a long-distance picture and on closer examination of the photo, I saw something that had eluded me at the time. Sitting just below the brilliantly colored western tanager male sat the very inconspicuous female—nearly invisible next to her exuberantly colored mate.

Wheeler Road crossing. The crossing is marked with signposts and the continuation is equally well marked. From here the trail leads southwest and up the narrow valley for a bit before doubling back along the headwaters of the Nehalem River. For the next mile it follows the Nehalem River, eventually crossing Cochran Road. On the south side of the bridge is the trailhead for the Gales Creek Trail. But for this walk, stay on the north side

Trailhead to the Triple C Trail, just opposite the entrance to the day-use area of Reehers horse camp.

of the bridge and proceed along the Triple C Trail, which continues just across the road.

Nehalem Bridge. After crossing Cochran Road follow the continuation of the trail up and along the side of the Nehalem for a half mile, weaving between huge old logs, nurse trees, and the mushrooms that thrive in this shaded and moist environment. It was here, along the shaded banks of the

Nehalem River in 1854, that Joshua Elder plotted a rudimentary trail that would later be used as the basis a direct wagon road between Salem and Astoria. Due to the constant flooding and rearrangement of soil along this upland stream, it is impossible to see much evidence of any road today. However, if you follow the existing Triple C Trail, it eventually rises and returns to the signpost situated in the day-use area where you started this hike. In all, it's a gentle but satisfying jaunt.

Animals to Avoid

I recently was given a treatise on "Logging Road Layout and Related Subjects" typed by Bull Durham in 1997.[1] If I thought that this obscure treatise might be the next best seller, I was disappointed. Mostly it was about the finer points of laying out truck roads through the forest. But then the voice of the writer pierced through the technicalities and I was captivated.

On page one he starts off with this choice piece of advice: "After the office interview have the client take you to the property and show you what he knows: roads, line crossings, line tags, mean dogs, crazy hermits, and hostile widows." Now that changes the proposition a bit . . .

But Durham isn't about to go charging into the lair of any slavering dogs or pernicious widows lying in wait. "Don't think of a project as an unfriendly foe and don't attack it. You should caress it and surround it." "Sneak up on it," he advises, "get to know the property intimately...the more you know of her secrets the more she will cooperate and the less pitfalls she'll have for you to stumble over." They sometimes talk about lonesome cowboys, but I've never, until now, considered the possibility of a lonesome surveyor making amorous advances on his special stand of timber.

But my favorite piece of advice that Durham gives us, after his many years in the field, is contained in the section entitled "Animals to Avoid." After quickly listing bears, elk, deer, skunks, feral dogs, rabid bats, and even pot farms, he warns of two particularly dangerous beasts in the forests. Would it be cougars, spiders, bees, or log-truck drivers? Nope, none of those.

His first warning is about "Game Hunters (Homo Stupidus)"! He categorizes them as "unpredictable, may shoot at anything." "They go a little nuts at hunting season," he confides. "Avoid whenever possible; stay in your vehicle," he advises. As a final caution he adds, "Don't wear bright colors to give them a target."

But it was his final choice of fearsome and dangerous beasts that really floored me. He relates a story emanating "a few years ago" from Coos County. It seems that

> the rigging crew on a yarding job were setting chokers down in a draw where they turned up a Salamander…some of the boys dared the newest member of the team to bite the head off of the Salamander. The boy took the dare, bit the head off, went into convulsions and died before anything could be done for him.

Now there's advice I wouldn't have thought to include in a manual on how to build logging roads. I'm sure it prevented lots of convulsions among the engineers.

Notes

1. Bull Durham, "Logging Road Layout and Related Subjects" (Vernonia, OR: Longview Fiber files, 1997).

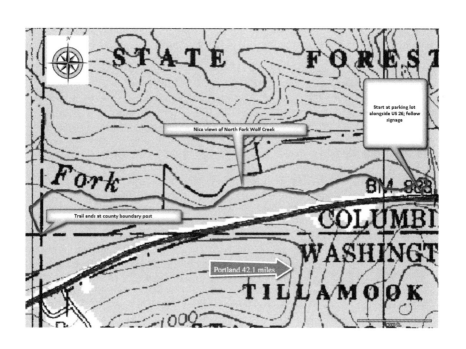

27. Four County Point Trail

BRIEF DESCRIPTION: The official brochure from the Tillamook State Forest claims that this is the only place in Oregon where you can stand simultaneously in four separate counties: Tillamook, Clatsop, Columbia, and Washington. Personally, I find this enticement a most unconvincing reason to visit. Focusing on some obscure cartographic anomaly entirely misses the point of this trail. Once you're out in the woods and listening to Wolf Creek as it meanders past you'll surely appreciate the real attraction of this short hike in the Coast Range.

DISTANCE: 1 mile

ELEVATION CHANGE: 40 feet

TRAIL CONDITION: Relatively flat and well maintained

APPROXIMATE DURATION: 45 minutes round trip

TRAVEL TIME FROM PORTLAND TO TRAILHEAD: 45 minutes

DRIVING DIRECTIONS: From the Sylvan exit (exit 71B), take US 26 west for 42.1 miles. A highway sign gives ample warning that there is a hiking trail ahead. Just as the road turns and begins to ascend you will spot the newly constructed trailhead with enough parking spaces to accommodate at least a dozen cars.

Trailhead for the Four County Point Trail alongside US 26.

TRAIL LOG: The trail winds through a Douglas fir forest mixed with vine maple, salal, Oregon grape, and sword ferns. North Fork Wolf Creek runs alongside, providing beautiful streamside vistas. Follow the trail down and around before heading uphill parallel to the road.

This is a nice hike for visitors. It will add an hour to your daylong beach excursion, but will give them a lovely impression of our deep forests—something at least as dramatic as our beautiful coastline.

The Wreck of the 104

About forty-six miles out of Portland on the Sunset Highway (US 26) we reach an important junction on the way to the coast. Unless a restroom is of immediate relevance, hardly anyone notices the Sunset Rest Area. But look out for this spot next time you pass by on the way to the coast. It might surprise you to know that for almost seventeen years this nondescript forested vale served as the gateway through which almost twenty million board feet of wood were hauled from the slopes above the Salmonberry River.

It all began in 1917 when the Oregon-American Lumber Company bought the Dubois tract, one of the last of the prime timber tracts (twenty-two thousand acres) on the Oregon coast. It lay high up on the crest of the rugged Coast Range, sheltering huge stands of old-growth timber that fronted out over the vast Pacific Ocean. The quality of the standing timber was beyond all standards that had been encountered before. The majority of the trees in the Dubois tract were between 300 and 600 years old, but one hoary survivor was recorded as having reached the advanced age of 838 years, surviving at least twelve major forest fires and dating back to the time of the Crusades. In the end, the Dubois tract turned out to be one of the most productive stands ever harvested, albeit under very rugged harvesting conditions.

In those heady days of the postwar reconstruction period, timber companies were rapidly increasing their labor force and were "highballing" production. These were the days of "boomers," "short stake artists," gyppos, career loggers, railroad builders, and railroad engineers. But as this story relates, harvesting logs near the ceiling of the Coast Range was a bodacious undertaking.

In early June 1948, the Oregon-American Lumber Company was operating along a rim of forested peaks that loomed over the Lower Nehalem River.

On June 3, they had just completed the installation of a three-hundred-ton Lidgerwood yarder that would enable them to extract valuable wood out of the very steep canyons in the Cronin Creek watershed. Released from their onerous job of pushing and pulling the gargantuan Lidgerwood into place, the Shay locomotives were now busy shuttling equipment up to the rim so that the massive loads the Lidgerwood was collecting could be transported down to Camp Olson and eventually to the mill in Vernonia.

At about 8:30 a.m., the 104, a Shay "lokie," was bringing an empty oil car and thirteen big carloads of logs down a narrow sinew of iron rail lines snaking along the rim of Windy Gap. Below the slowly descending train, clouds flowed over the Coast Range, turning the peaks into islands floating on a vast ocean of fog. And above the creeping train the clear blue sky was so close the engineers were tempted to tackle it with their skyline.

For the last twenty-five years Oregon-American had managed to haul several million board feet of wood out of the Coast Range without a serious railroad accident. And considering the tenuous network and rickety trestles that held this delivery system together, this was no trivial achievement. Yet as the train slowly sank through the blanket of clouds and maneuvered its way toward Camp Olson, that good fortune was about to change.

The train was inching its way down the steep grade of Line Spur 26. About a mile from Camp Olson, it was forced to stop because the section foreman was making repairs to the track. The braking process brought the train to a halt on a fairly steep slope near the junction with Spur 26-8. In the locomotive were Jeff McGregor, the engineer; Jerry Manning, the fireman; and Frank Willis, the timekeeper. Three brakemen were riding farther back among the carloads of logs. Everything seemed to be in order, and there was no apparent cause for concern.

After a short wait the section foreman completed his work and waved the train on. But from the moment the train began to move it was clear to those who witnessed the event that the locomotive was picking up speed too quickly. It continued to accelerate at an alarming rate, and as it rounded the bend near the 26-8 junction, the train jumped the tracks on the curve and immediately overturned.

This is where it gets a bit gruesome. George Lee, the head of the construction crew, described the scene with brutal frankness.

> The engineer wasn't alive when I got there. He got halfway out
> the cab window and that's as far as he made it. He was cooked.
> You don't get two hundred pounds of live steam goin' on you and

survive. The timekeeper 'ol Frank Willis, he was just squashed right between the boiler and the tank. The other guys, they weren't squashed, they were just cooked.[1]

The five that rode the ill-fated train accounted for more than 120 years of railroad logging experience. Yet the incident barely slowed down this high-balling[2] operation and the Oregon-American was intent on keeping to its schedule. By Monday they planned to have the scene cleared and enough trains moving to keep up the twice-daily delivery of thirteen carloads of lumber to the sawmill. The 104 was eventually repaired and rejoined the service. The same cannot be said of Jeff McGregor, Jerry Manning, and "ol' Frank Willis."

Notes

1. Kamholz, Blain, and Kamholz, *The Oregon-American Lumber Company*, 272.
2. Brix and Pentilla, *The Brix Logging Story*, 88 (see chap. 21, n. 3). One logger described this high volume-logging strategy as, "Get the logs out, if you want to keep your job. Do it safely if you want to keep your life."

The Pacific Ocean—at last!

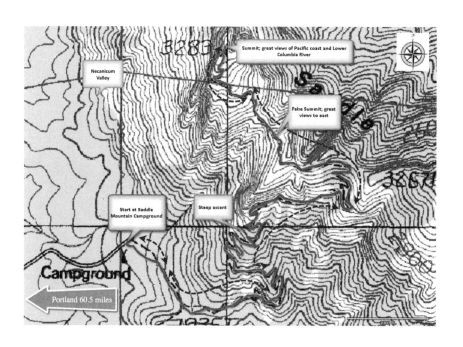

HIKING FROM PORTLAND TO THE COAST

28. Saddle Mountain Ascent

BRIEF DESCRIPTION: The hike up Saddle Mountain is one of the most iconic on the north coast of Oregon. From the summit elevation of 3,283 feet this peak provides excellent views of the entire northern coastline extending from Tillamook all the way up the Clatsop Spit to Astoria and its famous Astoria Column. Despite its popularity this trail can be quite strenuous for those not used to hiking. Be sure to carry enough water in the dry season. There are a few trickling springs along the way to keep your canine friends hydrated. This trail can attract quite a crowd on a sunny summer's day, so it is advisable to attempt this climb during the week or later in the season, especially when the fall foliage is at its brightest.

DISTANCE: 5.9 miles round trip

ELEVATION CHANGE: 1,600 feet

TRAIL CONDITION: Well-maintained hiking trail with some steep stretches

APPROXIMATE DURATION: 2–3 hours

TRAVEL TIME FROM PORTLAND TO TRAILHEAD: About 1 hour, 15 minutes

DRIVING DIRECTIONS: From the Sylvan exit (exit 71B) on US 26, head 60.5 miles west. Travel north on Saddle Mountain Road for 7 miles to reach the base of the trail. (The turnoff to Saddle Mountain Road is 14 miles east of Seaside.)

TRAIL LOG: The trail ascends from the east side of the parking lot at an elevation of about 1,700 feet. Two-tenths of a mile into the hike a side trail offers some nice vistas and a good look at Saddle Mountain looming overhead. For those not inclined to tackle the incline, this little side trail may be just the ticket. Hiking is not for everyone, so this detour may be a pleasant diversion for those unable or unlikely to go traipsing up mountains just because they're there.

The lower portion of the trail wanders up through a mixed alder and hemlock forest. It's well shaded as the trail twists through the chest-high undergrowth so typical of these Pacific-facing slopes. About a half mile in, at an elevation of about 2,000 feet, the trail turns and heads west, ducking into two ravines before resuming a westward traverse. A half mile farther, reach the next ridge at an elevation of 2,250 feet. Here the trail begins to zigzag up a bony spur. A half mile of crisscrossing the ridge finally brings you up to a ledge (2,600 feet) with spectacular views both east and west.

The trail follows the ridge on a gentler slope until it turns and heads west, just short of 2 miles into the hike. Given the mountain's profile one might say that you're crossing the low point in the saddle and approaching the elevated pommel. A quarter mile on, begin to climb to the summit, or the front of the saddle. This final ascent on sometimes slippery rocks takes you up to an elevation of 3,283 feet.

From there it's clear what the fuss was all about! (At least if it's not a cloudy day...)

The views wrap around the northern Oregon coast, all the way from Tillamook up the Columbia River to Cathlamet and even as far north as the beaches of Willapa Bay. What you're seeing is the first stretch of sandy shores on the northwestern Pacific coastline. North of here the Pacific coastline is an uninviting place with its battered rocks and massive trees that stretch all the way to Alaska. It's south of the Columbia River that our Pacific coastline changes, gradually losing its rocky edges and storm-ravaged conifers to settle into the gentle sweeps of coastline we associate with California's beaches. From Saddle Mountain you can see this gradual change from Willapa Bay in Washington all the way down to Neahkahnie Mountain to the south.

While traversing the interior, I've frequently found myself looking west into the late afternoon sun to see Saddle Mountain framed in the bright sky. The vantage points from which I have regarded Saddle Mountain are scattered across the Coast Range from Buck Mountain to Elk Mountain, and even Rogers Peak. From Saddle Mountain's peak I can look back into the green carpet at the countless promontories, clear-cuts, and clifftops where I've paused to search for a glimpse of this iconic peak. And now I am at my destination overlooking the Pacific Ocean. Here I finally reached the vantage point that I had looked forward to, and in so doing I can see the end of the trail laid out before me—right up to the edge of the Pacific Ocean.

Settling the Necanicum River Valley

Henry and Andrew Makela, two Finnish fishermen from Astoria, first spotted the Necanicum Valley while on a hunting trip in 1891. With their newly anglicized surname of Hill (the English translation of *makela*) they decided to homestead the valley. According to their descendants, the community never had more than about fifty inhabitants, or about ten families. It was, for all concerned, a mere "hamlet," hence its name to this day.

Approaching the summit of Saddle Mountain.

School was held in one of the homes until 1908, when the community built a new schoolhouse and hired Marie Pottsmith, a twenty-six-year-old teacher earning tuition to attend the University of Oregon. She packed her bags and proceeded by train from Salem to Portland. A steamer then transported her to Astoria, and from there she traveled by wagon down to Seaside.

There she learned that to reach the hamlet whose inhabitants she was to instruct would require a further twelve miles of rough inland travel to reach the village of Necanicum, and from there she would have to travel another eight miles on horseback into the mountains to reach her new home.

In her journal she recorded how one of the old-timers had informed her: "The postman waited here as long as he could before he drove to Necanicum with the mail. They don't have any electric lights out there and they have to travel early. He wanted to get back before dark." Another helpful soul then volunteered: "The people in Hamlet are Russian Finns and you have to eat black bread and sour milk and maybe you've got to sleep with some of the kids, too." Not to be too encouraging, he added, "There are cougars up in those mountains!" He failed to mention the packs of gray wolves that were then ravaging the farms along the Clatsop Spit.[1]

The next day saw Marie heading inland from the beach on a heavy buggy with her bags stowed alongside. At Necanicum she met up with the mail carrier, on whose horse she made the final eight miles up the muddy track. On the way they overtook a team of packhorses heading the same direction with the factory-made furniture that, according to the mail carrier, was intended to furnish her room—it was the first professionally made furniture to reach Hamlet. Until then the Finns had made all their furniture locally.

The community, it turned out, was not much more than the schoolhouse and several farms nearby, each with their 160 acres of homesteaded land. School was taught from 8:00 a.m., with scant time for lunch and recess, so that the kids could help with the haying and huckleberry picking. On one occasion she and another local women trekked six miles up a rough trail, scrambling over fallen logs and pushing the ever-encroaching foliage aside to reach the town of Elsie, where her companion had friends she wanted to see.

In her journals Marie relates the tribulations of the pioneer women, recounting how they took care of the homestead when the men were off fishing every summer and fall. Single-handedly they raised the kids, tended the livestock, and withstood the rigors of a pioneer life that left little room for respite.[2] In the fall they'd put up a barrel of corned beef, a barrel of salt pork, and one of sauerkraut. In the root cellar they'd keep barrels of apples, potatoes, and other vegetables. From the ceiling hung cabbages, onions, and sometimes, corn.[3] A sheep would provide enough wool for socks, mittens, and, in more remote locations, even underwear!

Bringing in a herd of cows lost in the fog along the Necanicum could result in a damp night spent sleeping rough in Oregon's primeval gloom. Childbirth meant an arduous horseback journey all the way to Astoria, or as happened, giving birth by the side of the track and waiting while the husband rushed the newborn babe to the nearest farmhouse and returned with help to transport his supine wife to safety.

But there was also warmth and human kindness to be found in these wild stretches along the Necanicum. Up near where Mail Creek enters the Necanicum, a Clatsop called "Indian Louis" had cleared some land and built a cabin of cedar shakes. A large fireplace, suitable both for warming the snug cabin and for smoking his venison, occupied one end of the small cabin. Louis's smoked meats were much prized by his downstream neighbors and many remembered visits to his cabin on Mail Creek with great fondness.[4]

Notes

1. Hanson, *Life on Clatsop*, 17 (see chap. 17, n. 3).
2. Friedman, *Tracking Down Oregon*, 35 (see chap. 10, n. 1).
3. Hanson, *Life on Clatsop*, 53.
4. Ibid., 52.

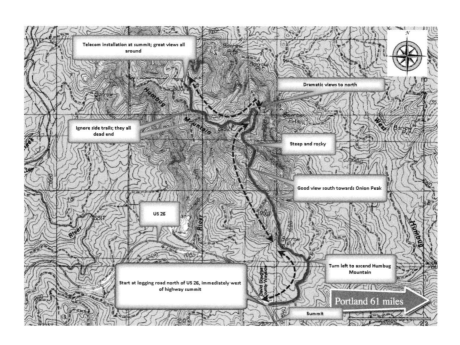

Telecom installation at summit; great views all around

Dramatic views to north

Ignore side trails; they all dead end

Steep and rocky

Good view south towards Onion Peak

US 26

Turn left to ascend Humbug Mountain

Start at logging road north of US 26, immediately west of highway summit

Portland 61 miles

Summit

HIKING FROM PORTLAND TO THE COAST

29. Humbug Mountain Ascent

BRIEF DESCRIPTION: This is a great hike if you're staying in Cannon Beach or Seaside. It's only about 14 miles from Seaside, is easier to access than Saddle Mountain, and is seldom frequented. The directions to the trailhead will shed some light on why so few people choose this trail. But those who do choose this hike will be rewarded with a dramatic view of the coast and of Saddle Mountain itself, located just north of Humbug Mountain. There is a radio and cell phone tower at the summit, but aside from those industrial intrusions the walk is wild, steep, and graced with craggy vistas.

DISTANCE: 7.05 miles

ELEVATION CHANGE: 1,313 feet

TRAIL CONDITION: Mostly graveled logging roads, though at times it gets steep and rocky

APPROXIMATE DURATION: 3–4 hours depending on your conditioning

TRAVEL TIME FROM PORTLAND TO TRAILHEAD: 1 hour, 10 minutes

DRIVING DIRECTIONS: Take US 26 westbound from the Sylvan exit (exit 71B) for almost 58 miles to the summit of the Coast Range at Humbug Mountain. As you cross the summit the left side of the highway has been clear-cut and a gated road climbs the highest ridge heading south. The highway bends right as it crests the top. About 1,000 feet past the summit a small logging road cuts back into the slope on the right side of the road. Due to the angle it is not easy to see this logging road, so slow down after cresting the top of the hill and look carefully for a road on your right. There is some space alongside this narrow road to park, but be careful not to block the roadway. About 100 feet into the forest is a blue gate with the usual signage pertaining to recreational user rights.

SPECIAL ATTRIBUTES: Portions of the route are quite dramatic and there is much game on these steep slopes. If your dog has any kind of hunting instinct it might be best to use a leash since there could be dramatic temptations all around. On one hike we had a young elk cow run right through the middle of our group.

NOTE: There is also a much better-known Humbug Mountain located near Port Orford. That coastal promontory has its own dedicated state park. The Humbug Mountain described in these pages is owned by private timber interests and doesn't enjoy the protection, stewardship, and publicity of its more famous namesake on the southern Oregon coast.

TRAIL LOG: From the gate, follow the road uphill. Ignore the left-hand option that leads down the northeast face of Humbug Mountain about 0.6 miles into the hike. Stay left and keep climbing. About 1.25 miles up, begin traversing the southern face of Humbug Mountain, passing through a stand of older trees (they could be stumps by the time you get there). At the top of the climb up the south face you will be able to look south and see distinctive Onion Peak, which dominates the skyline above Cannon Beach. In the foreground is Sugarloaf Mountain, which looks like someone poured the contents of a bag of sugar out on the ground.

From here the road hugs the increasingly rocky terrain as it crawls uphill and turns left to begin traversing the northern face all the way to the ridgetop, located at an elevation of 2,468 feet. This summit ridgeline runs for about a mile in an east-west orientation. The highest point of the mountain is actually located just above where the road first crests the summit ridge, but access to this height is difficult and the views are less dramatic than from the western end of the ridgetop, where the radio facilities are located. The views from that installation are magnificent, especially the view of neighboring Saddle Mountain.

The return trip is simply a retracing of the ascent, taking care not to twist an ankle as you navigate the steep grade, especially on the east face of the mountain's rocky crown. Though Humbug Mountain is about 460 feet shorter than Saddle Mountain, its ascent is quite dramatic, with terrific views in all directions. The trailhead is accessible right from US 26 and does not require a long detour on an access road. Even more rewarding is the absence of people on this ascent, resulting in a more satisfying experience and more interaction with wildlife. This is one of the great undiscovered hikes—easily accessible and remarkably short given the elevation gained.

Following the Golden Rule

The early 1800s were a time of social experimentation. Today, it's hard to see that idealism in the faded daguerreotypes and the stern visages that stare out at us from that far edge of modernity. This was the period when the Shaker communities were founded, the Amish established their ways of life, and the utopians were trying out new ideas for societal arrangements.

Humbug Mountain on a blustery fall day.

These were heady ideas and they found adherents among the newly arrived German immigrants that were flooding into the country. One of these immigrants was Wilhelm Keil, a young Prussian who arrived in New York in 1831. Dr. Keil was fascinated by the fusion of social experimentation with the growing body of scientific knowledge. It wasn't long before he joined the Methodists at their newest commune near Pittsburgh.

With his deep-set blue eyes, his fringe beard, and his intellectual passion, Dr. Keil quickly became an acknowledged leader among the Methodists. So when he proposed founding a new community on the Missouri frontier, many followed him west. The Bethelites, as the new group called themselves, were an industrious lot and soon erected a self-sufficient community with gristmills, sawmills, a pioneer wagon-building business, and a highly prized whiskey called the Golden Rule. But Missouri was getting crowded, and Dr. Keil realized that secular influences were threatening the survival of his Methodist community. So in 1854 he announced plans to establish a new colony in that distant country named Oregon.

Thirty-four identical wagons were soon under construction, and by 1855 they were ready and packed with all that might be necessary to establish a new colony. Dr. Keil's eldest son, Willie, was chosen to drive the lead wagon.

But here's where our story takes a dramatic twist from the usual Oregon Trail stories. Only days before the anticipated departure, young Willie fell ill and died! It was a wrenching dilemma, as Willie had been one of the most enthusiastic proponents of the move to Oregon. With his dying son in his arms, Dr. Keil vowed that Willie would make the journey across the wide prairies all the way to Oregon. Even this tragedy would not delay Dr. Keil's carefully laid plans.

Under normal circumstances, one might want to consider the grieving father's final promises to his dying son as sentimental hyperbole, but Dr. Keil was a man of his word. Without a moment's hesitation he ordered the Bethelites to construct a hearse, complete with a lead-lined coffin into which he laid Willie's body. And to prevent the decomposition of his corpse along the long and dusty route, he had the settlers fill the coffin with Golden Rule whiskey, effectively pickling young Willie for all eternity!

So, with Willie's hearse in the lead, the great column of thirty-four wagons rolled out of the gates of the compound, exactly on schedule. Behind them came the settlers' standard-bearer, who carried a uniquely Prussian artifact, a *Schellenbaum* that tinkled gaily as it was borne along. Next came a phalanx of horns, flutes, fiddles, and drums, followed by an orderly procession of settlers—all headed into the distant sunset.

Crossing the Missouri, they met retreating wagon trains whose would-be emigrants told of atrocities ahead. It seems that the Sioux had decided to wage war on the inexorable stream of settlers encroaching on their homelands. Several expeditions had already perished. But Dr. Keil was unperturbed. God would watch over them, he assured his followers. He trusted in the Almighty's wisdom and protection, and on they went—passing more and more panicked settlers running for cover.

By mid-June, the convoy reached Fort Kearney, near the Platte River. Here again, they were admonished to turn back. But Dr. Keil's response was resolute: "The Lord will guide us and preserve us," he insisted.

They didn't have to wait long for the first signs of trouble. Two days out from the fort, a small band of Sioux approached. But instead of attacking the convoy, they indicated that they were curious about the coffin at the head of the procession. Dr. Keil quickly ordered the elaborate casket opened, and as the Sioux approached he had the band strike up one of Martin Luther's famous hymns.

At first the band hesitated, but then the first notes of the hymn came wafting over the waiting procession. Soon the tentative sounds of the fiddles and flutes pierced the prairie silence. With mounting confidence the drums and tubas burst forth. And finally, a chorus of voices rose in a crescendo that filled the silent plains with music—the likes of which no Sioux had ever heard.

The natives were astounded. Not only was this whiskey-soaked deity clearly an instrument of powerful magic, but the accompanying chorales of the Bethelites were utterly bewitching. When the song was over the Sioux made it clear they needed an encore, and so the trembling settlers launched into several German folk songs. Surprised to see that they were still alive, they took heart and finished the impromptu concert with a lusty German drinking song. As dusk fell and the singing subsided, the Sioux vanished into the vast expanses of prairie that surrounded the wagon train. Everyone gave a deep sigh of relief, but wondered what was next.

At Fort Laramie, the commander was insistent that they either return to the East or stay encamped around the fort. But once again Dr. Keil demurred and insisted, "The Lord will watch over his own." There was no stopping Dr. Keil, and the settlers marched past the fort singing their German hymns to the accompaniment of the tinkling Schellenbaum. The soldiers watched them leave with dread in their hearts, because they knew that no wagon trains had survived the next leg of the journey.

Two days later along the Laramie River, the outriders reported Sioux approaching from several angles. The party halted as the warriors become visible along the tops of the ridges. Endless rows of mounted warriors stood silhouetted all along the tops of the hills that surrounded them. It was on these remote slopes of Wyoming, amid the smoke of campfires and the noisy bustle of the livestock, that the fearsome Sioux approached. Dust clouds arose from the lines of Indian ponies as they descended down through the arid chaparral to where the settlers waited.

Tensions were strung as tight as a fiddle's strings, but Dr. Keil was ready. He guided the oncoming warriors into two rows so that they could pass by on either side of Willie's whiskey-filled coffin. And as they did so the settlers burst into song. They were accompanied by the confident sounds of horns, drums, tubas, and fiddles as the choir joined in to give a spirited rendition of Luther's hymns.

On and on came more Sioux. Riding silently past the coffin, hundreds of war-painted warriors gazed reverently into Willie's coffin. Apparently, the entire Sioux nation had halted their prairie war so that they could witness the passage of this powerful whiskey-soaked deity as it traversed their ancestral lands to the accompaniment of angelic songs. Given the carnage of that summer's fighting, it is almost impossible to visualize these battle-hardened warriors settling back on their tired steeds to listen to the settlers singing "A Mighty Fortress Is Our God" as if their very lives depended on it.

And through the gathering dusk, the Sioux warriors sat as if mesmerized by the unfamiliar sounds of the guitar, the booming of the kettle-drums, and the steely whispering of the German zithers. They marveled in puzzlement at the birdlike calls delivered by the flutes and clarinets. And even the occasional jingling of the Schellenbaum's bells reminded them of the delicate sounds of trickling water.

And then there was the singing.

These German pioneers were steeped in the traditions of German choral singing—from its roots in the harmonic arrangements by Hildegard von Bingen, to the intricate scores of Johann Sebastian Bach, and even the rollicking drinking songs of the Bavarian Oktoberfest. The Sioux had never experienced this kind of music and were awestruck when the singers began their harmonized renditions of John Wesley's well-known hymns. After that they sang an assortment of popular German lieder, some popular Rhenish melodies, some Prussian marches and Bavarian folk tunes, and even an Italian cantata. Through the long, hot afternoon the musicians scoured their repertoires for peaceful tunes to soothe the hearts of their fearsome visitors. However, in the end it was the rollicking German beer-drinking songs that captured the hearts of their audience. Calling for more, the Sioux grinned through their war paint as the singers reprised the roistering verses of "Ach, Du Lieber Augustin," bringing the concert to a climax that would have done any Oktoberfest orchestra proud.

By morning the Sioux had vanished, but from that time on, they would appear leading lost cows back to the Methodist pioneers. They would leave freshly killed venison on the trail. Even after Dr. Keil's group crossed the Rockies, word of their special status had preceded them, and the Nez Perce, Cayuse, and Paiutes welcomed them effusively. Although the summer of 1855 was one of the worst years on the Oregon Trail, Dr. Keil's wagons suffered no harm as they traveled across two thousand miles of wilderness to their destination on Willapa Bay.

By October, Dr. Keil's thirty-four wagons had finally reached the Columbia River, and by November they had descended the Lower Columbia to reach Willapa Bay, where their scouts had been busy building structures to house the new colony. Upon their arrival their first act was to extract young Willie from his bath of Golden Rule whiskey and finally put him to rest in the salty soil of Willapa Bay. His grave can still be found there, even though the colony abandoned that site due to the nearly constant rain. Eventually, they resettled in the Willamette Valley where they established the successful colony of Aurora in 1857.

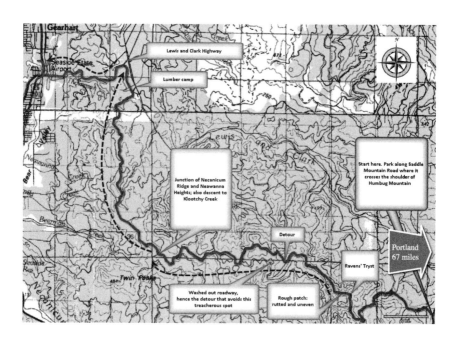

Gearhart

Lewis and Clark Highway

Lumber camp

Seaside State
Airport

Junction of Necanicum
Ridge and Neawanna
Heights; also descent to
Klootchy Creek

Start here. Park along Saddle
Mountain Road where it
crosses the shoulder of
Humbug Mountain

Detour

Portland
67 miles

Ravens' Tryst

Twin Peaks

Washed out roadway,
hence the detour that avoids this
treacherous spot

Rough patch:
rutted and uneven

30. Ridge-Runner's Delight

BRIEF DESCRIPTION: This final trail is best suited for bicycles due to its length. After a short downhill stretch, the route ascends a ridge that parallels US 26. From the summit this route runs 13 miles along the top of this ridge—all the way to the coast—and then turns and parallels US 101 before dropping down between Seaside and Gearhart. The views on this trail are panoramic and amazing. The road is in pretty good condition. After the initial ascent, the almost constant downhill grade means hardly any pedaling is needed! Look out for deer and bears in this segment; they're more frightened of you than the reverse. Be sure to consult the map since many of the turns are similar and it's easy to descend in the wrong place. The route is exhilarating as you zip down the ridge, dropping from 2,200 feet in elevation down to sea level. Breathtaking views and a ride to write home about!

DISTANCE: 18.7 miles

ELEVATION CHANGE: 2,200 feet. Enter the logging road network at 1,365 feet in elevation. Descend to 1,180 feet before ascending 921 feet to reach the ridgetop at an elevation of approximately 2,150 feet. Eventually this trail descends to the coastal plain, crosses US 101, and terminates at the Pacific Ocean (elevation 0 feet).

TRAIL CONDITION: A short path through the forest leads to a well-maintained graveled logging road network.

APPROXIMATE DURATION: 4.5 hours

TRAVEL TIME FROM PORTLAND TO TRAILHEAD: 90 minutes to the pull-off at Saddle Mountain Road. Add 45 minutes or so to drive to the Necanicum estuary, leave the second car, and return to the starting point.

DRIVING DIRECTIONS: Start by dropping off a shuttle car in Seaside. A good spot is in the business facing the estuary on the west side of US 101.

In your second car, take US 26 east about 15.5 miles and turn left (north) onto Saddle Mountain Road. Drive up Saddle Mountain Road for 3.1 miles and pull off on the left side of the road before reaching the shoulder of Humbug Mountain (just beyond where the road makes a virtual figure eight). There is a shallow pull-off area on the west side of the road. The trail leads west into the forest to a three-way intersection on a nearby logging road.

SPECIAL ATTRIBUTES: Ridge-Runner's Delight covers the last 18 miles to the coast, and what a ride it is!

TRAIL LOG: All locations are measured from where the trail begins in the parking area. Be certain to set your bike odometer or GPS device at the start of the trail.

Take the short trail from the parking pullout on Saddle Mountain Road through a narrow strip of older trees on the verge of a younger forest. The trail is clearly visible on the west (left) side of the road as it meanders slightly downhill along the shoulder to the edge of the canopy. Follow this path to an intersection of three logging roads at an elevation of 1,365 feet.

Take the right fork; it proceeds north and winds downhill. On the way down, you will pass a poorly maintained side road coming in from the north (right side), and you will also pass an intersection with a well-maintained road leading downhill on your left. Soon thereafter, you will encounter a T in the road. Take the right-hand option and head north. This road will drop down, eventually crossing a small stream flowing north. This is the lowest point on the route; it's all uphill for the next few miles!

Right after crossing this small stream the road begins to climb. To the left a logging road appears to climb steeply up the ridge immediately to the south. This is the road to the top of the ridge. It's a strenuous 2.2 miles, gaining 921 feet in elevation, and is made more difficult if you push a bicycle. I am not athletic enough to ride all the way up, though I'm sure most mountain bikers would scoff at my unimpressive stamina. We can talk about this when they reach the far side of sixty birthdays.

The trail leads uphill through a middle-aged alder forest for what seems like an eternity before reaching the summit. Although the road crosses several side trails, it's easy to discern the main route. This road is also well used by the elk and deer as evidenced by frequent scat and continuous prints. Eventually, the road turns abruptly uphill to the right, bypassing a side spur that continues briefly on the level. Follow the road up and around the end of the ridge. As you emerge from the climb the road opens up to the south, affording the first spectacular views of the mountains south of US 26. From here the road levels out a bit, rising only about 377 feet over the next mile; it crests at 2,150 feet about 2 miles from the base of this climb (4.07 miles from the start).

On my first ascent an elk took exception to our approach and challenged us. Suddenly, a deep sonorous bugle reverberated through the trees from a short distance away. I may not have appreciated the entire nuanced message, but it was enough to stop me in my tracks. At that point we decided that some audible response in English might suffice to convince the overly territorial elk lord that we were not interested in his harem. Given that

Saddle Mountain as seen from near Ravens' Tryst.

hunting season was in full swing, our massive challenger evidently thought better about showing himself. He was close enough so that when he thundered away we could feel his hoofbeats resonate through the forest floor.

At the top of this ridge you'll be treated to a panoramic view of Saddle Mountain. It was not always thus; in my early ascents the forest grew thickly all around and we could not see the narrow ridge that reached out toward Saddle Mountain. But when I returned, the narrow forest path had been opened up by a clear-cut that exposed much of the northern face of this ridge—and provided a stunning view of Saddle Mountain to the north. At the summit of the road a narrow ridge was now clearly visible toward Saddle Mountain. All around this narrow ridge great numbers of ravens were swooping and diving in great abandon.

Watching the performance I couldn't avoid naming this place "Ravens' Tryst" since it seems to be a favorite location for the ravens during their mating season. Witnessing these aerial love antics left me gasping as the birds locked together while plunging down the cliffs and swerving through the crags and chutes. If I am ever reincarnated, I hope it's not as a raven, because that might be a short-lived experience when my efforts to mate with my black-winged bride result in a feathery mess plastered against a cliff face.

From Ravens' Tryst along the Necanicum ridge. Just beyond Ravens' Tryst the road narrows as it traverses the north side of the ridge. This bumpy and uneven track is the roughest part of the route. Thereafter the road quickly widens and develops a gentler grade. Just short of 5 miles from the trailhead a road comes up the southern flank to meet the ridgetop road from the left. Continue along the ridgeline. About 5.95 miles from the trailhead (at an elevation of 1,891 feet) the mainline road turns left as a logging platform or clearing appears on the right. This clearing also provides an expansive view to the north.

Continue to follow the original mainline down the ridge for another quarter mile or so (6.25 miles from the trailhead) to a more recently constructed road on the right that straddles the ridgetop. This newer road was built after the original mainline was washed out in the 1997 storm. Instead of proceeding downhill along the ridge on the original mainline, turn and cross the ridge on the new road. It continues for about 1.6 miles before rejoining the original mainline road again. As you descend this newer detour, look north for a spectacular view of Saddle Mountain.

At the return to the mainline (about 7.85 miles from the trailhead), turn right and continue to head west along the ridge. You'll soon begin to see the coastal mountains to the south. This cluster of mountains rises up in a triangle between US 26 to the north, the Nehalem River to the east, and Nehalem Bay to the south. To the east, Kidder's Butte is one of a pair of peaks exceeding 2,200 feet in elevation. In the immediate foreground is the aptly named Sugarloaf Mountain—a perfect sugar cone that reaches 2,680 feet in elevation. And in the distance, a distinctive peak with what appears to be two horns reaches up to 3,057 feet. This is Onion Peak, named by the Native Americans for the delicious onions that are said to have grown in the saddle between the peaks. Beyond Onion Peak lie Ecola State Park and the Pacific Ocean.

Two-thirds of a mile onward (about 8.5 miles from the trailhead), pass a road on the right that leads up to an old radio facility located on one of the high points overlooking the Pacific. The next intersection follows about 0.9 miles farther (9.4 miles from the trailhead). There the road turns to the left, while two side roads head north. One's instinct is to start heading north at this point, but these roads only lead down into the valley and do not follow the ridgeline. So follow the turn to the left and stay on the mainline road. This road will go south to circle around a major promontory.

The next major intersection is the strategic turn at which you'll reach the end of the ridge and arrive at the Neawanna Heights facing Seaside and the expanse of the Pacific Ocean. At 10.35 miles from the trailhead, enter an intersection with several tributaries. The road to the left leads steeply down into the Klootchy Creek basin. Do not descend this way, but before proceeding let me digress for just a moment to pay tribute to our region's older residents.

Nearly 750 years ago a Sitka spruce was sprouted and began its quest for sunlight, water, and longevity. During its long existence it battled torrential storms and weathered fire and pestilence, ultimately becoming the world's largest spruce tree. Growing alongside Klootchy Creek, the "Klootchy" spruce grew to the prodigious height of 206 feet. But sadly, it was badly damaged in the storms that wracked the coast in 2007 and had to be cut down. To put its longevity into perspective, Kublai Khan became the ruler of the Mongol Empire at the time that this tree began to reach up into the sky!

Back at the top of the slope, turn your attention away from the Klootchy Creek basin on the south side and begin to follow the road that leads north across the slope overlooking the town of Seaside. This portion of the trip is delightful as you coast for 1.7 miles parallel to the coastline. Pass several roads ascending the slope on the right. At just over 12 miles from the trailhead, the road curves to the northeast and passes two lightly used roads: one heads off to the left, and the other to the right. Proceed straight on the main road and pass over the crest of the hill to descend the backside (eastern slope) of the hills.

From here, simply stay on the main track and descend along the eastern face of these hills. Eventually, you will pass by the site of a lumber camp and from there a short road takes you out to the Lewis and Clark Highway. In all, the gliding path down this long slope is about 3.85 miles long, but due to the slope and smooth surface it will all fly by in a blissful blur.

Do be careful to avoid hitting any animals that might also be using these roads. We almost ran over a bear on one occasion. Once you reach the Lewis and Clark Highway it's a gentle climb of about 0.5 miles to the summit. The trip culminates in a smoothly paved road that runs for almost 2.5 miles down off these final hills, swinging back and forth in wide loops as it brings you safely to the intersection with US 101 just to the north of the Necanicum Bridge.

From that intersection you need only ride north for about 0.1 mile on US 101 to reach the business facing the estuary on the west side of US 101 where you parked your car. The entire trip was less than 19 miles from the trailhead to the ocean and 15 miles of it was downhill.

Gone-to-the-Spirits

The view from the top of Saddle Mountain is breathtaking. It looks out over a long ribbon of coastline and the vast ocean beyond. Located midway down the long western coastline of North America, this is a *special* place! North of the Columbia River, Washington's craggy cliffs define a wild coast. To the south, Oregon's sandy beaches soften the landscape. In between, the Columbia River carves a deep channel out of the interior and disgorges such a torrent of water that approaching ships are often tossed about and occasionally crushed in the gigantic surf.

Currents and forces that arise in the vastness of the Pacific Ocean buffet the spit of land on which Astoria is built. Yet this feisty American outpost became an early destination for fur traders and British and Americans trading along the northwest coast. Settlers arrived, coming all the way around the tip of South America. Native Americans sidled up to the wharf in Astoria, paddling from as far away as the Rocky Mountains. Even sworn competitors and declared enemies mingled at this lonely outpost—sometimes with surprising consequences.

But no story of Astoria could be complete without telling of the extraordinary events that transpired in the weeks following June 15, 1811. On that sunny day, the local Chinooks escorted "two strange Indians" into the fort at Astoria.[1] Remarkably, the man and his wife were both attired in the long robes of deerskin favored by the tribes living on the eastern slopes of the Rockies.[2]

Eventually it was learned that this tall Algonquin-speaking native was known as Gone-to-the-Spirits, or, in the Kootenai language, Kauxuma Nupika. They were carrying a letter for John Stuart, who at that time was trying to descend the Fraser River in British Columbia. The intrepid couple had canoed all the way down the Columbia River from its icy springs high in the Canadian Rockies. But along the way they'd managed to take a wrong turn and thus became the first to navigate the entire length of the Columbia. Although David Thompson is usually accorded this honor, the historical record clearly documents the arrival of the Kootenai Indians in Astoria more than two weeks earlier.[3]

No sooner had this Kootenai warrior arrived than the Americans realized what an amazing source of information had stumbled into their fort. Kauxuma Nupika was an absolute intelligence coup. Not only could he confirm the details of how and where the British fur traders were operating, but it appeared that this couple had managed the perilous journey from the top of the Continental Divide down the Columbia River, through the territories of countless tribes, all the way to the tiny American outpost at the mouth of the mighty river. If this couple could manage such an epic journey, then it must also be possible for the Astorians to ascend the river to its source.

One of the Astorians, Alexander Ross, calls out the intelligence value as follows:

> Among the many visitors who every now and then presented themselves, were two strange Indians, in the character of man and wife, from the vicinity of the Rocky Mountains.... The husband was a very shrewd and intelligent Indian, who addressed us in the Algonquin and gave us much information respecting the interior of the country.[4]

The Americans were thrilled, even as they remained puzzled by the mannerisms of Kauxuma Nupika. The interrogations lasted several days since the dialogue required a serial translation through several indigenous languages before the Astorians could understand it. What they learned was invaluable. Even as Kauxuma Nupika was being debriefed, the Astorians began to prepare their own expedition up the river.

The Astorians were literally packing the canoes when someone spotted a canoe coming down the river. Seated in the stern was what appeared to be an English officer; at his back fluttered the Union Jack. It was David Thompson, the renowned North West Company explorer. Despite the fact that they were commercial rivals, Thompson and his Nor'Westers were warmly welcomed. At some point during their stay the Astorians told Thompson about the recent arrival of the Kootenai couple from the Rockies. Taken to meet the visitors, Thompson immediately recognized Kauxuma and exposed him as the "woman" who had married his aide, Boisvert. Ultimately, he told them, he had been forced to expel Kauxuma from Kalispell House when his "overbearing presence became disruptive."[5]

Tarrying only five days in Astoria, David Thompson quickly provisioned his canoes and set out to make the long trip back up the Columbia and across the Continental Divide. Before leaving, he did agree to guide the Astorian David Stuart and eight of his men to where they planned to build an outpost at the base of the Okanagan River. But they weren't the only fellow travelers.

When he heard that a party was headed back up the Columbia, Kauxuma Nupika and his wife approached Thompson, seeking his protection during the journey upriver. Despite his misgivings, Thompson agreed to include them in his entourage—a decision that made the Nor'Westers' own passage considerably more dangerous.

Not only was Thompson aware of the disruptions that Kauxuma was capable of fomenting, but he was also well aware of Kauxuma's reputation as a seer and prophet. In July of 1809, Thompson had encountered Kauxuma on Rainy Lake near the Upper Columbia River and reported that

> She [sic] had set herself up for a prophetess and gradually had gained, by her shrewdness, some influence among the natives as a dreamer, and expounder of dreams. She recollected me before I did her, and gave a haughty look of defiance, as much to say, I am now out of your power.[6]

Apparently, after being expelled from Kalispell House, Kauxuma had returned to his tribe and announced that European medicine had succeeded in changing him from a woman into a man. He soon assumed a new name, took to wearing men's clothing, carrying weapons, and participating in horse-thieving raids. He tried to attract a female partner, but the women in his village were unresponsive to his advances. Finally, he attracted the companionship of a woman who had been abandoned by her husband. Their romance intensified and soon they were inseparable. But over time the flame of love flickered, turning into an acrid plume of jealousy and violence, which had to be quelled by Kauxuma's brother and the tribal elders.

It was during this time that Kauxuma began to develop a threefold prophetic narrative that he circulated throughout the Northwest. For starters, he said that Europeans were bringing smallpox and it would kill them...soon. Following that, he predicted that two giants would appear and would turn over the earth, burying all the native peoples and their lodges. And to cap it off, he predicted that most Native Americans would simply die. All along his journey down the Columbia River, Kauxuma had retailed this nightmare scenario to every village he visited, leaving the tribes in considerable turmoil.

If Thompson needed proof of the vitriol Kauxuma had left in his wake, it was forthcoming before they even entered the Columbia Gorge. Here's how Thompson describes the encounter in his journal:

Having proceeded half a mile up a Rapid, we came to four men who were waiting for us ... the four men addressed me, saying, when you passed going down to the sea, we were all strong in life, and your return to us finds us strong to live, but what is this we hear, casting their eyes with a stern look on her [the "man woman"], is it true that the white men ... have brought with them the Small Pox to destroy us; and two men of enormous size, who are on their way to us, overturning the Ground, and burying all the Villages and Lodges underneath it; is this true, and are we all soon to die. I told them not [to] be alarmed, for the white Men who had arrived had not brought the Small Pox, and the Natives were strong to live, and every evening were dancing and sing-ing... At all which they appeared much pleased, and thanked me for the good words I had told them; but I saw plainly that if the "man woman" had not been sitting behind us they would have plunged a dagger in her [sic] . . .[7]

Not only did Kauxuma have more than four years of experience with the English and Scottish fur traders, but he had also spent considerable time with the French Canadian voyageurs. Through this latter associa-tion he had been imprinted with the opportunistic culture of the French Canadian trappers, who excelled at manipulating the credulous natives to their advantage.[8] But this incident near the entrance to the Columbia Gorge clearly demonstrated that Kauxuma's prior messages of doom were rebounding back on him—with likely mortal consequences.

Realizing he was in danger, Kauxuma's tune changed dramatically. Soon he was spreading hope and promising appealing visions of the future. He predicted "a complete change in the face of the country."[9] Kauxuma Nupika was widely believed to have supernatural powers, so the people listened when he said, "the present race of white inhabitants...would be removed."[10] He asserted boldly that fertility would replace the current ste-rility. Instead of threatening visits by fearsome giants, Kauxuma now an-nounced that the great white chief was about to inundate the natives with everything they wanted.[11] There was no more mention of smallpox and death. Instead his message held out hope and promises of unimaginable largesse by the great chief of the Europeans. In their gratitude for these glad tidings the local tribespeople now showered the Kootenai couple with gifts as they continued to make their way up the Columbia River.

Kauxuma and his wife parted ways with David Thompson about 535 miles upriver from Astoria, at the confluence of the Okanagan River. At this junction, we get one final glimpse of Gone-to-the-Spirits and his Kootenai wife. The expedition reports that they were last seen ascending a long slope trailing twenty-six packhorses heavily laden with all manner of tribal wealth. From various sources, we continue to hear of Kauxuma's activities until he was finally killed by a Blackfoot raiding party.

Yet for all his infamous connivances, Gone-to-the-Spirits was undoubtedly an unusually complex personality whose boldness was matched only by his uncanny prophetic abilities. It seems almost like denial that we continue to ignore Kauxuma's insights, which turned out to be more accurate than anyone might have guessed.

Notes

1. Alexander Ross, *Adventures of the First Settlers on the Oregon or Columbia River, 1810-1813* (Lincoln: University of Nebraska Press, 1986), 101.
2. Gabriel Franchere, *Eyewitness to Astoria* (Astoria, OR: Moffit House Press, 2011), 64.
3. Ibid., 64.
4. Ross, *Adventures of the First Settlers*, 101.
5. Robert Clark, *River of the West: Stories from the Columbia* (New York, NY: Harper Collins, 1995), 69
6. "Kaúxuma Núpika," Wikipedia, last modified Feb. 17, 2016, http://en.wikipedia.org/wiki/Kauxuma_Nupika/.
7. Claude Schaeffer, "The Kutenai Female Berdache: Courier, Guide, Prophetess, and Warrior," *American Society for Ethnohistory,* vol.12, no. 3 (Summer 1965), 193–236.
8. Ross, *Adventures of the First Settlers*, 153.
9. Schaeffer, "The Kutenai Female Berdache."
10. Ibid.
11. Ibid.

Index

C

Calapuyans, 26, 83, 84, 94, 97, 168

Calhoun, Deputy, 57

California, 95

calk boots, 133

camas lilies, 32, 46

Camp Divide, 147, 148, 150, 151,

Camp Eight, 65, 67

Camp McGregor, 138, 151, 152

Camp Nine, 204, 219

Camp Olson, 235

Camp Wilkerson, 73

canoe Indians, 46

Cannon Beach, 245–246

Cape of Mendocino, 199

Capehorn Mountain, 99, 107, 115, 123

Capehorn Traverse, 107–108, 116, 124

Carcus Falls, 7

Cascades, 54, 93

castaways, 199

Cater Road, 73

Cathlamet, WA, 102

Cathlapotle, 19, 46

Cayuse Indians, 93, 101, 251

Cedar Creek, 74

Chakonweiftei village, 94

chanterelles, 24, 32, 44

Chapanakhtin village, 94

Chapman, Fred, 62, 64, 65

Chapman, Simco, 62, 64, 65

Charbonneau, Toussaint, 118

Chatakwin village, 94

China, 95

Chinook jargon, 47, 96

Chinooks, 26, 32, 45, 46, 47, 49, 56, 93, 109, 111, 156, 198, 258

Chipewyan, 96

Chewan, Chief, 84

Civil War, 169

Civilian Conservation Corps (CCC), 140, 152

Clackamas Indians, 93, 102

clamons, 47, 48

Clark and Wilson Timber Co., 65, 67

Clatskanie, OR, 126

Clatskanie Indians, 62, 84, 111

Clatsop County, 58, 137, 141, 166, 233

Clatsop Plains, 199

Clatsop Spit, 239, 242

Clatsops, 55, 84, 93, 111, 199

Clear Creek, 147, 148

Coast Range, 10, 13, 85, 140, 155, 169, 183, 184, 185, 191, 223, 224, 233

Coast traders ("coasters"), 47, 94, 111

Cochran Fire, 178

Cochran Pond, 82, 117, 126, 168, 175, 192, 194, 197

Cochran Road, 170, 192, 227–229

Coffee Creek, 185

Colville, WA, 166

Comcomly, Chief, 47

Conley, William, 187

Conservation Fund, 9

Convoy, The, 112

Columbia County, 65, 73, 81, 84, 85, 137, 141, 233

Columbia River, 18, 26, 46, 51–52, 55, 73, 93, 95, 126, 166, 186, 199, 240

Comanches, 109

Cook Creek, 175

Coon Creek Road, 68, 81, 85

Cornelius, Abe, 40

Cortez, 109

cougar, 24, 69, 74

Cowaniah, Chief, 94–96

Cowlitz formation, 149

Cowlitz Indians, 111

Cowlitz River, 45

Coyote Corner, 218

Crabapple Creek, 58

Cree, 96

G

Gales Creek, OR, 155, 160, 167, 168
Gales Creek Campground, 155, 159
Gales Creek Trail, 228
Gearhart, OR, 253
General Land Office, 169
Gentry, William, 28
Gilkison Road, 24, 31, 37
Gillihan Road, 17
Gilmore Logging Company, 179
Gilmore Road, 173
Ginger Creek, 138
Glenwood, OR, 155
Golden Rule (whiskey), 248
Gone-to-the-Spirits, 258, 262
gonorrhea, 111
Gourlay Creek, 37, 38
Gourlay Mainline, 39
GPS device, 11, 52
grange dances, 85–87
Gravelle Brothers Trail, 163–164
Gray, Captain Robert, 95, 200
Grays Harbor, WA, 198
grebes, 18
Green Mountain, 168
Greenman, Judd, 152
grouse, 46
Grouse Lane, 52, 89
Gunners Lake, 55
gyppo logging, 177–181, 222

H

Hadley's Landing 16, 17,
Haller, Major, 103
Hamlet, OR, 169, 241
Hancock Timber Co., 62
Hastings, Warren, 120
hats, 47
Hawaiians, 20, 95, 96
Hawkins Road, 67
Hay, Keith, 9
Heimuller Road, 52, 89, 90,

hemlock, 44, 62, 65,
Hennig, Don, 209
Hillsboro, OR, 93
Hinduism, 34
HMS *Raccoon*, 165–166
Hodges, Randy, 156, 160, 161,
Hoffman family, 90
Hoffman Road, 89, 91,
Holbrook, Stewart, 133
Holy Old Mackinaw, 133
Homestead Act, 78
honey mushrooms, 32
Honolulu, HI, 95
Horseshoe Trail, 82
huckleberries, 43–44,
Hudson's Bay Company, 21, 84, 92,
    94, 95, 165–166
Humbug Mountain, 245, 253
Humbug Mountain State Park,
    245–246
Huntington, Eunice, 128
hypothermia, 12, 40–41

I

Idaho, 96, 109
Illahee, 48, 49
"Indian Louis," 243
influenza, 110, 120

J

Jackson Creek, 23, 24, 26
Jardine, Ray, 159
Jarvis, Ed, 145
Jeppesen family, 90
Johnson, Mrs., 187
Johnston, Bob, 24, 29
Jones Creek Campground, 173
Joy Creek Nursery, 25

K

Kalama, WA, 102
Kalispell House, 260
Kamholz, Ed, 225

Weller family, 90

western tanager, 228

West Hills, 53

West Oregon Logging Company, 178, 179

Westport, OR, 84

Westport Slough, 76

West Road, 52

Weyerhaeuser Co., 9, 13, 14, 148

Wheeler, OR, 211

Wheeler Cut-off Road, 193, 204, 218,

Wheeler Pond Road, 192, 197, 204, 205, 218, 219

White Salmon River, 93

Whitman Mission, 101

Wickiup Mountain, 73

Wilark Camp, 67, 69,

wildfires, 139

wild ginger, 32

Wild Salmon Center, 195

Willamette River, 18, 55

Willamette Valley, 26, 46, 83, 92, 93, 94, 166, 186, 251

Willapa Bay, 46, 198, 240, 251

William's Creek trestle, 100

Willis, Frank, 235–236

Wilson River, 82, 183

Wilson River Road, North Fork, 173

Wilson River Trail, 183, 184

Wilson River Wagon Road Trail, 163, 164

Windsor, Henry, 128

Windy Gap, 224

Winship, Captain Nathan, 84

Winthrop, Theodore, 102

Wobblies, 177

Wolf Creek, 140, 187, 188, 195–197, 224, 233, 234

Wolf Creek fire, 152

Wood, Sidney, 76

Wood's Landing, 76

Woodson, OR, 73, 76

Works Progress Administration (WPA), 140

Wyeth, Nathaniel, 20

Wyoming, 249

Y

Yakimas, 102

Yankton, OR, 78, 85

Yeon Avenue, NW, 132

Yeon Building, 134

Yeon, Jean Batiste, 132

Yoakum, Finis, 53

Youngs Bay, 101